BRIDGESTONE 90

TECHNICAL HANDBOOK

BS BRIDGESTONE TIRE CO., LTD.

Tokyo, Japan

INTRODUCTION

Welcome to the world of digital publishing ~ the book you now hold in your hand, was printed using the latest state of the art digital technology. The advent of print-on-demand has forever changed the publishing process, never has information been so accessible and it is our hope that this book serves your informational needs for years to come. If this is your first exposure to digital publishing, we hope that you are pleased with the results. Many more titles of interest to the classic automobile and motorcycle enthusiast, collector and restorer are available via our website at www.VelocePress.com. We hope that you find this title as interesting as we do.

NOTE FROM THE PUBLISHER

The information presented is true and complete to the best of our knowledge. All recommendations are made without any guarantees on the part of the author or the publisher, who also disclaim all liability incurred with the use of this information.

TRADEMARKS

We recognize that some words, model names and designations, for example, mentioned herein are the property of the trademark holder. We use them for identification purposes only. This is not an official publication.

INFORMATION ON THE USE OF THIS PUBLICATION

This manual is an invaluable resource for those interested in performing their own maintenance. However, in today's information age we are constantly subject to changes in common practice, new technology, availability of improved materials and increased awareness of chemical toxicity. As such, it is advised that the user consult with an experienced professional prior to undertaking any procedure described herein. While every care has been taken to ensure correctness of information, it is obviously not possible to guarantee complete freedom from errors or omissions or to accept liability arising from such errors or omissions. Therefore, any individual that uses the information contained within, or elects to perform or participate in do-it-yourself repairs or modifications acknowledges that there is a risk factor involved and that the publisher or its associates cannot be held responsible for personal injury or property damage resulting from the use of the information or the outcome of such procedures.

WARNING!

One final word of advice, this publication is intended to be used as a reference guide, and when in doubt the reader should consult with a qualified technician.

TECHNICAL HAND BOOK

INDEX

Page

1. OUTSTANDING FEATURES OF BRIDGESTONE 90
    1. 1 Main Features of the Engine 1
    1. 2 Outstanding Features of the Frame 2

2. SPECIFICATIONS 3

3. PERFORMANCE 6

4. ENGINE
    4. 1 Dismounting and Mounting Engine in Frame
        A. Care to be observed 10
        B. Dismounting Engine 10
        C. Mounting Engine 13
    4. 2 Disassembling and Assembling Engine
        A. Matters that require special attention 13
        B. Disassembling Engine 13
        C. Inspection 16
        D. Assembling Engine 16

5. CONSTRUCTION OF ROTARY DISC VALVE ENGINE
        A. Description 18
        B. Rotary Disc Valve Timing 19
        C. Disassembling 19
        D. Inspection 19
        E. Assembling 19

6. CONSTRUCTION OF CYLINDER AND PISTON
        A. Description 20
        B. Disassembling 21
        C. Assembling 22
        D. Cleaning 22
        E. Inspection 23

7. CLUTCH
        A. Construction 24
        B. Clutch Functions 24
        C. Clutch Adjustment 25

        D. Disassembling Clutch 26
        E. Assembling 26
        F. Inspection 27

8. TRANSMISSION
        A. Construction 28
        B. Mechanism 28
        C. Disassembling 32
        D. Inspection 32

9. KICK STARTER
        A. Construction 33
        B. Operation 34
        C. Disassembling and Assembling 34
        D. Inspection 34

10. CARBURETOR
        A. Design and Operation 36
        B. Functions of Various Parts 39
        C. Adjustment 40

11. FRAME
        Frame structure 43

11.1 Handle Bar
        A. Remove Handle Bar 43
        B. Assembling 43

11.2 Front Fork
        A. Operation 45
        B. Disassembling 46
        C. Inspection 46
        D. Assembling 46

11.3 Rear Frame and Rear Suspension
        A. Construction 48
        B. Disassembling 48
        C. Inspection 48

11.4 Front and Rear Wheels
        A. Description 49
        B. Removing Front Wheel 49
        C. Removing Rear Wheel 50
        D. Inspection 50
        E. Assembling 50
        F. Removing Tire 51
        G. Mounting Tire on the Rim 51
        H. Cautions 51

11. 5 Brakes
- A. Description 53
- B. Disassembling 53
- C. Inspection 53
- D. Assembling 53

11. 6 Fuel Tank and Seat
- A. Description 54
- B. Removing 54
- C. Inspection 54

11. 7 Air Cleaner
- A. Description 55
- B. Removing 55
- C. Inspection 55
- D. Installing 55

11. 8 Exhaust System
- A. Removing 56
- B. Inspection 56
- C. Installing 56

11. 9 Footrest and Stands
- A. Removing 56
- B. Inspection 56
- C. Installing 56

11.10 Main Frame
- A. Construction 58
- B. Disassembling 58
- C. Inspection 58
- D. Assembling 58

12. ELECTRICAL EQUIPMENT

12. 1 Ignition System
- A. Contact Breaker 60
- B. Condenser 60
- C. Spark plug 62
- D. Flywheel Magneto 63
- E. Testing Ignition Coil 63

12. 2 Charging System
- A. Coil for Charging 63
- B. Silicon Rectifier 64
- C. Battery 64

12. 3 Wiring Diagram .... (Facing Page 64)

13. INSPECTION AND MAINTENANCE

    A. Daily Check Procedure ···65
    B. Periodic Checking ···65
    C. Periodic Greasing ··66
    D. Inspection and Maintenance Storage ···67

14. TROUBLE SHOOTING ···72

1. OUTSTANDING FEATURES

Bridgestone 90 belongs to the class of regular motorcycles perfected by concentrating the know-how and technical skill of Bridgestone's engineers.
Incorporating many features, such as styling and superlative finish, comfortable riding position and stability, and powered by a two-stroke rotary disc valve engine, it gives matchless performance.

1. 1 Main Features of the Engine:

A **Rotary Disc Valve System:**
The rotary disc valve system for intake of fuel, gives stable high torque from low to high speeds and quick and smooth acceleration from a standing start.

B **Kick Starter:**
Regardless of transmission in any position, kick starting is possible by simply operating the clutch lever, that is, quicker starting is effected by disengaging the clutch and kicking the pedal without the need of putting the gear first in neutral.

C **Four-Speed Rotary Transmission:**
The four-speed rotary transmission enables gear changes to be effected smoothly and a high speed in high gear of 95 km/h (60 M. P. H) or more is possible.

D **Carburetor:**
The carburetor is completely enclosed in the transmission case for protection against dust and water, the need for which had long been a problem for two-cycle engines.

E **Little Vibration:**
Attention has been paid especially to perfect balancing of the crank shaft, to minimize engine vibration which communicates to the frame.

Riding comfort is assured at any speed in low or high gear.

1.2 Outstanding Features of the Frame:

A **Telescopic Front Fork with Oil Damper:**
The adoption of a telescopic front fork with oil damper assures great stability even at high speeds on rough roads.

B **Maneuverability:**
Exceptional stability in maneuvering even on rough roads because of ample road clearance and banking angle.

C **Light and Strong Frame:**
This permits safety, easy riding and handling.

D **Braking Performance:**
Extra wide brake hubs 130 mmϕ (5.12ϕ inch) and the completely watertight drums assure efficient braking.

2. SPECIFICATIONS

*Engine :

(1)	Type :	2-stroke, Single Cylinder.
(2)	Piston Displacement :	88 cc. (5.39 cu inch)
(3)	Bore & Stroke :	50 mm × 45 mm (1.97 × 1.77 inch)
(4)	Compression Ratio :	6.8 : 1
(5)	Max. Brake Horse Power :	7.8 HP/7,000 rpm.
(6)	Max. Torque :	0.85 kg-m/5,000 rpm.
(7)	Air Intake System :	Rotary disc valve.
(8)	Starting System :	Kick Starter.
(9)	Charging System :	A. C. Magneto.
(10)	Ignition System :	Flywheel Magneto.
(11)	Ignition Timing :	22° before T. D. C.
(12)	Spark Plug :	N. G. K. B-7H.
(13)	Carburetor :	AMAL Type, VM 15 SC.
(14)	Fuel Mixture :	20 (gasoline) to 1 (motor oil SAE No. 30)
(15)	Transmission Oil :	0.6 litre (0.158 US gal.) in transmission case SAE No. 20 in winter or SAE No. 10W/30 in all seasons.

*Performance :

(1)	Max Speed :	95 km/h (60 mph)
(2)	Climbing Ability :	1 in 3
(3)	Fuel Consumption :	75 km/1 (177 mpg/20 mph) at 30 km/1 paved flat test road.
(4)	Min. Turning Radius :	1.8 m (70.8 inch).
(5)	Acceleration :	13.0 seconds (Standing start 0-200 m)
(6)	Braking Distance :	6 m at 35 km/h (20 feet, at 22 mph).

*Frame & Suspension :

(1)	Frame Type :	Pressed Steel, Backbone Type.
(2)	Front Suspension :	Telescopic Fork with Hydraulic Damper.
(3)	Rear Suspension :	Swinging Arm with Hydraulic Damper.

*Transmission:

- (1) Clutch : Manual, Multiple discs in oil bath.
- (2) Transmission : 4 speed constant-mesh gear and foot control.
- (3) Gear Ratio : Primary (Herical Gear); 1 : 3.95

  Gear Box :   1st 1 : 2.77
                      2nd 1 : 1.72
                      3rd 1 : 1.23
                      4th 1 : 0.924

  Secondary (Chain) :   1 : 2.43

  Total Gear Ratio :   1st 1 : 26.58
                                  2nd : 1 : 16.51
                                  3rd : 1 : 11.81
                                  4th : 1 : 8.86

*Dimensions, Weight:

- (1) Overall Length : 1,830 mm (72.0 inch)
- (2) Overall Width : 660 mm (26.0 inch)
- (3) Overall Height : 970 mm (38.1 inch)
- (4) Saddle Height : 750 mm (29.5 inch)
- (5) Wheel base : 1,160 mm (45.7 inch)
- (6) Road Clearance : 150 mm (5.9 inch)
- (7) Tire Size (Front) : 2.50-17, 4 ply
             (Rear) : 2.50-17, 4 ply
- (8) Tire Pressure (Front) : 1.6 kg/cm^2 (22.8 lbs/in^2)
             (Rear) : 2.0 kg/cm^2 (28.4 lbs/in^2)
- (9) Caster : 63°
- (10) Trail : 80 mm (3.15 inch)
- (11) Banking Angle : 45°
- (12) Dry Weight : 79 kg (174 lbs)
- (13) Fuel Tank Capacity : 7.0 l (1.85 US gal.)
  Including 1 litre (0.264 US gal.) reserve
- (14) Front Brake : Right Hand
- (15) Rear Brake : Right Foot

*Electrical Equipment :

- (1) Head light : 6V-15/15W
- (2) Tail light : 6V-3W
- (3) Stop light : 6V-8W
- (4) Battery : 6V-4AH

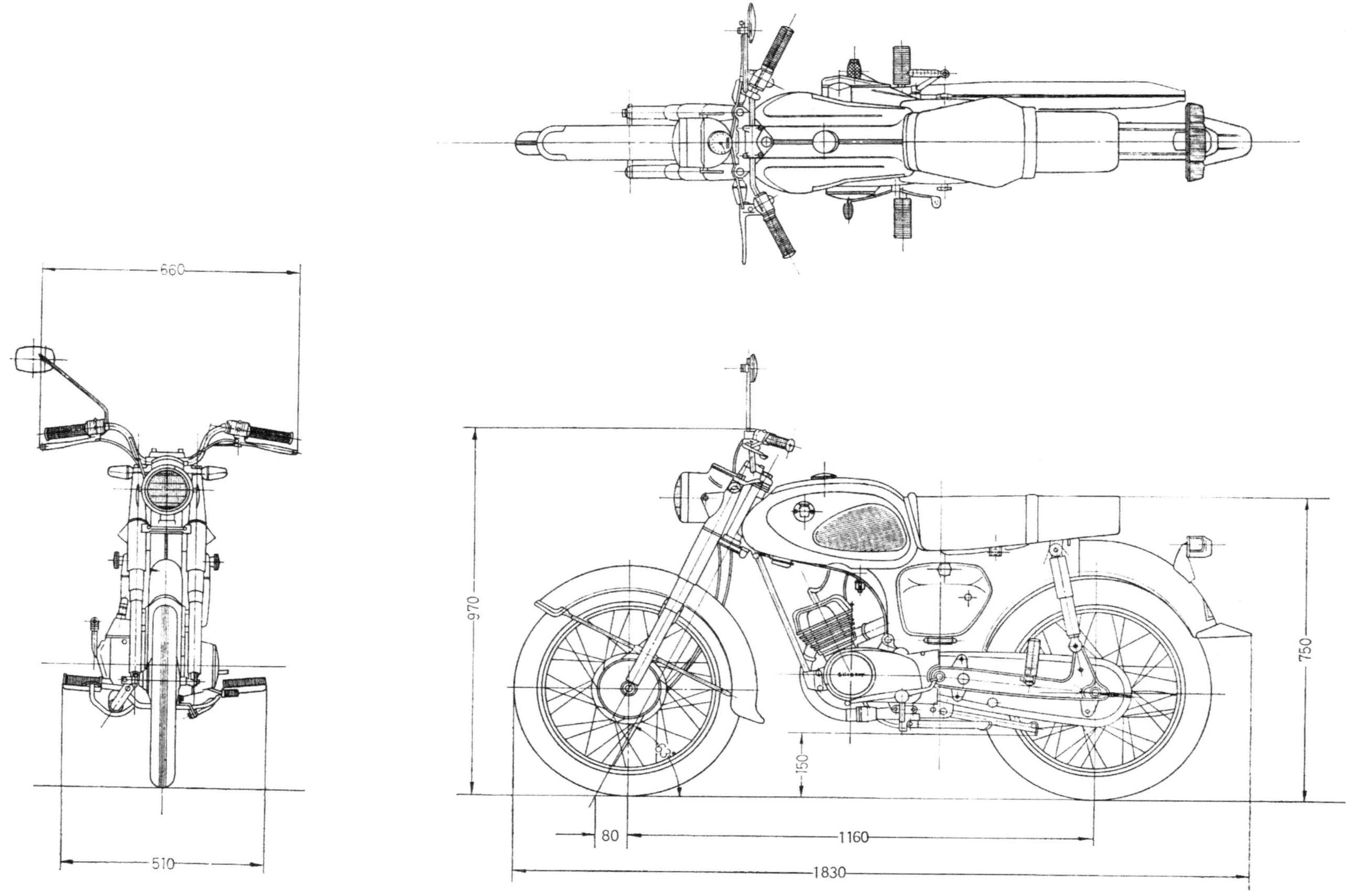

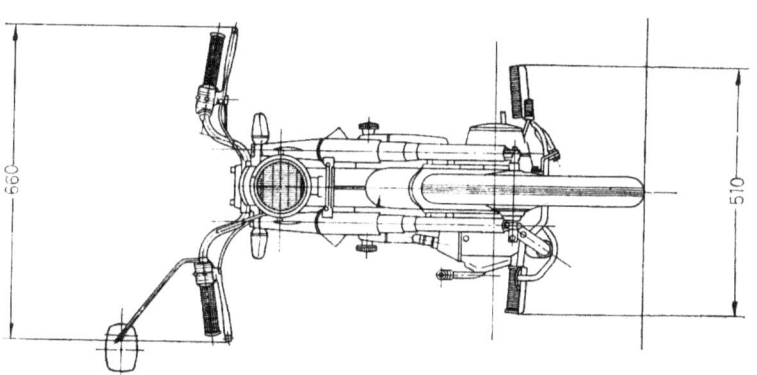

Top, side and front views of "BRIDGESTONE 90"

3. PERFORMANCE CURVE

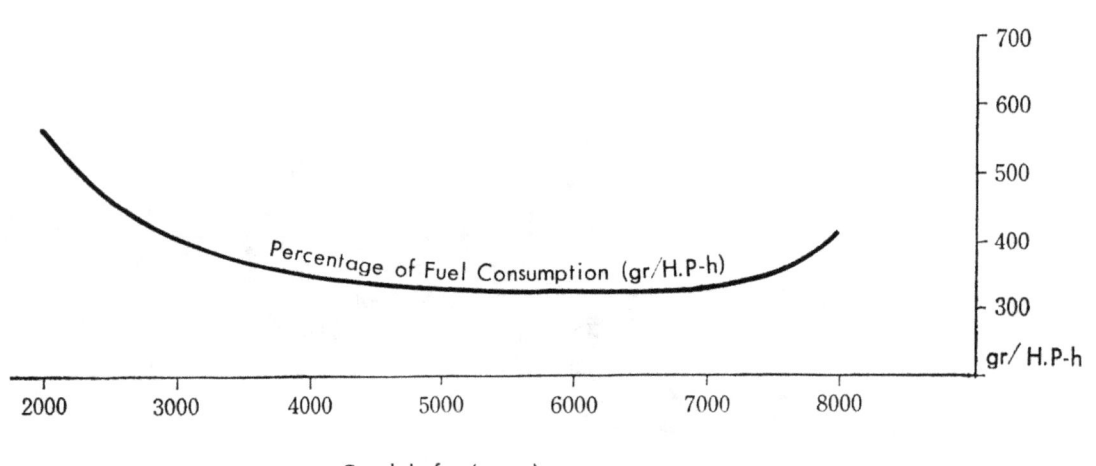

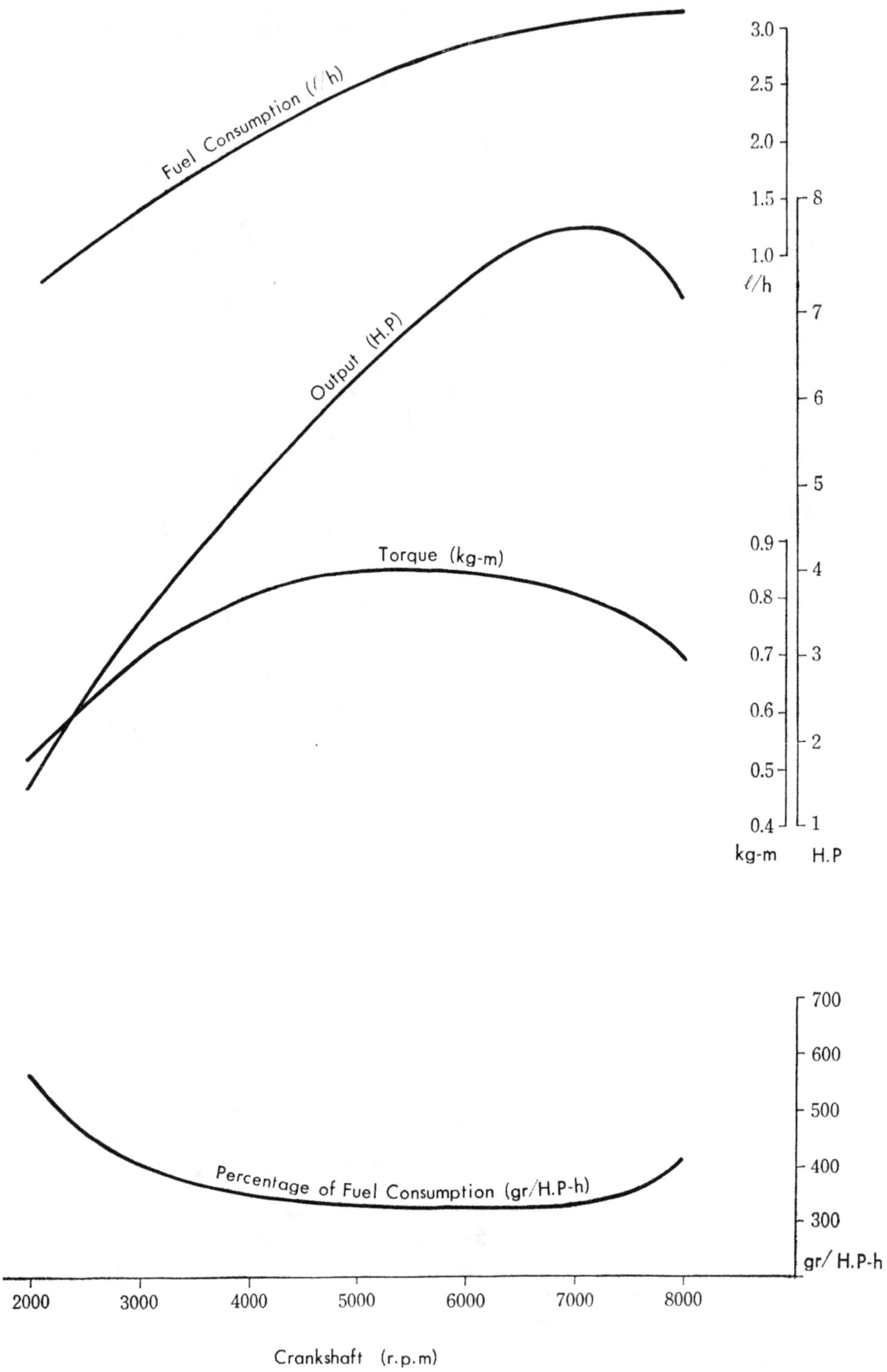

ENGINE/ROAD SPEED

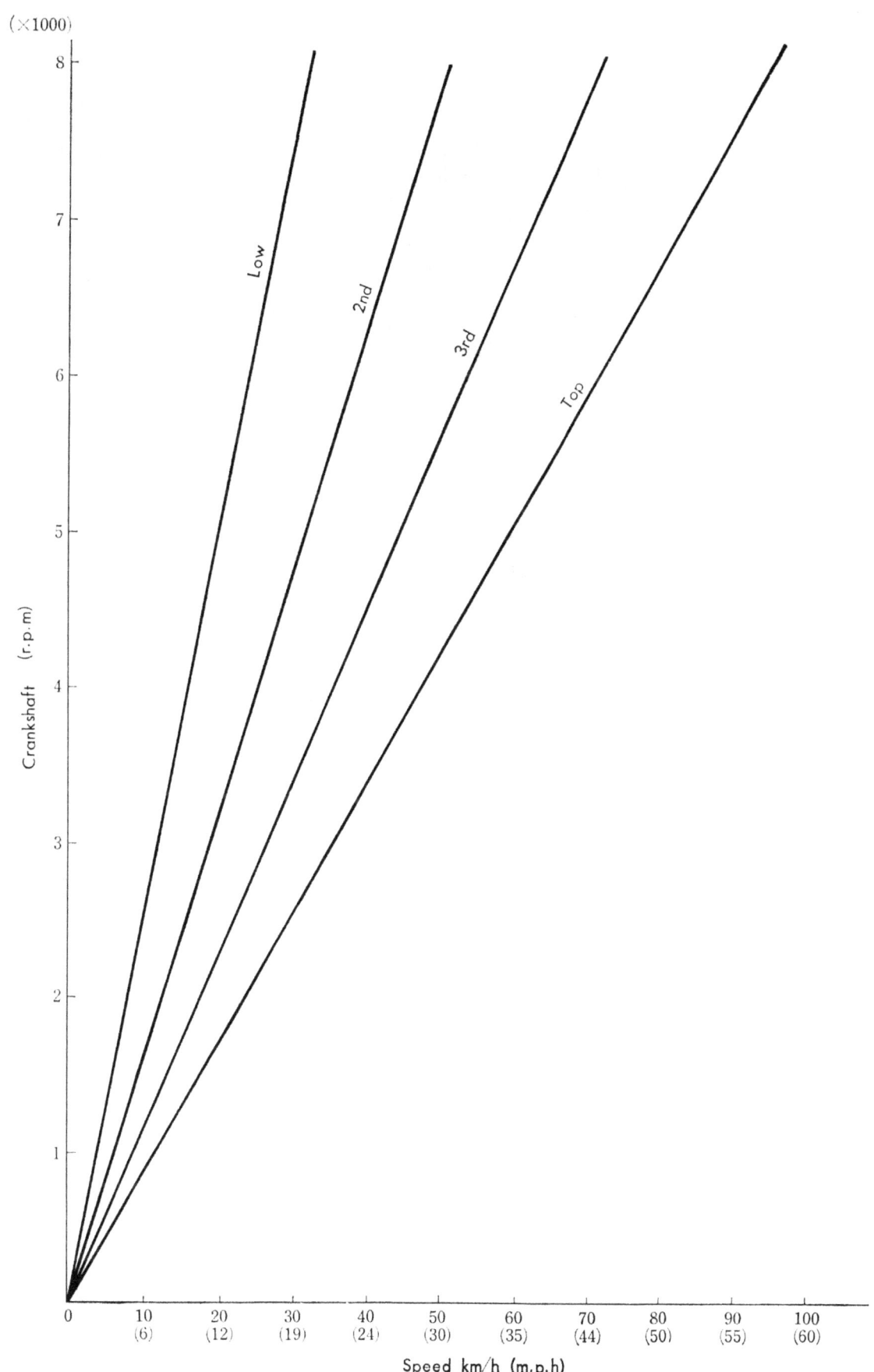

4. CROSS SECTION OF ENGINE

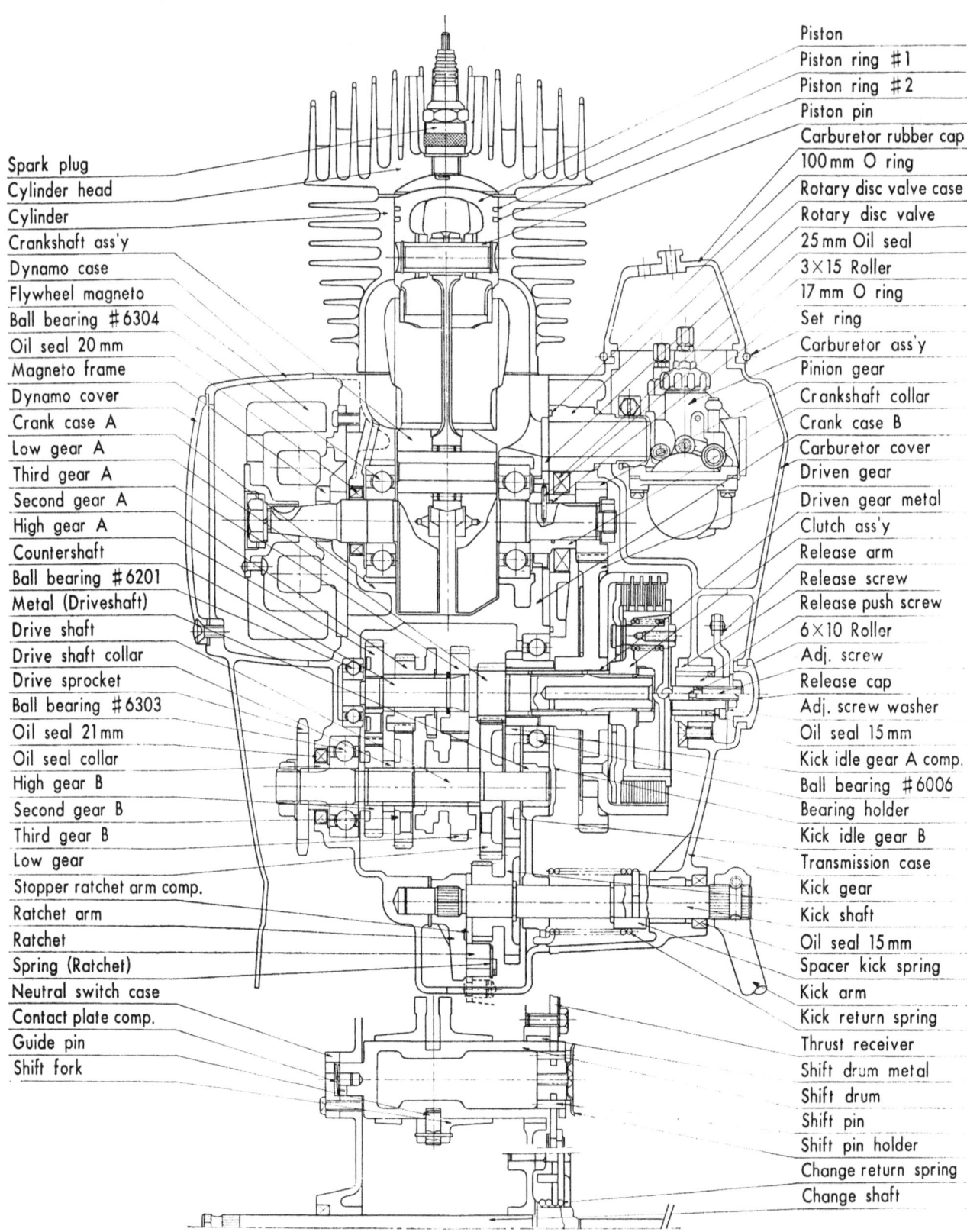

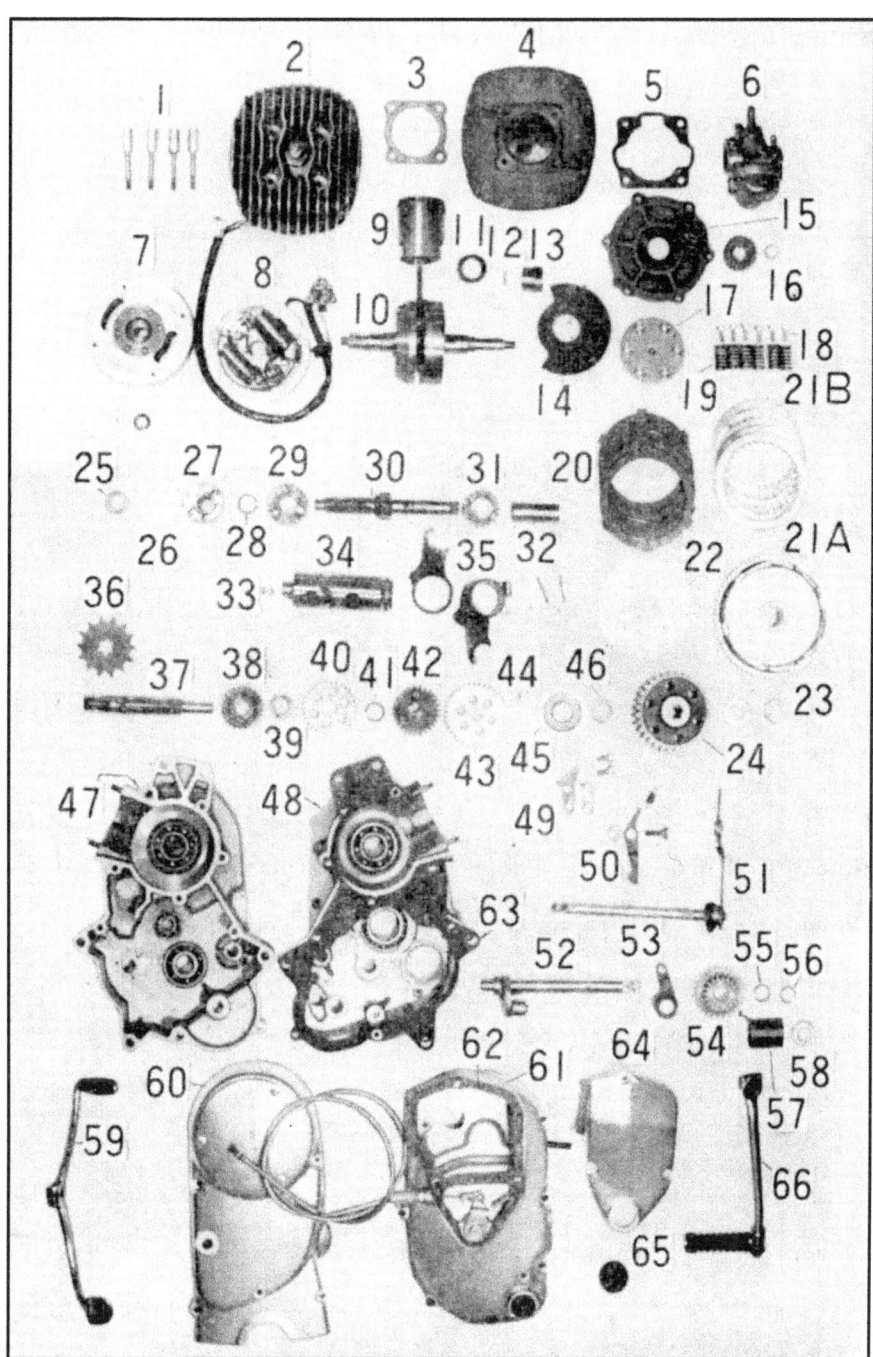

Engine Components

1. Nut (Cylinder Head)
2. Cylinder Head
3. Gasket (Cylinder)
4. Cylinder
5. Packing (Cylinder)
6. Carburetor Ass'y.
7. Flywheel
8. Frame Ass'y.
9. Piston
10. Crankshaft Ass'y.
11. Shim
12. 3×15 Roller
13. Crankshaft Collar
14. Rotary Valve Complete
15. Rotary Valve Case
16. Pinion Gear
17. Set Plate
18. 5×15 mm Hex. Bolt
19. Clutch Spring
20. Clutch Facing
21. A Clutch Outer Plate
    B Clutch Inner Plate
22. Pressure Plate
23. Driven Gear Complete
24. Clutch Braket
25. 12 mm Thrust Washer
26. Top Gear A
27. Second Gear A
28. Circlip 17 mm
29. Third Gear A
30. Countershaft
31. Kick Idll Gear A
32. Idle Gear Metal
33. Contact Plate
34. Shift Drum
35. Shift Fork
36. Drive Sprocket
37. Drive Shaft
38. High Gear B
39. Drive Shaft Collar
40. Second Gear B
41. Circlip 17 mm
42. Third Gear B
43. Low Gear B
44. 13 mm Thrust Washer
45. Kick Idle Gear B
46. 13 mm Thrust Washer
47. Crank Case A
48. Crank Case B
49. Thrust Receiver
55. Drum Stopper
51. Changeshaft Complete
52. Kick Shaft
53. Stopper Ratchet Arm
54. Kick Gear
55. Circlip 15 mm
56. Circlip 15 mm
57. Kick Return Spring
58. Spacer Kick Spring
59. Change Pedal
60. Dynamo Case
61. Transmission Case
62. Packing (Carburetor Cover)
63. Packing (Crank Case)
64. Carburetor Cover
65. Release Cap
66. Kick Arm

4. 1 Dismounting and Mounting Engine in Frame:

A. Care to be observed

(1) Be careful not to damage the insulation of the various lead wires.

(2) Be careful not to damage the frame or engine when handling bolts, nuts and tools.

B. Dismounting Engine:

(1) Tools necessary.

(2) Remove two hexagonal bolts (8×32) of the down tube (frame stay), loosen hexagonal bolt (8×32) at the top of down tube, and push tube forward (Fig. 2).

(3) Remove clamp nut of exhaust pipe with a clamp nut removing tool and remove exhaust pipe and gasket.

(4) Let clutch cable adjuster have full play and remove cable from the clutch lever. (Fig. 3 & 4)

(5) Remove hexagonal bolt (6×25) of kick arm and detach kick arm.

(6) Remove fuel pipe from the side of cock after shutting of fuel cock.

(7) Remove rubber cap from carburetor by pulling it up.

(8) Remove carburetor cover by removing one (6×25) and three (6×14) bolts.

(9) Pull out carburetor by removing rubber plug using a driver. (Fig. 5)

(10) Take off side cover on left side of frame, remove battery rubber band, disconnect ⊕ and ⊖ terminals of battery, and remove battery.

(11) Disconnect main switch lead wires and flywheel magneto wires from the terminals.

(12) Remove high-tension terminal plug cap from spark plug.

(13) Take off change pedal by removing hexagonal bolt (6×20) of change pedal. (Fig. 7)

(14) Take off dynamo case by removing three (6×35) and two (6×25) dynamo case fitting screws.

(15) Remove two (6×10) screws on lower half of chain case.

(16) Remove chain connector link and lift the chain off the drive sprocket. Join up the chain temporarily so that the connector will not get lost.

(17) Place a block (support) under the engine, remove one (3×114) footrest bolt, one (8×106) and one (8×102) hexagonal bolts, then pull out the engine. (Fig. 8)

Fig. 1. Tools necessary.

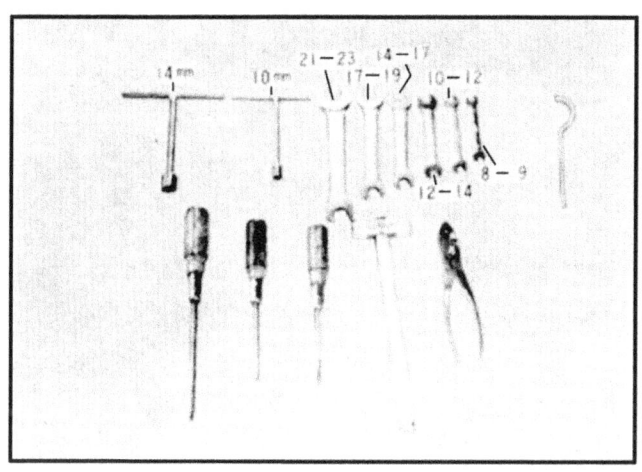

Fig. 2. Pushing away down tube (stay).

Fig. 3. Clutch cable adjuster.

Fig. 4. To remove clutch cable first pull and then detach.

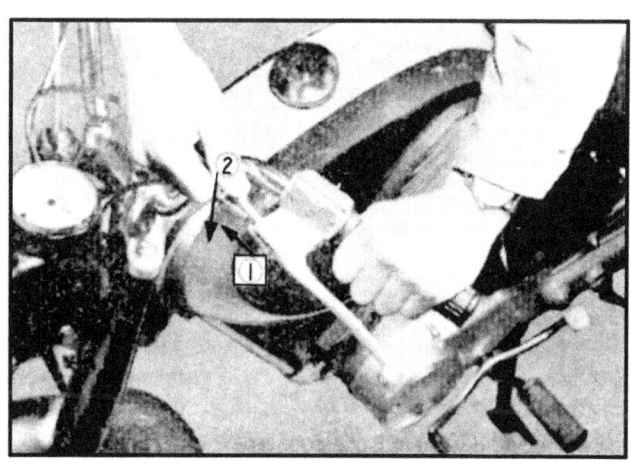

Fig. 5. Pulling out carburetor.

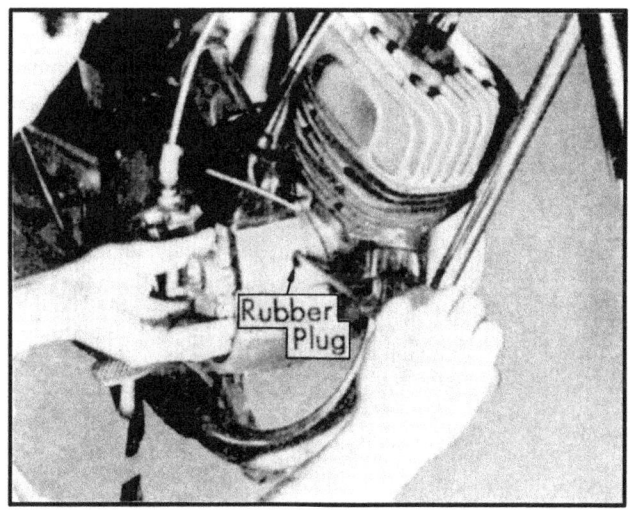

Fig. 6. Removing battery.

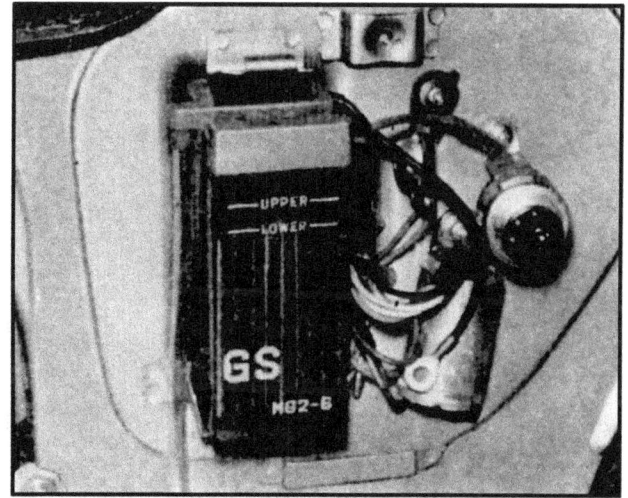

Fig. 7. Taking off change pedal.

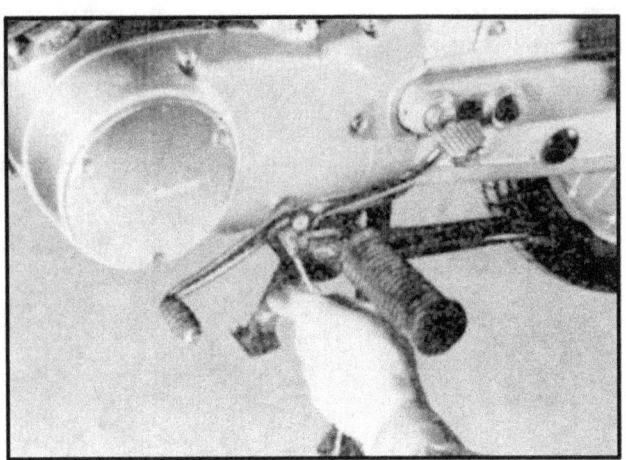

Fig. 8. Dismounting engine

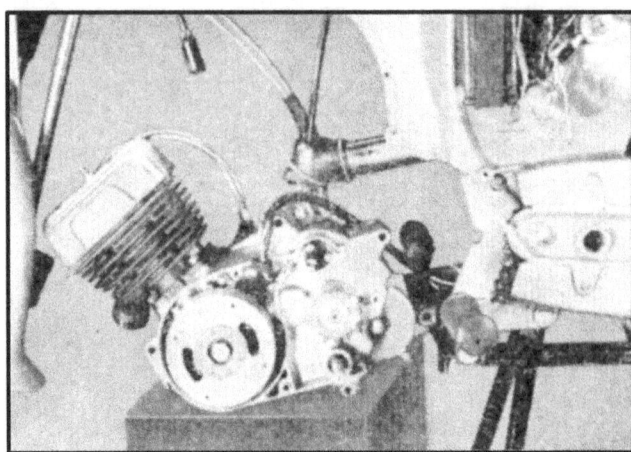

Fig. 9. Link of chain connector

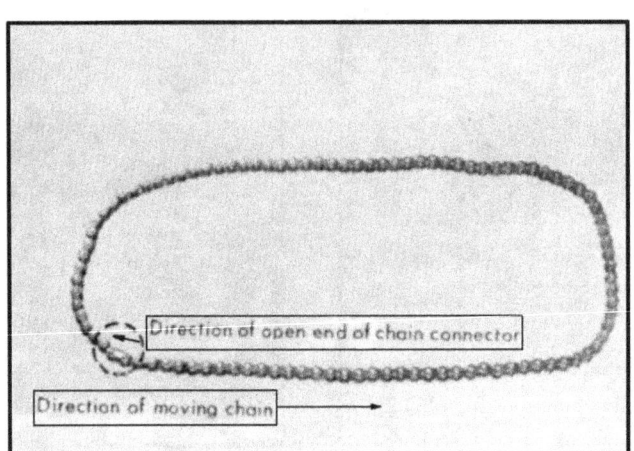

Fig. 10. Tools for Removing.

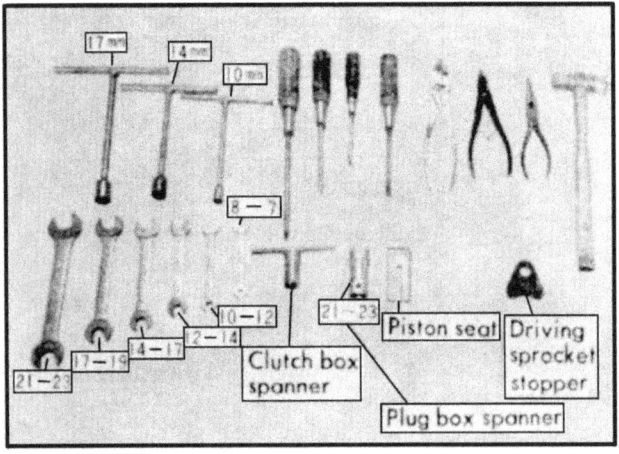

Fig. 11. Remove cylinder head.

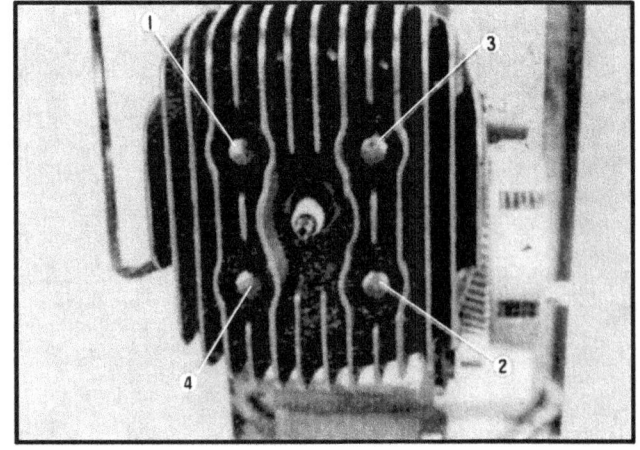

C. Mounting Engine:

(1) The engine should be installed in the reverse order of removal.

(2) To mount easily, first push in the upper rear part of engine's back part by raising the front slightly. Then return the engine to horizontal position and push in the back part.

* Be careful of the following points:

a) The chain connector should be linked with the open end pointing in the reverse direction of the moving chain. (Fig. 9)

b) Mount the carburetor securely.

c) See that the throttle valve works properly.

d) Set the clutch wire correctly.

e) See that the clutch works properly.

f) See that gas does not leak from the exhaust pipe and muffler joint.

g) See that all nuts, bolts and screws are tightened firmly.

h) See that the transmission is filled with the proper amount (0.6 litre = 0.158 U. S. gallons) of oil.

4. 2 Disassembling and Assembling Engine:

A. Matters that require special attention when disassembling and assembling engine.

(1) When removing or installing, use a wooden or plastic hammer and tap lightly and uniformly so as not to strain any part. (4. 2B. 20-25)

(2) When handling bolts, nuts, screws, tools, etc., exercise great care so that the component parts of gear, case, piston, cylinder etc. are not damaged or lost.

(3) When disassembling, take careful note of the position of the meshing gears and location of the many washers, and lay the parts out in an orderly manner, so that they may not get mislaid or confused when assembling.

(4) Be careful not to damage the case to prevent leakage of oil.

(5) Handling of the respective parts should be carried out carefully and neatly.

(6) The parts should be carefully cleaned.

B. Disassembling Engine:

(1) Tools required for disassembling engine. (Fig. 10)

(2) Loosen and remove diagonally four nuts of the cylinder head and remove cylinder head and gasket. (Fig. 11)

(3) Remove four hexagonal nuts holding down the cylinder, lift up cylinder gently, and remove cylinder packing. (Fig. 12).

(4) Place the "piston seat" under the piston, turn magneto section upward and remove magneto flywheel nut. Then pull out magneto flywheel with the magneto puller. (Fig. 13)

(5) Remove three (5×12) neutral switch screws, then the neutral switch and contact plate.

(6) Remove three (5×12) magneto frame screws and remove magneto frame. (Be careful to keep in mind the location where the magneto frame should be installed.)

(7) Loosen drain bolt on the under side of the engine and drain out transmission oil.

(8) Face upward the transmission case, take off transmission case by removing five (6×55), one (6×45) and two (6×35) screws.

(9) Remove diagonally and evenly the six (5×14) hexagonal bolts of the clutch set plate. (Fig. 14).

(10) Flatten the lock washer of the clutch setting nut, engage transmission with first gear, fit stopper (special tool) to the drive sprocket, and then remove the clutch assembly with 23 mm. box spanner. (Fig. 15)

(11) Flatten the lock washer of drive sprocket bolt, fit sprocket stopper and then remove drive sprocket with 23 mm. box spanner. (Fig. 15)

(12) Remove pinion gear with clutch box spanner (special tool), which can also be used for BS-50 and BS-7 models.
(Be careful of left-hand thread screw).

(13) Remove kick spacer and take out kick return spring. (Fig. 16)

(14) Remove drum stopper with 12 mm. wrench, and detach spring which is attached to drum stopper and case. (Fig. 17).

(15) Flatten the lock plate of thrust receiver and remove two (6×14) hexagonal bolts.

Fig. 12. Remove Cylinder

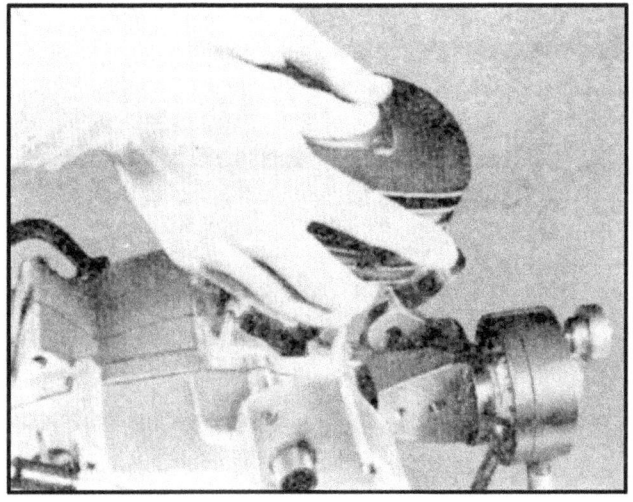

Fig. 13. Remove magneto flywheel

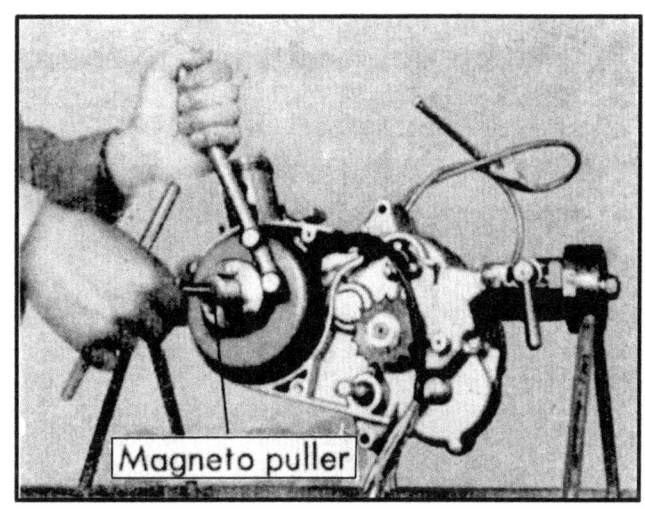

Fig. 14. Removing six bolts of clutch

Fig. 15. Fitting stopper to the drive sprocket

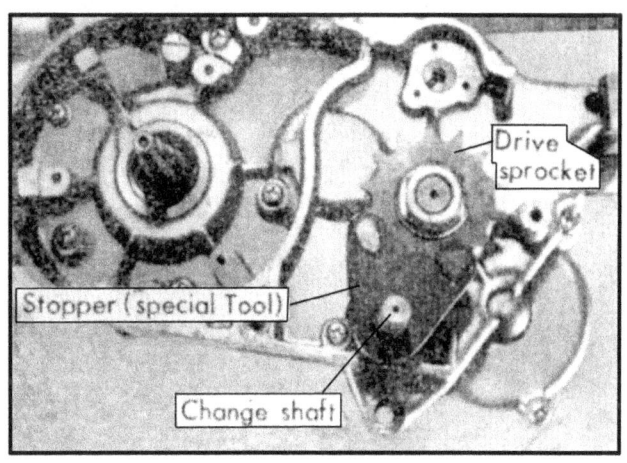

Fig. 16. Removing kick spacer and kick return spring.

Fig. 17. Mechanism of drum shifter

(16) Remove drum shifter from shift drum, and pull out change shaft assembly.

(17) Take off rotary valve cover by unscrewing six (6×20) valve cover screws. (Fig. 18).

(18) Pull out rotary disc valve.

(19) Remove crankshaft collar and knock out 3×15 pin.

(20) Face the magneto upward, unscrew four (6×45), four (6×55) and one (6×25) crank case A screws, and remove crank case.

(21) Take out the gears together with shift drum, counter shaft and drive shaft, as a unit, (Fig. 19).

(22) Face the transmission case upward, remove kick shaft circlip, and take kick shaft out of crank case.

(23) Remove kick idle gear A from crank case B.

(24) Remove gears from counter shaft and drive shaft.

(25) Take crankshaft assembly out of crank case B. (Be careful not to damage the lip of oil seal.)

(26) Remove packing of each case.

C. Inspection:

After dismantling, inspect each part comparing it with servicing standards.

D. Assembling Engine:

(1) The engine should be assembled in the reverse order of disassembling.

(2) When installing shift drum, connect spring first with case and stopper and then tighten stopper screw bolt. (Fig. 20, 21)

(3) After engine has been completely assembled, the point gap and ignition timing should be adjusted.
(Refer to P. 60 for adjustment procedure.)

SERVICE MEMO:

Fig. 18. Rotary Valve Cover

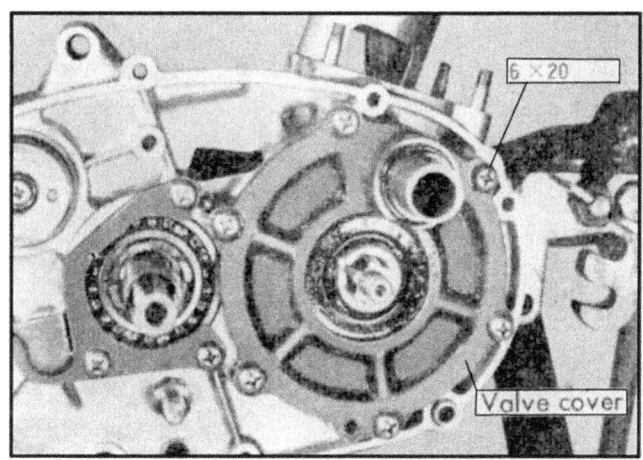

Fig. 19. Take out the gears.

Fig. 20. Connecting drum stopper spring

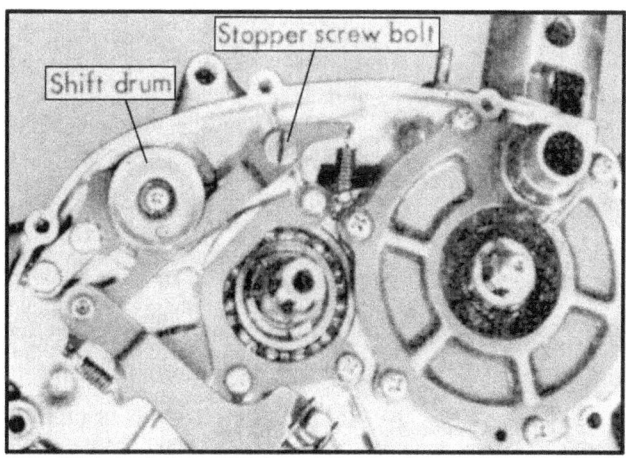

Fig. 21. Inserting stopper screw bolt

5. CONSTRUCTION OF ROTARY DISC VALVE ENGINE:

A. Description:

(1) The engine is a rotary disc valve type, in which a disc valve with a section cut out for fuel and air intake into the cylinder, is attached to the crankshaft and rotates with it (Fig. 22 & 23)

Fig. 22. Cross section of rotary disc valve engine

Fig. 23. Component parts of rotary disc valve

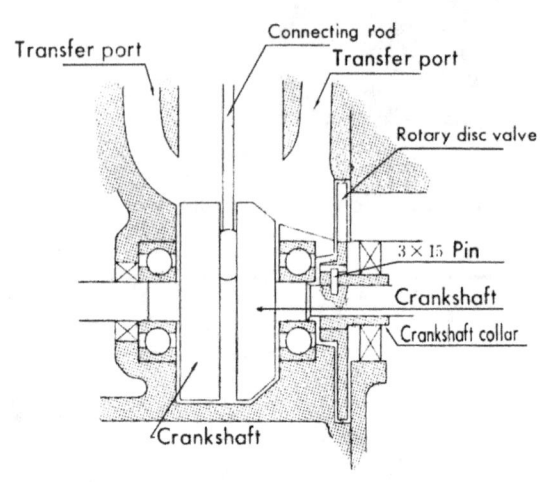
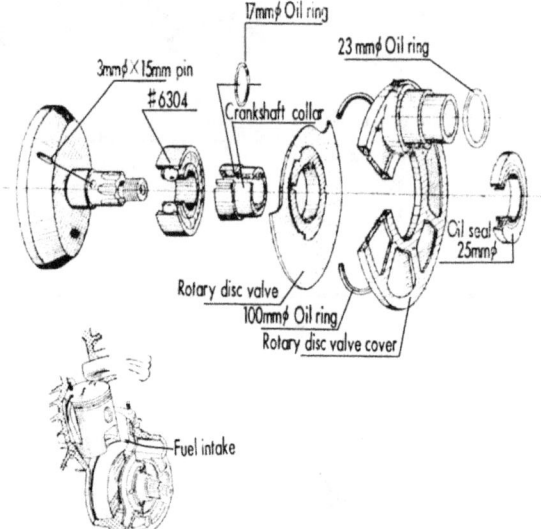

In the conventional piston valve type engine, suction of the fuel is limited by the position of piston at top dead center, whereas the timing of the Bridgestone rotary disc valve engine is determined solely by the size and shape of the cut-out area of the valve, and thus a better suction is obtained, and back flow of raw fuel to carburetor as in the case of piston valve engines in which the piston cuts off the intake port in its descent, is prevented.

Fuel consumption is thereby decreased and engine performance greatly improved.

2) Construction:

(1) The rotary disc valve is made of heat hardening phenol resin and the thickness of disc is 3 mm. (0.0118 inch)

(2) The disc valve is a sliding fit on the crankshaft, secured by a 3 mm. stop pin.
The bushing of the valve is of cast metal.

(3) Compression of the fuel is maintained by the disc valve rotating with the crankshaft closing the intake port and shifting tightly against the rotary valve cover fitted with O ring.

B. Rotary Disc Valve Timing:

Fig. 24. Start of intake:
107° before Top Dead Centre

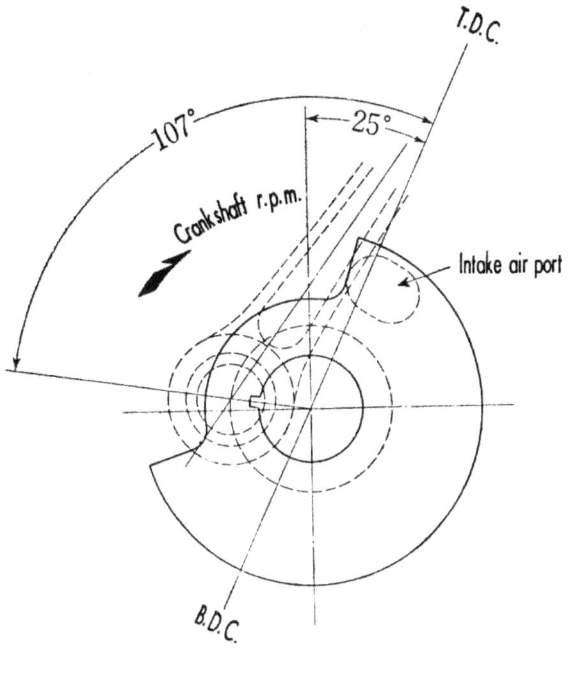

Fig. 25. Closing of intake:
49° after Top Dead Centre

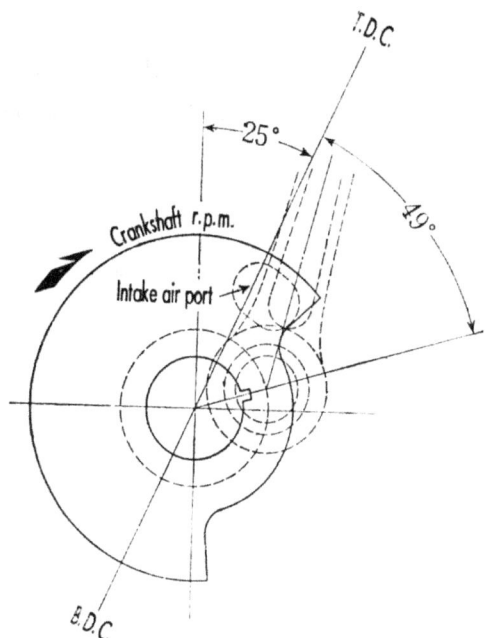

C. Disassembling:

Remove rotary disc valve according to the procedure described in earlier paragraphs (17, 18 and 19 of 4. 2. B).

D. Inspection:

1) Check to see if lip of oil seals is damaged or ineffective and replace if necessary.
2) Check whether O rings are damaged and replace if necessary.

E. Assembling:

1) Assembling can be performed in the reverse order of disassembling.
2) Fit 17 ⌀mm. O ring to inner side of crank shaft collar and 100 ⌀mm O ring into groove of valve cover.

SERVICE MEMO:

6. CONSTRUCTION OF CYLINDER AND PISTON:

A. Description:

A-1. Cylinder:

The cylinder is of high-grade cast iron and accurately finished by honing.

In the piston valve engine, the fuel is drawn through the intake port from the carburetor which is located outside, the flow being dependent upon the action of the piston, and therefore limited.

In the case of the rotary disc valve engine, the carburetor is encased in the transmission case and therefore no intake port in the cylinder is required, the intake of fuel being controlled by the opening and closing of the rotary valve.

Instead of the intake port, however, a third transfer or "boost" port is provided to obtain better scavenging. (Fig. 26 & 27)

Fig. 26. Fuel intake system.   **Fig. 27.** Cross section cylinder.

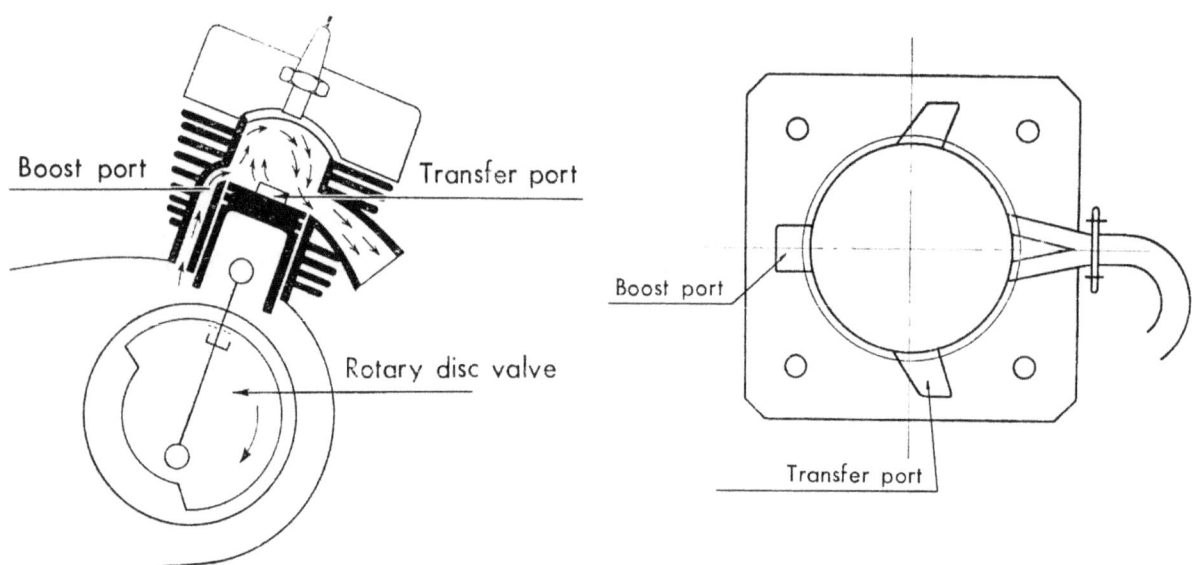

A-2. Piston:

The piston is of high silcon aluminum alloy with a low coefficient expansion and light specific gravity, and it has excellent wearing and heat proof qualities. (Fig. 28)

Note: The mark "EX" is cast on top of piston to correspond with the exhaust port.

Fig. 28. Piston

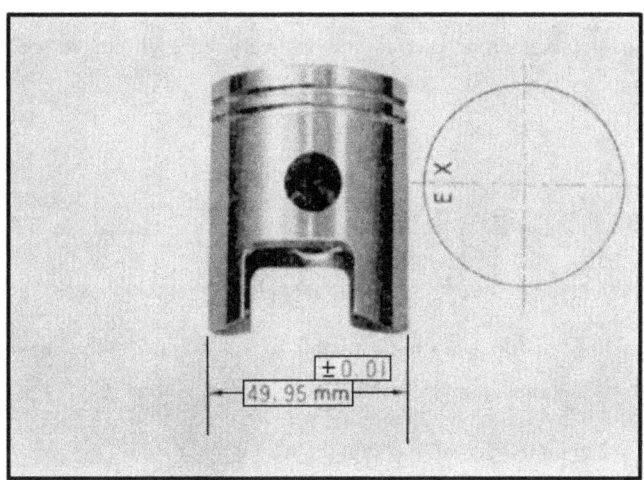

A-3. Clearance between Piston and Cylinder Wall.

The standard clearance between piston and cylinder wall is 0.09 mm.—0.11 mm. $\left(\frac{3.54}{1,000} - \frac{4.33}{1,000} \text{ inch}\right)$. (Fig. 29)

Fig. 29. Clearance between piston and cylinder wall

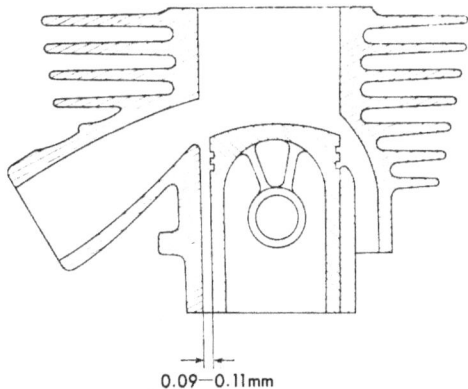

0.09—0.11mm

B. Disassembling.

(1) The cylinder can be taken off without removing engine from the frame. Disconnect high tension terminal and plug cap from spark plug and detach exhaust pipe by removing exhaust pipe clamp nut with a special tool.

(2) Take off cylinder head nut and remove cylinder head and gasket.

(3) Remove the hexagonal nut at four places at bottom of cylinder and remove cylinder gently lifting it.

(4) Before removing piston, cover the crank case opening with cloth to prevent dirt from entering into the crank case and then remove piston pin circlips.

(5) Remove piston pin with puller (special tool) and detach piston from connecting rod. (Be careful connectiing rod is not forced left or right.)

(6) Remove piston rings from piston and be very careful not to damage the rings or the piston.

C. Assembling :

(1) Replace piston rings on piston.

(2) The "EX" mark on the piston head should correspond with the exhaust port.

(3) Before inserting piston pin, heat piston in an oil bath to about 120°C (248°F.). Piston pin should be gently pushed in with the finger.

(4) Insert piston pin circlips at both ends of piston pin hole.

(5) After oiling with engine oil the cylinder wall and piston, set piston at bottom dead center and pressing down the rings in the grooves, slide cylinder into place carefully.

(6) Insert cylinder gasket and fit cylinder head to cylinder.

(7) Fit high tension terminal plug cap to spark plug and put back exhaust pipe.

Fig. 30. Sliding cylinder into place.

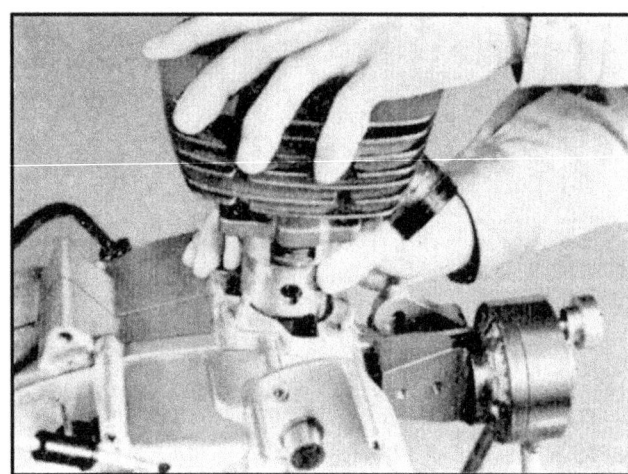

D. Cleaning :

Thoroughly scrub piston, piston rings and cylinder with gasoline or cleaning solvent to remove carbon deposits.

Pay particular attention to the cylinder intake and exhaust ports.

Where carbon deposit is heavy or hard, it is advisable to scrape it before cleaning. Use extreme care to avoid scratching the wall of the cylinder.

Clean piston ring grooves. After the parts are thoroughly washed, dry with compressed air. Force air through all passages in cylinder.

E. Inspection :

E-1. Insufficient Power :
(1) Rotate fly wheel with hand and if very little compression is felt, the cause may be either wear of piston rings or cylinder. Replace parts where necessary. (Refer to Service Standards Manual.)

(2) Check side clearance between piston and cylinder and see whether any part is damaged (such as burnt spots, stiff rings or scratches).

(Refer to Service Standards Manual.)

(3) Check for gas leakage through cylinder gasket and cylinder packing. Replace if unsatisfactory with new ones.

E-2. Knocking :
(1) Check clearance between piston skirt and cylinder wall. (Refer to Service Standards Manual).

(2) Check for tightness of piston pin. (Refer to Service Standards Manual).

SERVICE MEMO :

7. CLUTCH

A. Construction:

The clutch, which is of the wet multi-disc type, is mounted on the counter shaft of the transmission. It has five clutch friction discs and six clutch springs. The springs have the strength to withstand 50 kg. (110 lbs.)

Moreover, six shock absorbing damper rubber discs are attached to the driven gear.

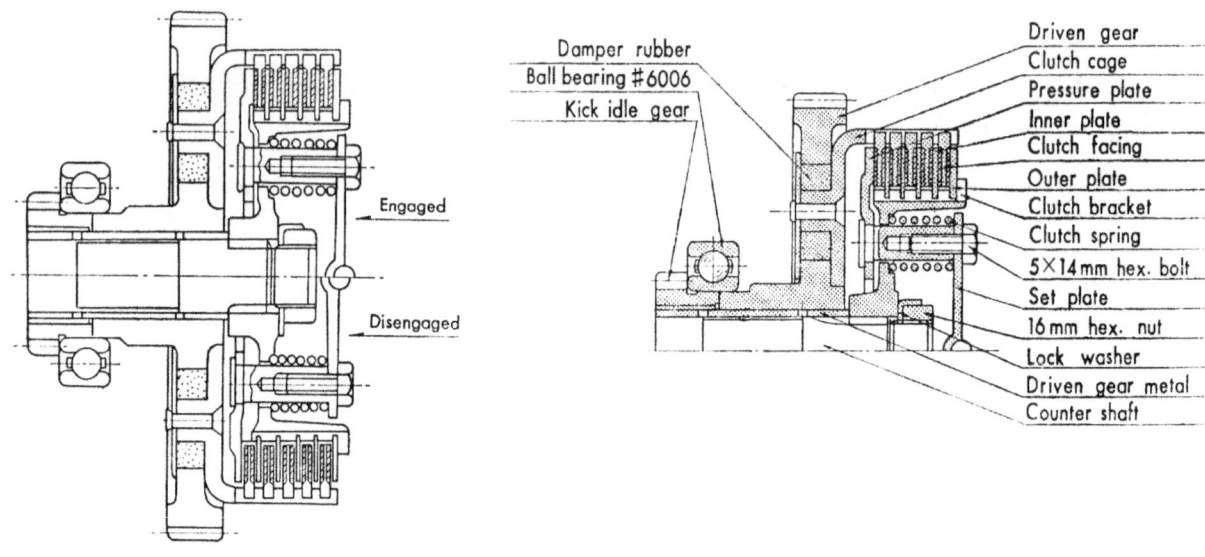

Fig. 31. General view of Clutch

Fig. 32. Sectional view of clutch

B. Clutch Functions:

The clutch is located between the engine and transmission to transmit or disconnect engine power.

Smooth transmission and cut-off of power is important especially in starting and gear changing.

B-1. Power Transmission:

The engine power is transmitted to the pinion on the crankshaft and the driven gear and rotates the clutch cage.

The clutch cage has six slots which hold in place the arms of the clutch facings, which, under pressure of the clutch springs cause the clutch inner and outer plates to come into solid contact and rotate as a unit.

The inner plates and outer plate fit into the spline of the clutch bracket, the clutch bracket fits into the spline of the countershaft, and the engine power is transmitted to the countershaft of transmission.

B-2. Cutting off the Engine Power:

When the clutch lever is depressed, the clutch wire lifts the release arm and the $6\phi \times 10$ roller, which is set by an adjusting screw, acts on the 7/32" ball of the clutch set plate.

When this set plate is pressed, the clutch springs are depressed and lose tension, causing the clutch discs to separate, cutting off engine power.

C. Clutch Adjustment:

(1) Adjustment is easily carried out with the cable adjuster.

(2) When satisfactory adjustment cannot be made in this way, remove rubber cap from carburetor cover, loosen lock nut with 10 mm. box spanner in the tool set, and adjust by holding down the lock nut and turning adjustment screw.

The play of the lever is lessened by turning the screw right and increased by turning left.

Fig. 33. Clutch Adjustment.

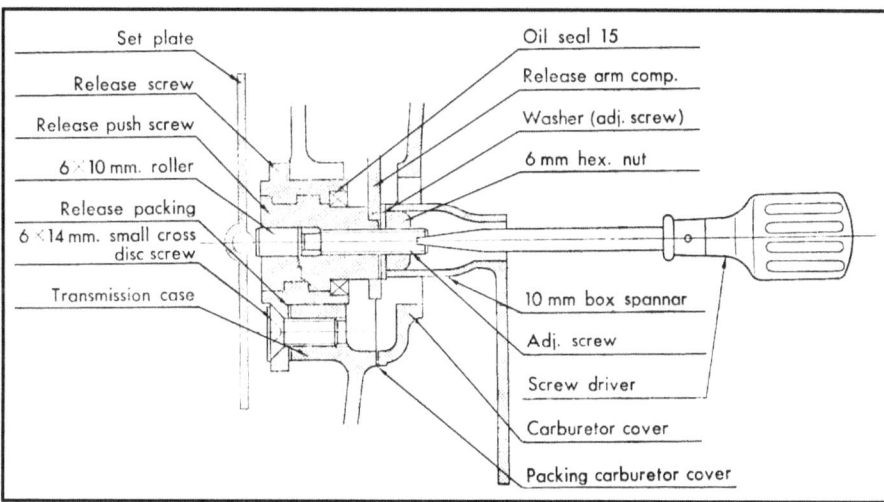

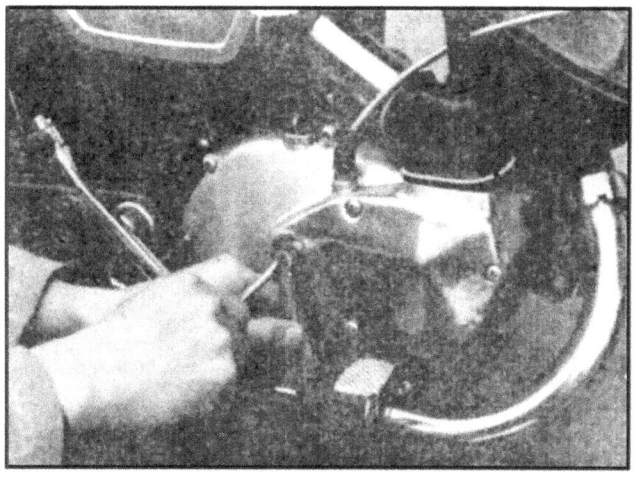

D. Disassembling Clutch:

(1) Follow procedure described under 4.2 B 8 for removing transmission case. (This work can be done by removing kick pedal, air pipe, carburetor cover and carburetor, without dismounting the engine.)

(2) Remove six (5×14) hexagonal clutch set plate bolts.

(3) Flatten lock washer of countershaft nut (16 mm. hexagonal nut), put transmission into first gear and insert a stopper in the drive sprocket, and remove clutch nut. (When engine is not dismounted from frame, remove nut after transmission is put into first gear and with the rear brake on.)

Fig. 34. Component parts of clutch.

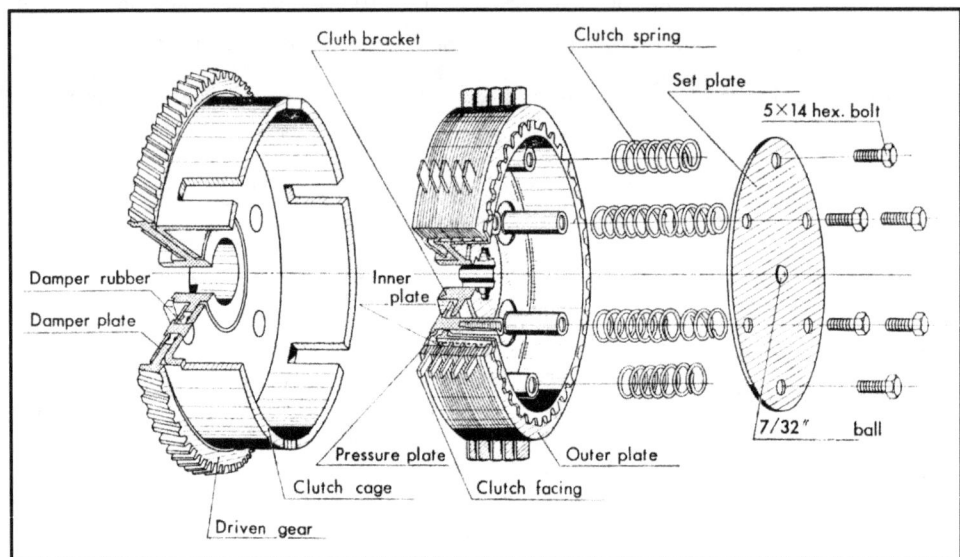

E. Assembling:

(1) Assembling can be done in the reverse order of disassembling.

(2) The facings and inner plates alternately contact with each other. The outer plate is thicker than the other plates.
(Thickness 2 mm. (0.012″)).

F. Inspection :

(1) See if there are any damaged serrations on the inner and outer plates, and worn or uneven plates.
(Refer to Service Standards Manual).

(2) Check for damaged arms on facings, worn on uneven.

(3) Check for irregularities in set plates, looseness of set bolts or weakened tension or breakage of return springs.
Adjust or replace any that are found to be unsatisfactory.

(4) Check release arm for wear, release screw, release push screw or 7/32" ball. Replace where necessary.

SERVICE MEMO :

8. TRANSMISSION

A. Construction:

The transmission is of the four-speed constant-mesh, rotary type, and all parts being encased in the transmission case, inspection is easy, and repair work and dismantling greatly facilitated.

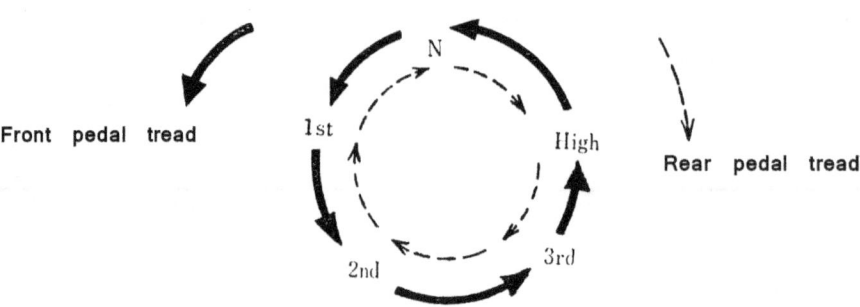

Fig. 35. Gear Shifting

B. Mechanism:

(1) The shift drum is maintained in a constant position by a thrust receiver. Pressing down the change pedal front or rear, the drum shifter on the change arm attached to the change shaft, turns the drum forward or backward one notch. The pedal is depressed approximately 11°, and as the drum rotates every 72°, the shift fork moves to left or right as the case may be, along the drum groove and clutch claws engage the corresponding sliding gears.

(2) Shift Arm Positions in Relation to Pedal Control.

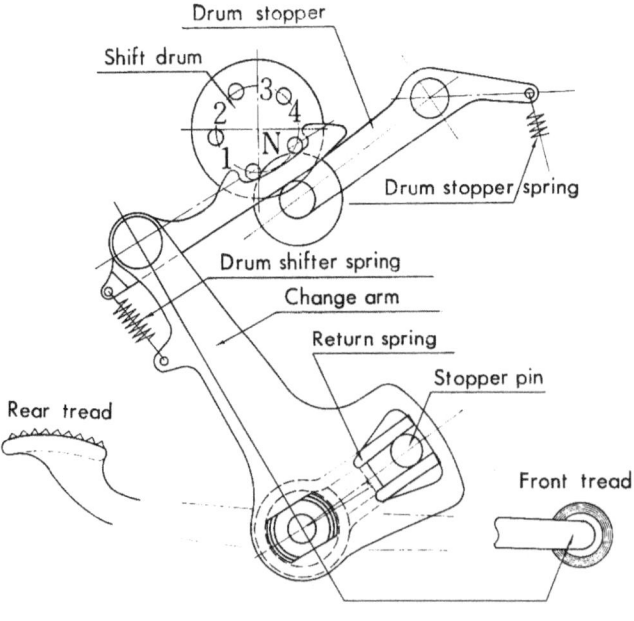

Fig. 36. Neutral Gear.

Fig. 37. Pedal pushed down front with foot once showing drum advanced one notch, (engaging 1st gear) 2nd, 3rd, High and Neutral follow in succession.

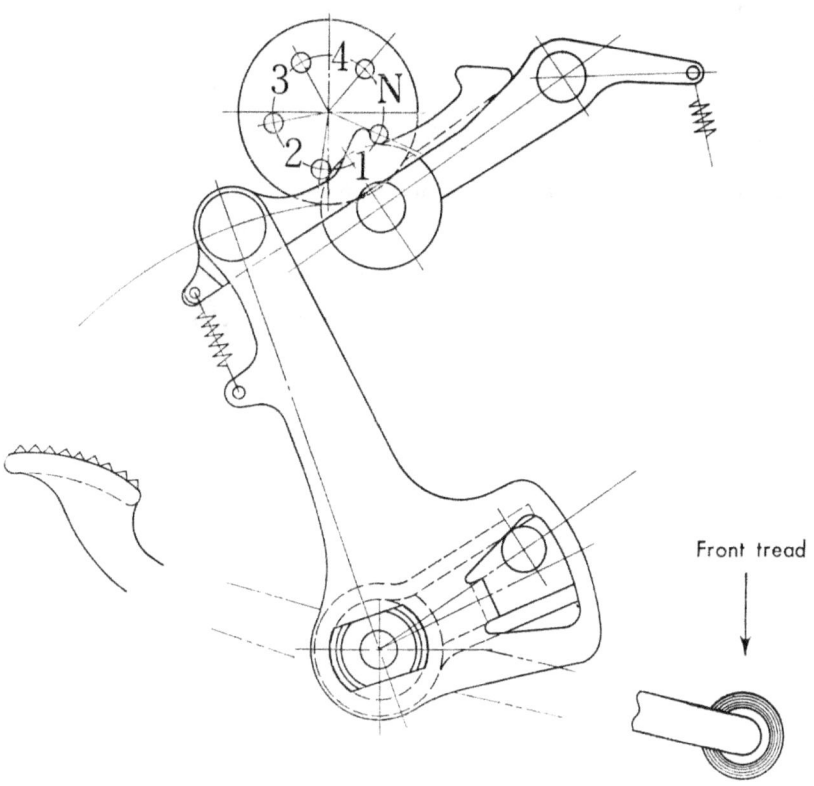

Fig. 38. Back pedal tread pushed down with foot once showing drum turned in the opposite direction and shifting gear in reverse.

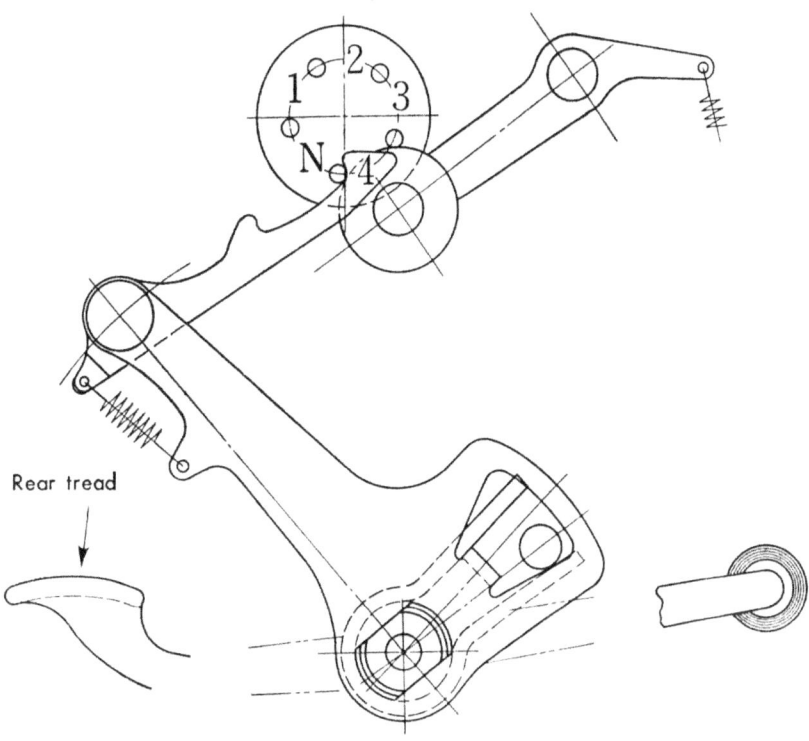

(3) Gear Manipulation and Gear Ratios.

NO. OF TEETH	COUNTERSHAFT	DRIVE SHAFT	TRANSMISSION GEAR RATIO
First Gear (Low Gear)	13	36	2.77
Second Gear	18	31	1.72
Third Gear	22	27	1.23
High Gear	26	24	0.924

The countershaft and First Gear A act as a unit, and Second Gear A slides on the countershaft spline. The Third Gear A and High Gear A turn freely on the countershaft. The Second Gear A engages with the dog claws on the Third Gear A and also with the High Gear A which has oval holes to engage the claws on the Second Gear.

The High Gear B and Third Gear B are spline fitted on the drive shaft. The Second Gear B and First Gear B turn freely on the drive shaft, and only Third Gear B slides both ways and engages with First Gear B or Second Gear B with claws.

Fig. 39. Transmission Mechanism in Neutral Gear Position.

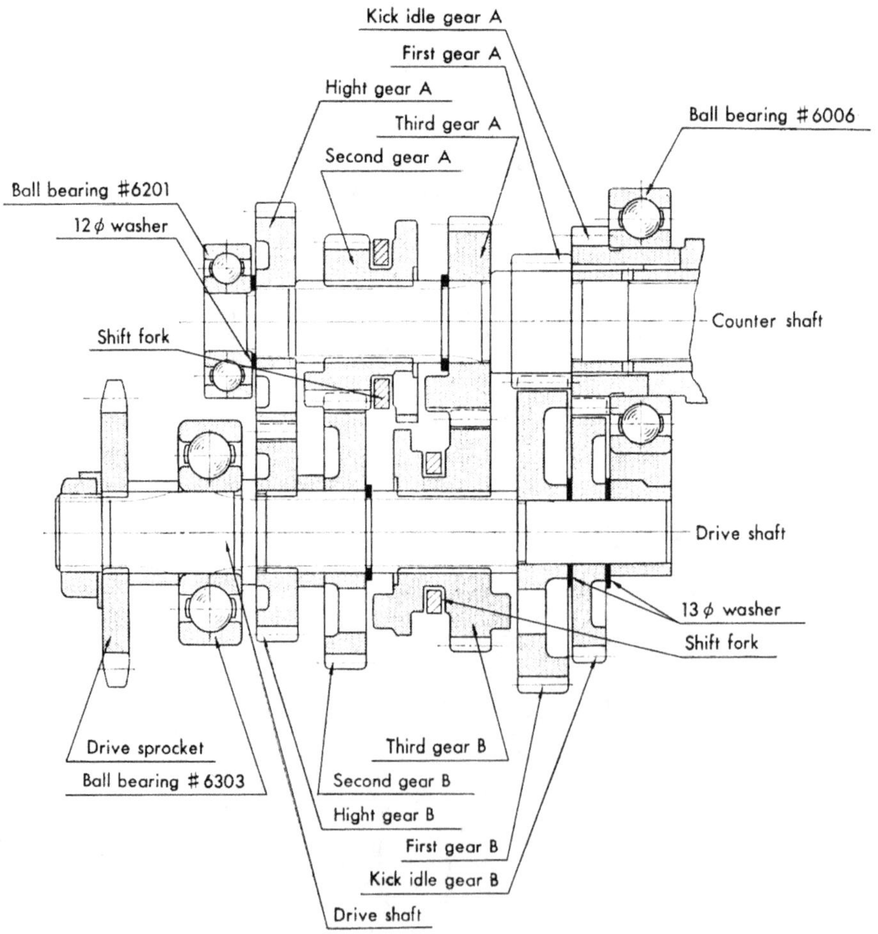

— 30 —

First Gear:

With the Second Gear A on the counter shaft remaining in position, the Third Gear B on the drive shaft slides to the right and the clutch claws engage with the First Gear B.

Engine power is transmitted in the order of driven gear—clutch—countershaft—First Gear A—First Gear B—Third Gear B—drive shaft and drive sprocket.

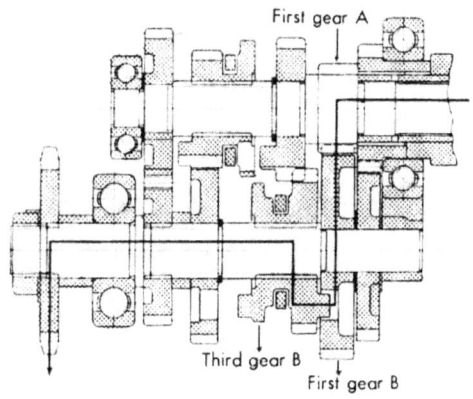

Fig. 40. In First Gear Position.

Second Gear:

The Second Gear A remaining in position the Third Gear B slides to the left and the clutch claws on this gear engage with the Second Gear B.

The engine power is transmitted in the order of driven gear—clutch—countershaft—Second Gear A—Second Gear B—Third Gear B—drive shaft and drive sprocket.

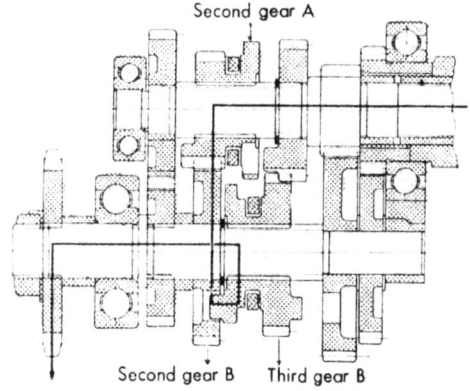

Fig. 41. In Second Gear Position.

Third Gear:

With the Third Gear B on the drive shaft remaining in position, the Second Gear A slides to the right and engages with the clutch claws on the Third Gear A.

The engine power is transmitted in the order of driven gear—clutch—countershaft—Second Gear A—Third Gear A—Third Gear B—drive shaft and drive sprocket.

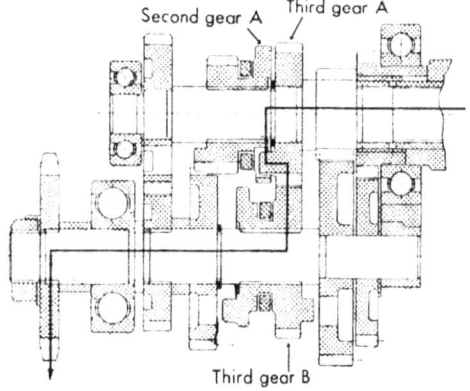

Fig. 42. In Third Gear Position

High Gear:

The Third Gear B remaining in position, the Second Gear A slides to the left and the dog teeth engage with the High Gear A.

The engine power is transmitted in the order of driven gear—clutch—countershaft—Second Gear A—High Gear A—High Gear B—drive shaft and drive sprocket.

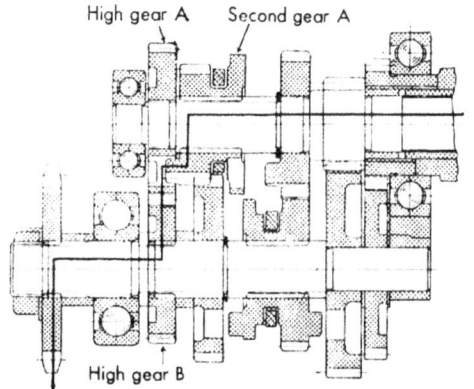

Fig. 43. In High Gear Position.

C. Disassembling:

Disassembling and assembling procedures are carried out in accordance with paragraph 4.2.

D. Inspection:

(1) Check for worn or damaged gears, splines, bearings and shafts.
(Refer to Service Standards Manual.)

(2) Inspect shift fork and drum grooves.
(Refer to Service Standards Manual)

SERVICE MEMO :

9. KICK STARTER

A. Construction:

On the Bridgestone 90, the new kick system (Primary Type) is equipped. In this method, the kick pedal can be used regardless of the transmission in any gear, by simply disengaging the clutch with the lever. It is therefore very convenient and the engine can be started quickly.

The kick Idle Gear A meshes with the driven gear, kick idle gear B meshes with kick idle gear A, and the kick gear meshes with kick idle gear B.

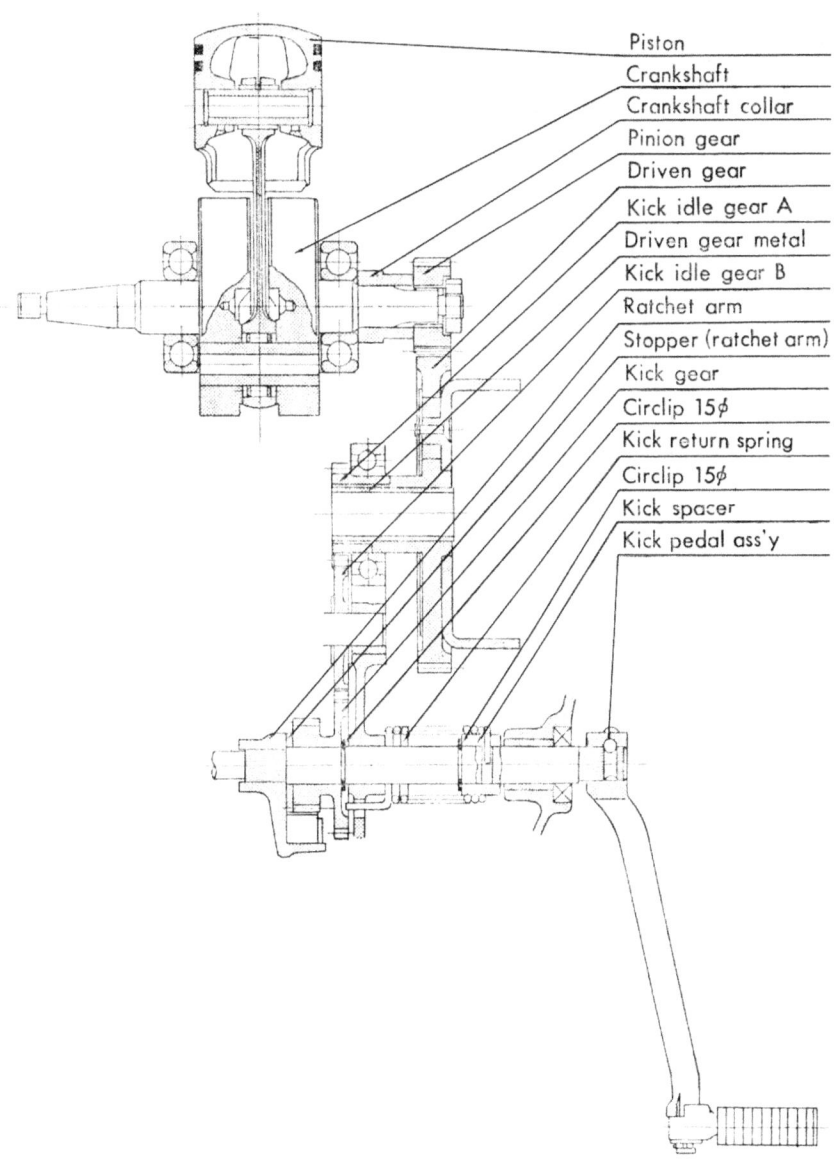

B. Operation:

B-1. In Cruising.

(1) Ratchet arm is turned counter clockwise, as shown, by the kick return spring.

(2) Ratchet is kicked up by the ratchet arm stopper counterwise as shown by arrow "B" in Fig. 45, and rachet and kick gear are held apart.

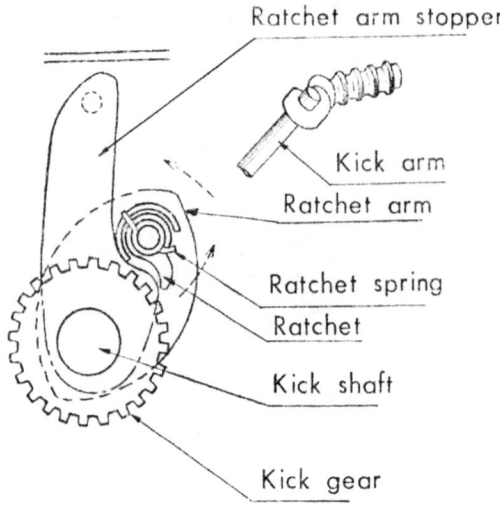

Fig. 44. In cruising position

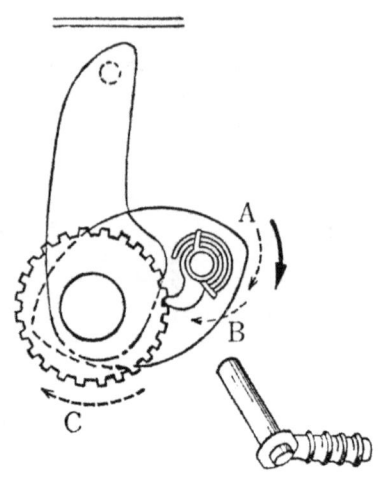

Fig. 45. In kicking position

B-2. To start

(1) Kick down kick-arm.

(2) Kick shaft and rachet arm turn clockwise as shown by arrow "A" in Fig. 45.

(3) Ratchet turns clockwise as shown by arrow "B" in Fig. 45, resulting from the pressure of ratchet spring, and mesh with the kick gear.

(4) Ratchet, which is in mesh, turns kick gear clockwise as shown by arrow "C" in Fig. 45.

(5) Since kick gear is always in mesh with kick idle gear B, the force created by turning the kick pedal is transmitted from kick gear, through kick idel gear B, kick idle gear A, driven gear and pinion gear, to the crankshaft and starts the engine.

(6) When the kick pedal is released, it is returned to its original position by the return spring and the ratchet is released automatically from the kick gear, and the kick gear rotates freely.

C. Disassembling and Assembling:

Performed according to procedure described in earlier paragraph 4. 2.

D. Inspection:

Check for worn or damaged gears and kick return springs.

SERVICE MEMO :

10. CARBURETOR:

A. Design & Operation:

(1) Principle:

The air entering through the air cleaner flows into the cylinder past the throttle valve.

The vacuum in the venturi (main bore) created by this flow of air causes the fuel in the float chamber to flow through the main jet into the needle jet and out into the passage to the cylinder intake port mixing with the air entering through the venturi, the fuel having been atomized by the air entering through the air jet (air bleed).

Fig.46. Carburetor

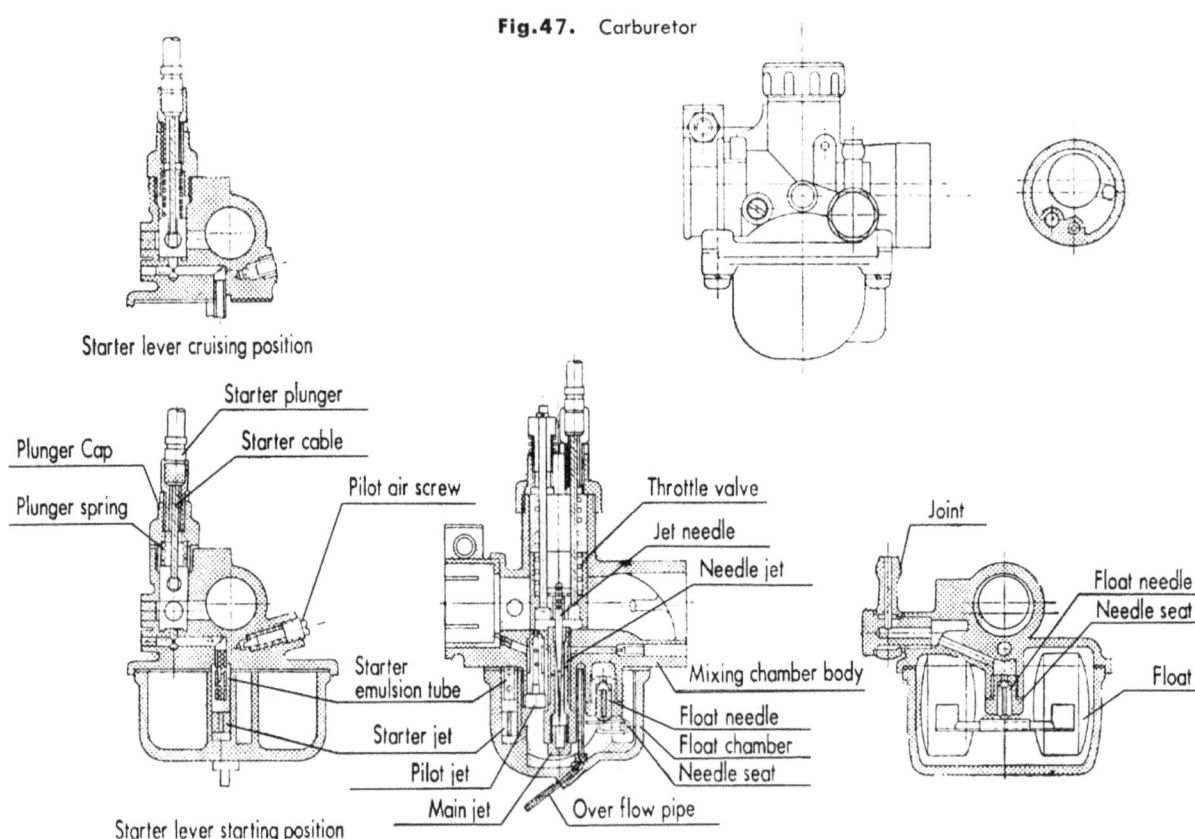

Fig.47. Carburetor

(2) Idling (Pilot Jet):

The vacuum caused by the engine suction draws fuel out of the pilot jet, and mixes with the air, which is controlled by an adjusting screw, entering from the pilot air hole.

This mixture flows out of the pilot outlet and is further mixed with the small amount of air entering through the venturi and then sucked into the engine as correct air-fuel mixture.

(3) Starting :

Pulling the starter lever raises the starter plunger. Kicking the kick-pedal with throttle grip in closed position, will create a vacuum in the intake port side of engine and draws fuel through the starter jet, mixing it with the air entering through starter emulsion tube.

This mixture flows out of the starter jet located at the rear of throttle valve and is further mixed with the air entering through the venturi and then sucked into the engine as correct air-fuel mixture for starting engine from cold. (Fig. 48).

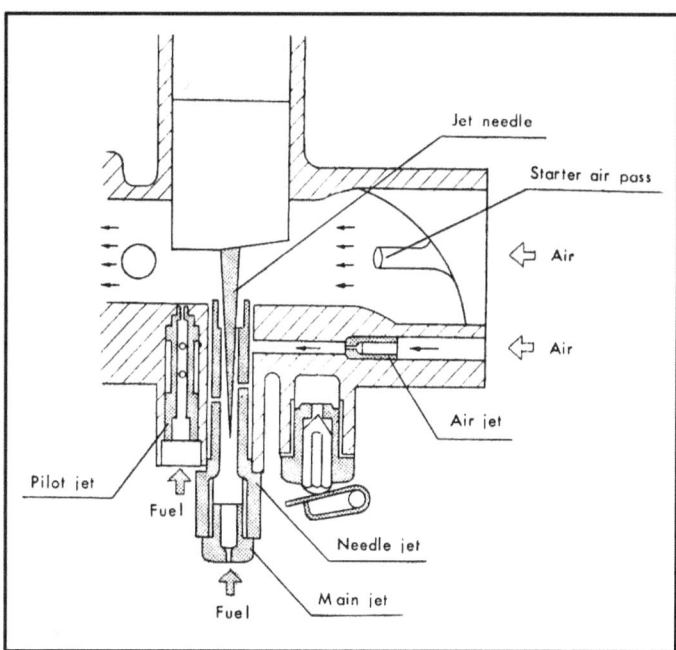

Fig. 48. Fuel Flow :

Fig. 49. Main Jet

Fig. 50. Needle Jet

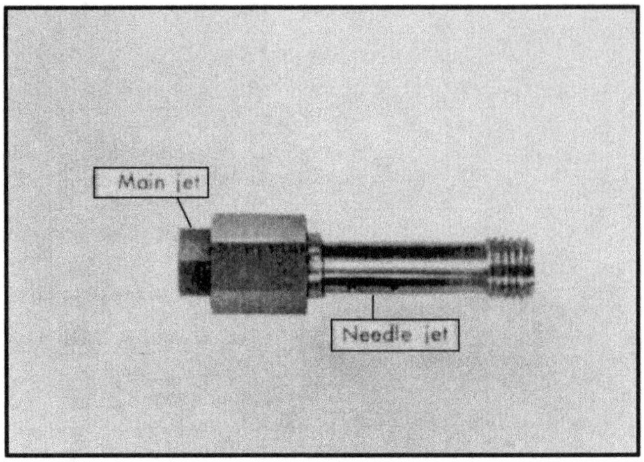

Fig. 51. Jet Needle

Fig. 52. Throttle Valve

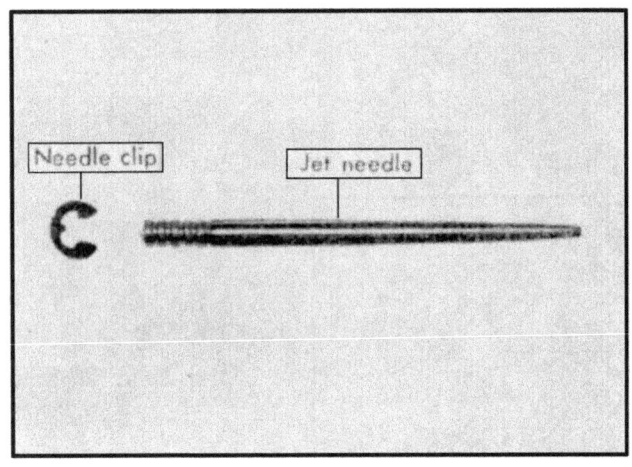
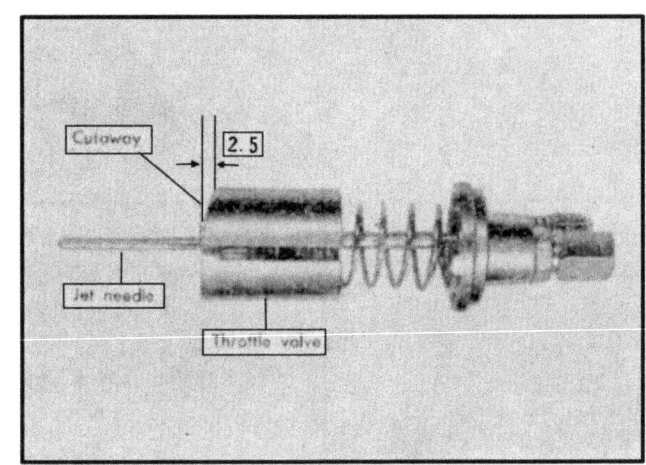

Fig. 53. Pilot Jet

Fig. 54. Air Screw

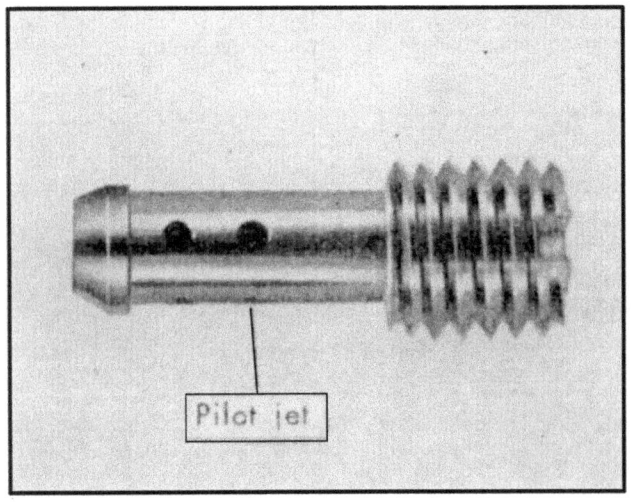
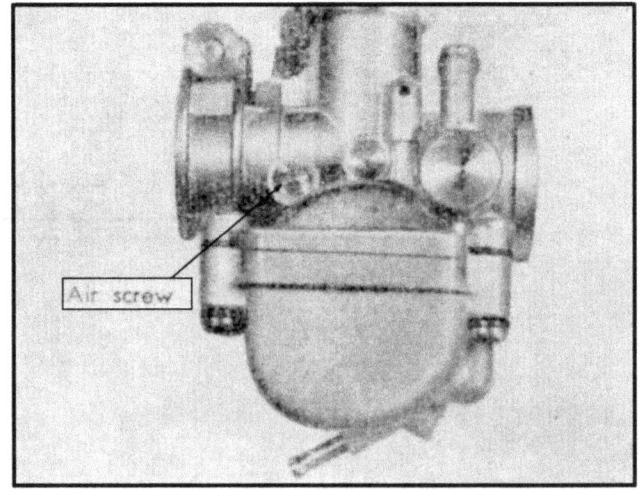

(4) Float chamber maintains the correct fuel level, the fuel flows into float chamber, the level of fuel being controlled by a float valve. As fuel enters, the float rises pushing up the float arm and cutting off the flow by the closing of the valve. As fuel level drops, the float also drops and the valve opens allowing the fuel to flow into the chamber. This process is repeated, maintaining the correct amount of fuel in the chamber proportionate to the amount consumed.

B. Functions of Various Parts:

(1) Main Jet (M. J.)

The main jet controls the fuel supply when the throttle is more than three-quarters open, but at smaller throttle openings although the fuel passes through the main jet the amount is diminished by the tapered needle jet.

Standard number of the main jet of this machine is No. 100.

(2) Air Jet (A. J.)

The air jet controls the flow of air entering the needle jet. The fuel passing through the needle jet mixes with the air coming in from the air jet.

(3) Needle Jet (N. J.)

With full throttle or at medium speeds, the fuel is first regulated by the main jet and the needle jet acting simultaneously. (Fig. 50)

(4) Jet Needle (J. N.)

The tapered jet needle attached to the throttle valve works in the needle jet and adjusts the air-fuel ratio at medium throttle 1/4 to 3/4 throttle opening.

The taper needle position in relation to throttle opening can be set according to the mixture required by clipping it to the throttle valve with the jet needle clip in one of the grooves.

The lower the groove, richer the mixture will be at 1/4–3/4 throttle.

The jet needle has five grooves No. 1 to No. 5 from top to bottom. The standard clip position of BS-90 is No. 3 (Fig. 51).

(5) Throttle Valve (C. A.)

The throttle valve is cut away on the inlet side and controls the flow of main fuel supply from 1/8 to 1/4 throttle opening. The extent of cut away is marked on the valve, viz. 2.5 for 2.5 m/m cut away. Thus, mark 3 indicates a weaker mixture and 2 a richer mixture (Fig. 52)

(6) Pilot Jet (P. J.)

At idling speed or cut down throttle, the pilot jet controls the flow of fuel mixed with air which enters through the air jet, and atomizes the mixture. (Fig. 53)

(7) Air Screw (A. S.)

The air screw controls the flow of air which mixes with the fuel passing hrough the pilot jet. (Fig. 54).

The standard adjustment of screw position is 1-1/2 turn back.

C. Adjustment:

Engine performance is mainly dependent on the proper functioning of the carburetor, i.e. its ability to adjust itself to the supply of the most suitable air-fuel mixture at any speed, from idling to the maximum engine speed. Thorough experiments and tests have been conducted by the carburetor maker and Bridgestone technicians, to produce the efficient carburetor fitted to the BS 90. As all the component parts have been correctly set by experts at the factory, it would be unwise to make casual adjustments.

In the event, however, of adjustment being inevitable, a careful check of the engine and component parts should be first made as indicated.

(1) Look for possible air leakage from carburetor adaptor connection.

(2) Replace all worn parts.

(3) Warm up the engine for 2 to 3 minutes before adjusting.

C-1. Adjusting Mixture Gas:

How to determine correct mixture.

(1) Too Rich

Exhaust fumes are white and heavy.

Engine runs irregularly.

Spark plug apt to be wet and coated with carbon.

(If the spark plug is too cold or running speeds very slow, change to a hotter plug.)

(2) Too Lean:

Idling is irregular.

Engine overheats easily.

Engine rpm irregular at a constant throttle opening.

Poor acceleration.

Spark plug electrodes dry and spotted with white deposit.

(If the spark plug is too hot or running speeds are very high, change to a colder plug.)

C-2. Adjusting for Various Speeds:

THROTTLE OPENING	TOO RICH	TOO LEAN
0 -1/8	Turn air screw back a little.	Turn in slightly air screw.
1/8-1/4	Use throttle valve with larger cut away.	Use throttle vale with smaller cut away.
1/4-3/4	Lower jet needle.	Raise jet needle.
3/4-Full	Use smaller number main jet.	Use larger number main jet.

C-3. Adjusting Fuel Level :

Loosen the four float chamber screws and remove float chamber.

Place the carburetor upside down.

Adjust the float position with the float arm. The bottom of the float should be 19±0.5 mm from the point shown in Fig. 55 with the float arm touching the float valve.

Fig. 55. Adjusting Fuel Level

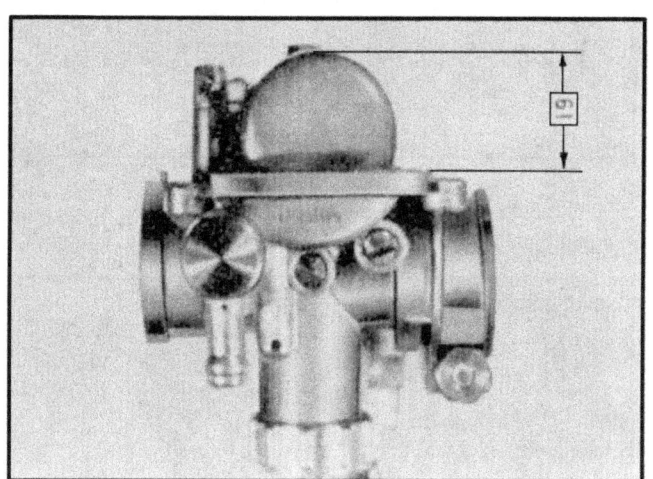

SERVICE MEMO :

Fig. 56. Tools necessary

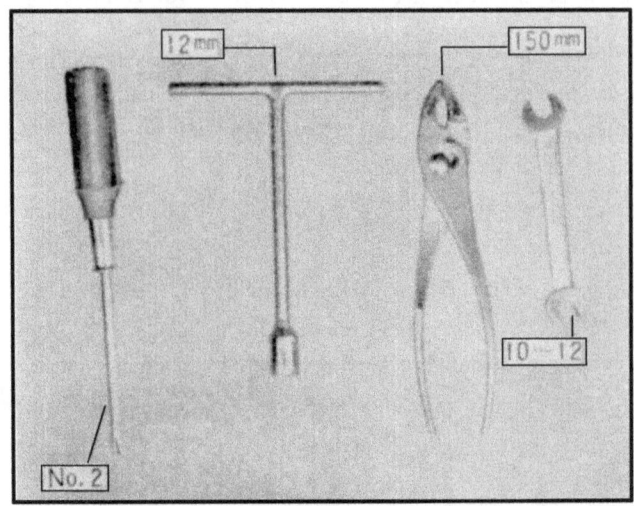

Fig. 57. Remove brake wire

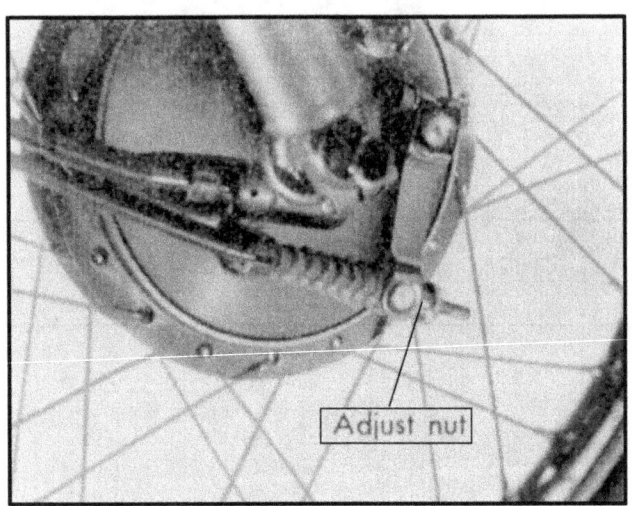

Fig. 58. Adjustment of Clutch Lever

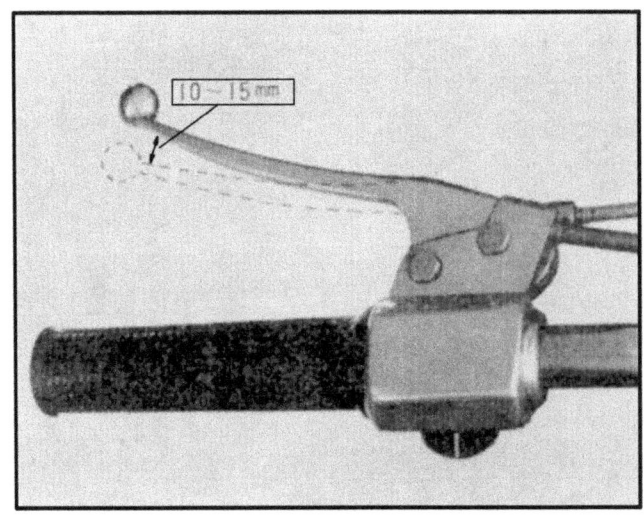

11. FRAME:

Frame Structure:

Frame is built with pressed steel plates backbone type, very rugged but light in weight.

And the telescopic fork with oil damper assures excellent suspension on any type of road.

11.1 Handle Bar:

A. Removing Handle Bar:

(1) Tools necessary (Fig. 56.)

(2) Loosen clutch cable to the limit of adjusting nut and remove from clutch lever.

(3) Remove adjusting nut of front brake wire, pull out of brake lever. (Fig. 57.)

(4) Remove carburetor mixing chamber top from body, and remove throttle cable while pressing down throttle valve spring.

(5) Take off (5×35) hexagonal nut of body starter lever, and remove starter cable from lever.

(6) Unscrew head light screw at left bottom of head cover and light rim, and remove wire harness connections from terminals.

(7) Take off steering head bolts, handle holder and remove handle assembly from front fork.

B. Assembling:

(1) Assembling is done in the reverse order of removing.

(2) Connect up all lead wires and adjust them. (Fig. 58)

SERVICE MEMO:

SERVICE MEMO :

11.2 Front Fork:

A. Operation:

The load or shock on the front fork is absorbed by oil cushion, coil springs and compressed air acting as a damper. The down stroke of the upper fork tube (cover) forces the oil in the lower tube through the oil plunger hole into the upper tube and the pressure (compression) increases as the plunger in the lower tube closes the hole.

The air in the upper tube is thus compressed by the filling oil, the coil springs come into action, the whole process acting as a damper.

As the load is released the process is reversed.

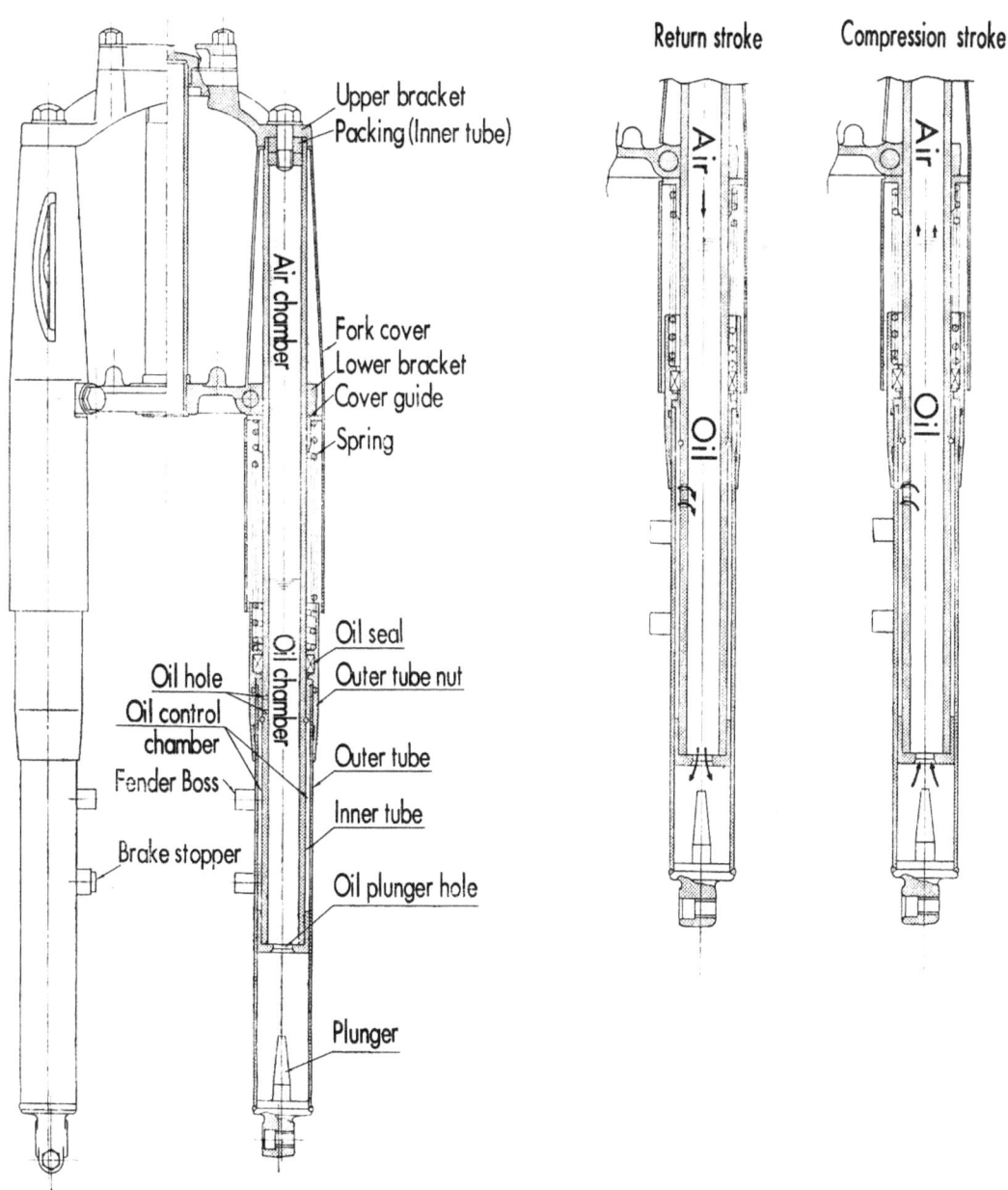

Fig. 59. Front Fork

Fig. 60.

B. Disassembling :

(1) Tools necessary. (Fig. 61)

(2) Handle bar is removed according to the procedure given in 11. 1 A.

(3) Take off two (8×16) hexagonal bolts of head cover, and remove head cover. (Fig. 62).

(4) Push aside front tension bar at hub end.

(5) Loosen (8×25) hexagonal bolt (bolt axle bracket) at bottom right of front fork and remove front shaft.

(6) Place a supporting block under the engine, raise the front fork and remove wheel assembly.

(7) Take off front mudguard by loosening four (6×8) hexagonal bolts.

(8) Remove upper bracket by loosening cap nut (32 mm) on upper part of steering head, and two hexagonal bolts (10×28) of the holder upper bracket. (Fig. 63)

(9) Loosen bolts of lower bracket, pull down front fork and detach.

C. Inspection :

(1) Repair or replace outer tube which is bent. (Refer to Service Standards Manual.)

(2) Replace upper bracket and lower bracket which are bent or have flaws.

(3) Adjust or replace parts which are the source of oil leakage or any springs which have lost tension.
(Free length of spring 168 mm.)

(4) Fill in the ratio of 6 and 4 with 135 c.c. fork oil in each fork tube. Mixture of No. 60 spindle oil (60 %) and No. 30 engine oil (40 %).

The fork oil can be drained from the draining hole at the bottom of fork tube by removing screw.

D. Assembling :

(1) Lay upper bracket washer on the fork cover, insert cover guide into outer tube while pressing it down with finger, insert outer tube into fork cover and screw in the front fork tool (special tool). (Fig. 64)

(2) Raise outer tube right up and tighten lower bracket bolt temporarily.

(3) After tightening the outer bracket temporarily, install upper bracket, tighten cap nut and upper brakcet temporarily.

(4) After loosening lower brakcet bolts, tighten upper bracket bolts and cap nuts uniformly. (Fig. 65)

(5) Tighten lower bracket bolts.

(6) Install outer parts in the reverse order of disassembling.

Fig. 61. Tools necessary

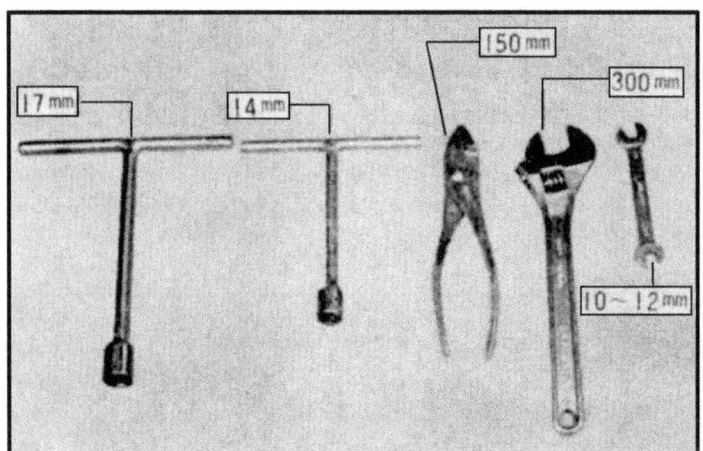

Fig. 62. Remove head cover

Fig. 63. Remove handle bar

Fig. 64. Raise outer tube with special tool.

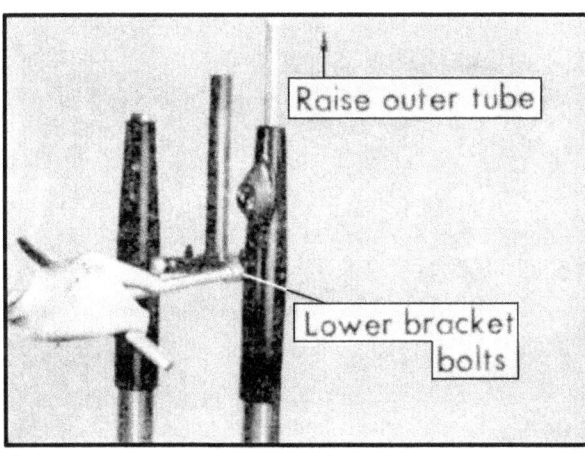

Fig. 65. Upper bracket.

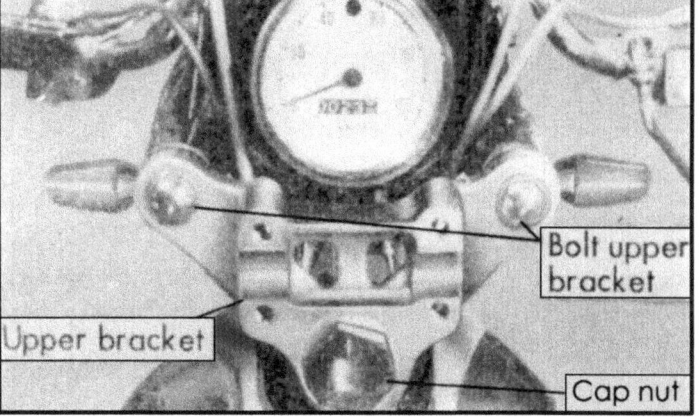

11.3 Rear Frame and Rear Suspension:

A. Construction:

The rear frame is built of pressed steel plate, and connected to the main frame by the rear frame shaft (bolt), and pivots on this shaft.

The rear suspension is fixed by bolts to the main frame and the upper end of the rear frame.

B. Disassembling:

Fig. 66. Tools.

(1) Tools necessary. (Fig. 66).

(2) Remove chain case and drive chain.

(3) Remove rear tension bar and rear wheel.

(4) Remove rear suspension by loosening four bolts.

(5) The rear frame will be detached by pulling out the rear frame bolt. (Fig. 67)

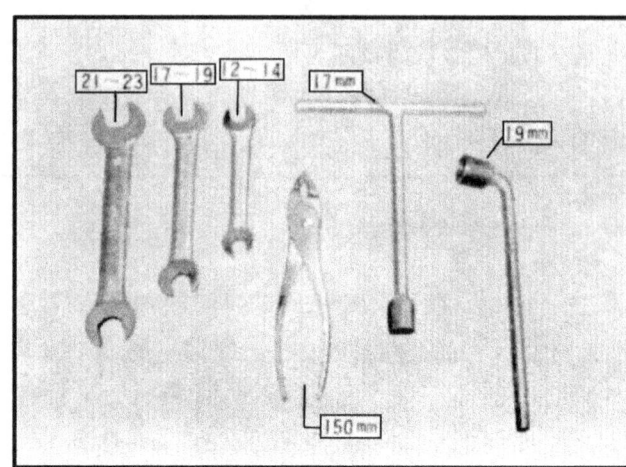

(6) The rear frame torsion rubber will come out by tapping with a plastic hammer. (Fig. 68).

C. Inspection:

(1) Check for bends or damage of frame and rear frame shaft (bolt).

(2) Check to see if torsion rubber is damaged and replace if necessary.

(3) Check to see if rear suspension is damaged or leaking and replace if necessary.

Fig. 67. Loose rear frame bolt.

Fig. 68. Rear Frame.

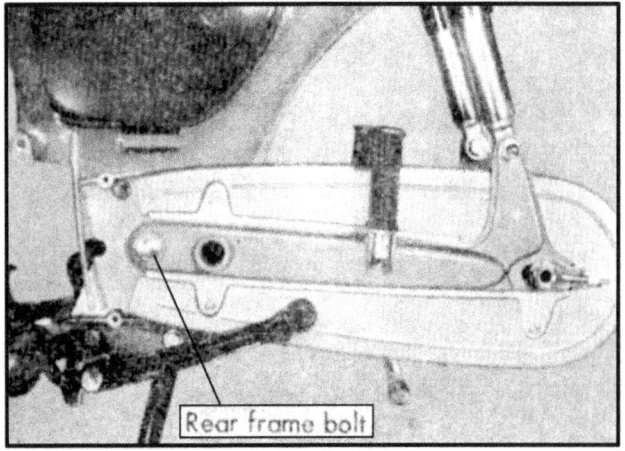
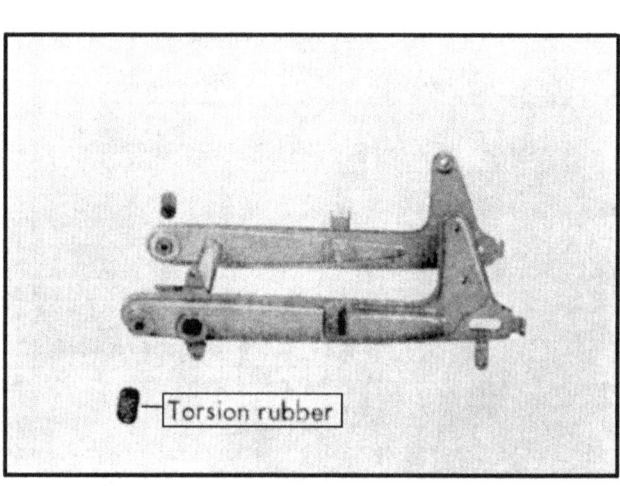

11.4: Front and Rear Wheels:

A. Description:

Both the front and rear wheels consist of tire tube, rims, spokes, etc.

Both tires are 2.50-17, 4PR and spokes No. 12 for front and No. 10 and No. 11 for the rear.

Brake hulbs are of aluminum alloy, 130 mm⌀.

Fig. 69. Construction of Tire

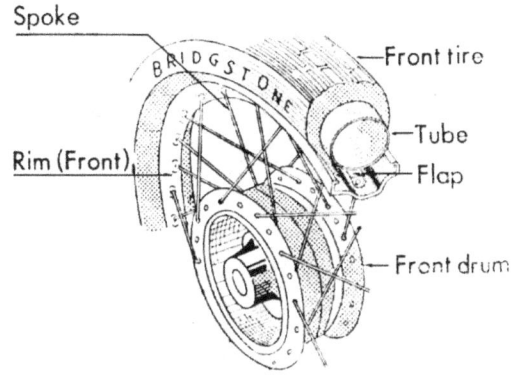

CORRECT AIR PRESSURES

	FRONT	REAR
1 passenger	1.6 kg/cm² (22.5 lb/in²)	2.0 kg/cm² (28.4 lb/in²)
2 passenger	1.6 kg/cm² (22.5 lb/in²)	2.1 kg/cm² (29.9 lb/in²)

1. FRONT WHEEL:

The front wheel has the brake on the right side of the machine. The speedometer unit is installed in the hub to keep out water and dust.

2. REAR WHEEL:

The rear wheel has the rear sprocket on the left side of the machine and the brake on the right side.

B. Removing Front Wheel:

Place a supporting block under the engine, loosen axle bracket bolt, remove front tension bar from the hub side, remove front shaft nut, pull out front shaft, raise front fork slightly, and detach wheel. (Fig. 70 - 71).

Fig. 70. Pull out front shaft.

Fig. 71. Removed Hub Cover

C. Removing Rear Wheel:

Lift the machine on its main stand, remove brake rod adjusting nut, remove tension bar from the side of the hub, remove rear shaft nut on left side (**The big nut need not be touched**), pull out rear shaft together with chain adjuster, and by removing rear hub collar the wheel will come off the drive flange on the right side.

Take out wheel by leaning machine to the left.

Fig. 72. Remove rear wheel.   **Fig. 73.** Remove rear wheel.

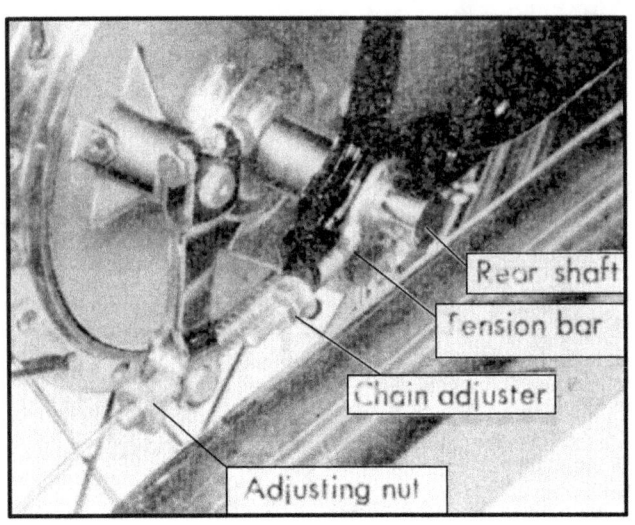

D. Inspection:

(1) Bent or deformed rim.

(2) Check to see if any spokes are loosen and tighten if necessary.

(3) Check to see if tires have any bad cuts or nails embedded and if necessary make repairs or replacements.

(4) Wash ball bearings of the hubs well and check for looseness and snatching action in idle running. Make replacements if necessary.

(5) Replace bent or damaged front and rear shafts.

(6) The speedometer gear should rotate smoothly. Apply grease if necessary. Also check pinion speedometer.

(7) Check if the oil seal is damaged, deformed or worn out. Replace if necessary.

E. Assembling:

Assembling is performed in the reverse order of disassembling.
Assemble after applying sufficient grease to ball bearings.

F. Removing Tire:

(1) When removing tire to repair punctures, bursts, etc., take off valve cap and with its top loosen valve core in the stem, to let air out.

After deflating, lay wheel on the ground as shown in Fig. 74 and press tire down with the feet. Detach bead of tire from rim, insert tire lever between rim and tire bead, and with the tire lever it out of the rim.

Fig. 74. Press tire down with the feet

Fig. 75. Insert tire lever

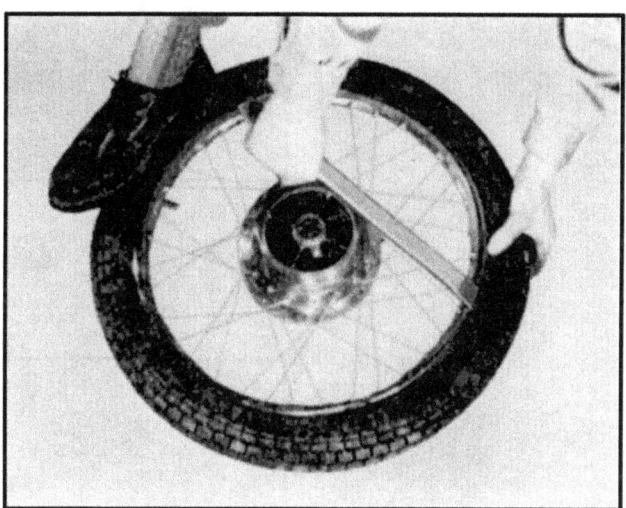

It would be more convenient to use two levers for this purpose. When one side of the bead is completely out of the rim, push in stem of tube valve and pull out tube.

After repairing tube, replace it in the tire, being careful to see that the valve stem is exactly centered in the hole of the rim.

G. Mounting Tire on the Rim:

To lever the bead on the rim, hook one tire lever on the rim and with the other lever gradually pull the bead over the rim.

H. Caution:

(1) As tire bead is a very tight fit on the rim, be careful not to put too much strain on it when mounting tire on the rim. Refer to 11.4 A on page 49 regarding correct tire pressure.

(2) Always choose the correct size (2.50-17, 4PR) tire or tube for replacement.

(3) After inflating, put soap water on the valve tip to check for leakage of air. If it is found to be leaking, tighten valve or replace it with a new one.

(4) When removing or putting back tube, be careful not to damage the screw thread of stem.

Fig. 76. Brake shoe and lining.

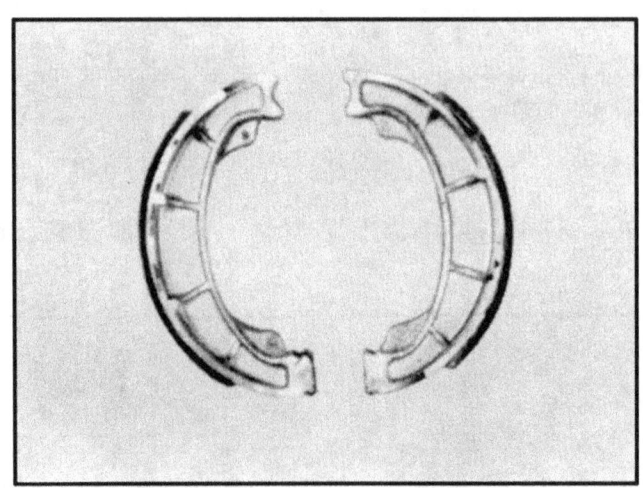

Fig. 77. Hub cover & shoes ass'y.

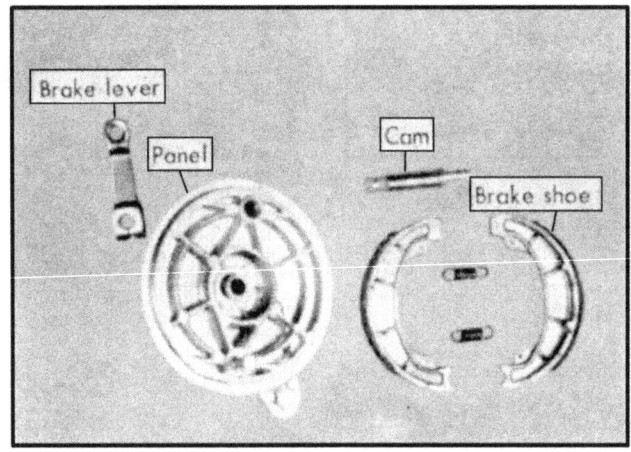

Fig. 78. Brake Cam.

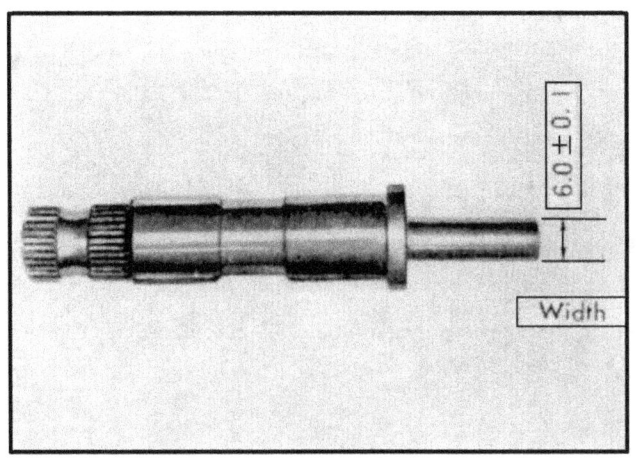

— 52 —

11.5 : Brakes :

A. Description :

The front and rear brakes are of the internal expansion type and operated by a lever and pedal respectively, and the brake shoes contact the drum by cam action. The brake linings made of asbestine woven are cemented on the shoes with a special adhesive agent. (Fig. 76).

B. Disassembling :

(1) By removing the wheel according to the procedure given in 11.4 B and C, the hub cover (front or rear hub) will be detached.

(2) Unhook springs from one shoe only, and both shoes can be detached.

Remove brake arm and cam after shoes are detached. (Fig. 77).

C. Inspection :

(1) Check brake cam for wear. (Fig. 78).

Refer to the Service Standards Manual.

(2) Check worn return springs (brake shoe) and replace if necessary.

(3) Replace shoe assembly when worn to the limit. Refer to Service Standards Manual.

(4) Replace bent or damaged oil seal.

D. Assembling :

Assembling is carried out in the reverse order of disassembling. When any particles are embedded in the surface of the shoe lining or if it is unevenly worn, roughen the surface with a rough sandpaper.

SERVICE MEMO :

11.6: Fuel Tank and Seat:

A. Description:

The fuel tank is located on the frame with the rear part fastened by two hexagonal bolts and the front insulated by rubber pads attached to the frame. (Fig. 79, 80).

The seat is hooked on to the fuel tank bracket pipe, and the brackets on the rear are fastened by two hexagonal nuts of rear suspension.

Fig. 79. Fuel Tank   **Fig. 80.** Frame

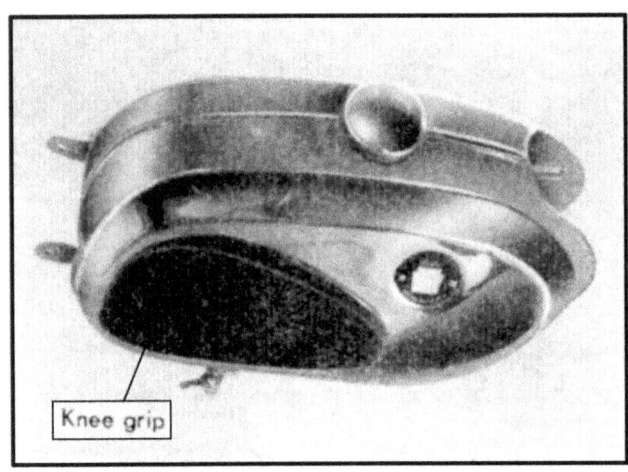 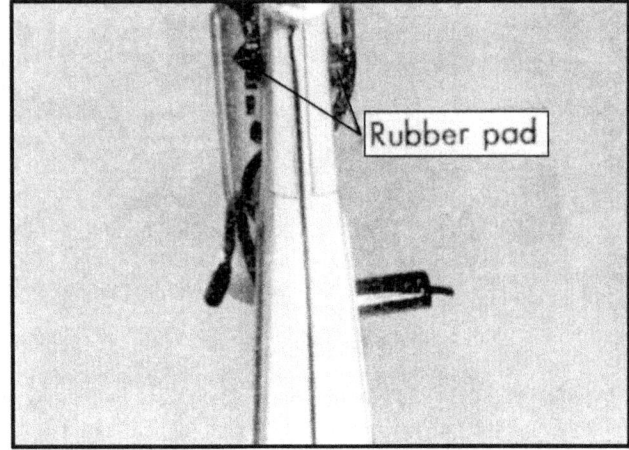

B. Removing:

Take off hexagonal nuts on the rear suspension and raise rear of seat slightly and unhook.

The fuel tank will be detached by taking off the two hexagonal bolts at the back and moving it to the rear.

C. Inspection:

(1) Replace front insulation rubber of fuel tank if it is worn or damaged.

(2) Replace fuel tank if there is any leakage.

(3) Replace tank cap packing if it is damaged or worn-out.

(4) Replace damaged pipe union or clips of drain pipe and fuel pipe if they are worn.

SERVICE MEMO:

11.7 : Air Cleaner

A. Description :

The air cleaner element is installed in the side cover (right) at center of left side of frame by two screws. The air sucked in here is filtered, and flows into the carburetor through the air hose. (Fig. 81)

Fig. 81. Air passage   **Fig. 82.** Remove Aircleaner

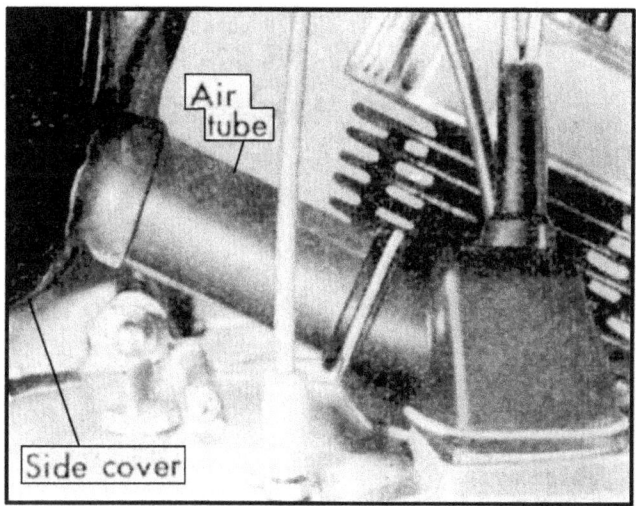
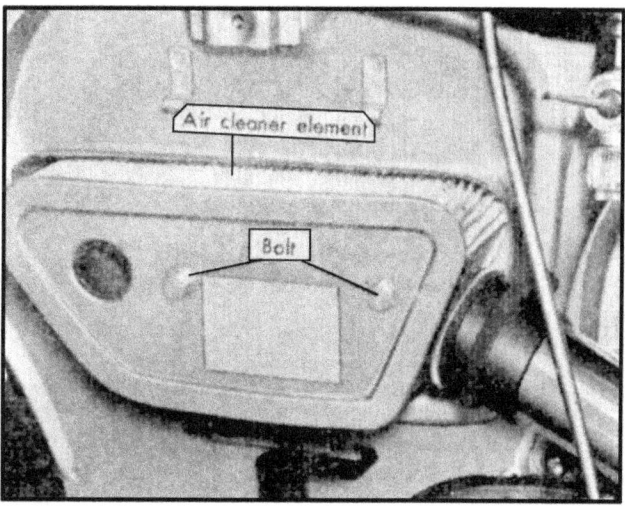

B. Removing :

Remove left side cover, joint rubber, and hexagonal nuts and the complete air cleaner assembly can be detached. (Fig. 82).

C. Inspection :

(1) Clean or replace air cleaner element periodically by compressed air or with soft hair brush.

(2) Replace joint rubber if it is damaged.

D. Installing :

Install in the reverse order of removing. However, special attention should be paid when installing air cleaner to see that no air is sucked in from any source other than through the air cleaner to prevent any foreign matter entering the carburetor.

SERVICE MEMO :

11.8 : Exhaust System :

A. Removing :

Remove muffler blind bolt nut on rear frame, and bolt and nut on muffler bracket, and then the muffler will come off by pulling it to the rear.

The exhaust pipe will detach by loosening clamp nut. (Fig. 83).

B. Inspection :

(1) Scrape off carbon from exhaust pipe and muffler periodically. (Fig. 84).

(2) When rubber joint is noticeably worn and causes gas leaks or when ring rubber joint or ring is worn out, make necessary replacements. (Fig. 85).

(3) When exhaust gasket is noticeably worn, make necessary replacements.

C. Installing :

Installing is carried out in the reverse order of removing.

11.9 : Footrest and Stands (Main stand and side stand) :

A. Removing :

(1) The footrest and side stand can be detached together by loosening engine bolt (8×114) and frame bolt (8×16). (Fig. 86).

(2) To detach main stand, suspend motorcycle with rope or lean it against the wall with the stand in position, take off cotter pin, take out stand tube by hammering, and the brake pedal will come off, after which the main stand can be removed from the spring. (Fig. 87).

B. Inspection :

(1) Check the outer diameter of stand tube and stand pipe, adjust or replace if necessary according to Service Standards Manual.

(2) Replace worn-out brake pedal return spring and main stand spring.

(3) Adjust or replace bent main stand and brake pedal.

C. Installing :

Install in the reverse order of removing, applying grease to working parts of main stand pipe and brake pedal.

SERVICE MEMO :

Fig. 83. Remove Exhaust Pipe

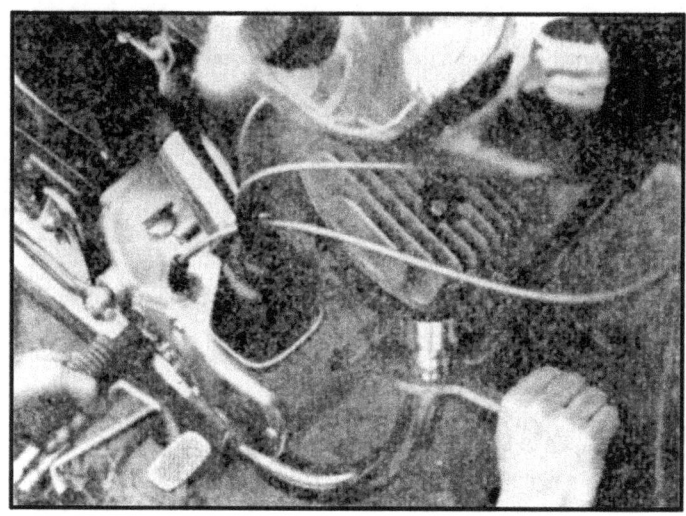

Fig. 84. Muffler.

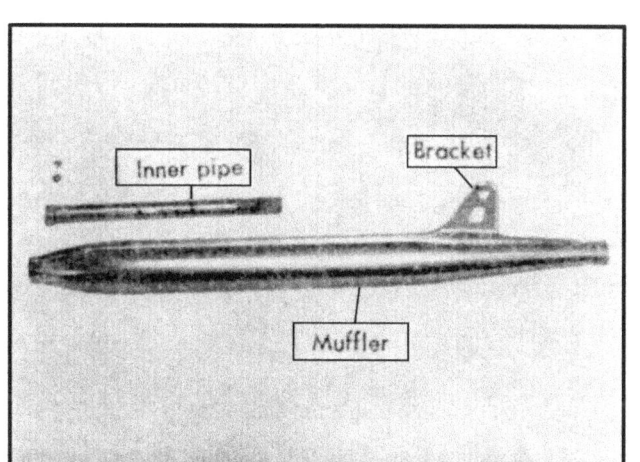

Fig. 85. Exhaust Pipe.

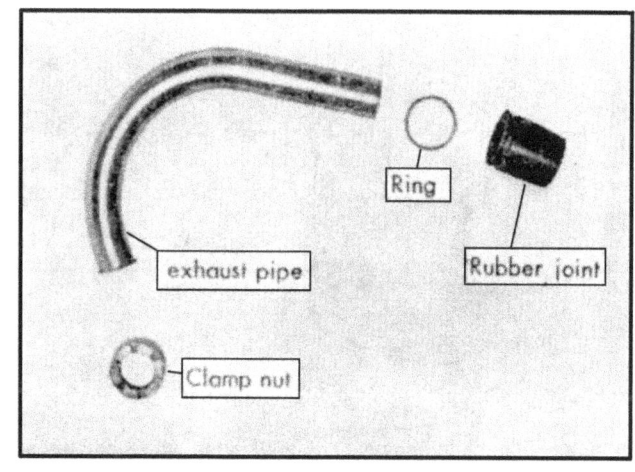

Fig. 86. Footrest and Side stand.

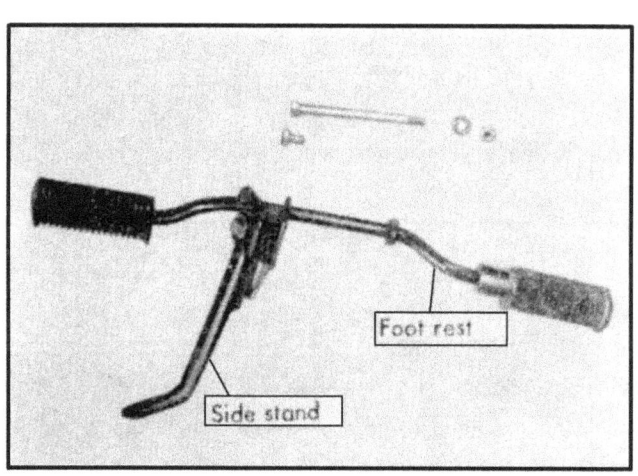

Fig. 87. Main stand & Brake pedal.

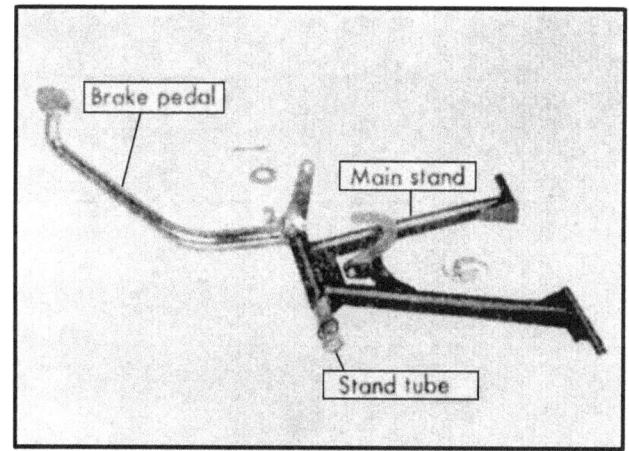

11.10: Main Frame

A. Construction:

The frame is built with pressed steel plate backbone type, very rugged but light in weight.

B. Disassembling:

Fig. 88 shows the frame after the engine and other parts have been dismounted.

Fig. 88. Main Frame.

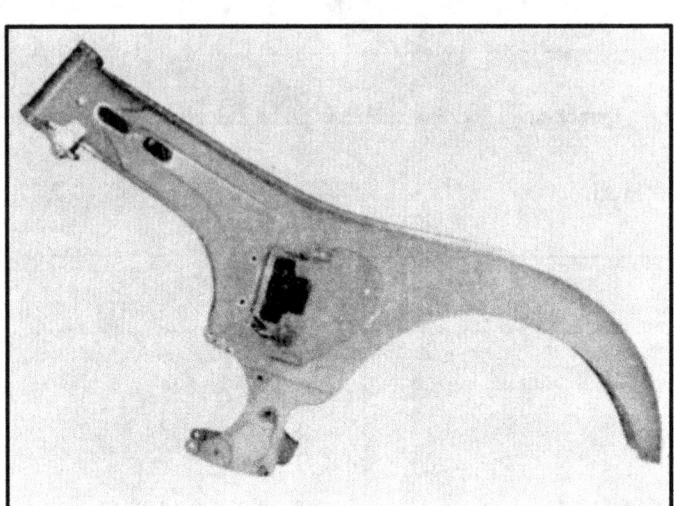

C. Inspection:

(1) Repair by welding (arc welding) where necessary and replace broken or damaged pipes.

(2) Check for any bends in frame and head. Replace frame if defect is too great.

(3) Check for wear of steel balls, and replace if necessary.

(4) Check for damaged or worn inner and outer races, and replace if necessary.

D. Assembling:

Assemble in accordance with procedure described in the previous paragraph.

SERVICE MEMO:

SERVICE MEMO :

12. ELECTRICAL EQUIPMENT:

12.1: Ignition System:

The ignition system consists of the magneto, condenser, ignition coil, contact breaker and spark plug.

A high voltage electric current of approximately 10,000 V. is created and conveyed to the spark plug.

A. Contact Breaker:

The contact breaker is mounted on the magneto frame and its actuating cam is on the crankshaft.

Adjustment and Repair: The contact points should be checked. If the points are rough, file carefully with a fine file or emery paper.

If the surface is very rough and uneven, take them out, and file lightly with an oil-stone. After this wash with gasoline and wipe clear with a rag before assembling.

Replace with new if perfect contact of the two points is not possible.

Adjusting Ignition Timing: The ignition timing of the engine is 22 degrees (22^{+1}_{-2} degrees) before Top Dead Center and point gap is 0.3–0.4 mm. (0.012″–0.016″).

(1) Take off dynamo cover and check point gap. (Fig. 89).

(2) Use flywheel magneto puller (special tool) and remove flywheel magneto. (Fig. 90).

(3) Loosen screw (2) and set point gap by turning contact breaker (1) 0.35 mm. (0.014″) with thickness gauge. (Fig. 91).

(When breaker is turned to the left, gap increases.)
(When breaker is turned to the right, gap decreases.)

(4) Then loosen magneto frame screws, turn the magneto frame left or right and set it as Fig. 91: when the notch on the flywheel meets the corresponding mark on the crankcase, the points should separate. (Fig. 92).

(When magneto frame is turned to the **left,** ignition is retarded.)

(When magneto frame is turned to the **right,** ignition is advanced.)

B. Condenser:

The condenser is mounted on the magneto frame, and absorbs the current generated when the contact breaker cuts out and assists the functioning of the ignition coil.

Fig. 89. Adjusting Ignition Timing.

Fig. 90. Remove Flywheel Magneto.

Fig. 91. Magneto Frame.

Fig. 92. Set the ignition timing mark.

C. Spark Plug:

The standard spark plug is used N.G.K. B-7 H whose sectional structure is shown in Fig. 93.

The gap of the spark electrodes should be adjusted to 0.6 mm-0.7 mm (0.024"-0.027").

Fig. 93. Spark Plug.

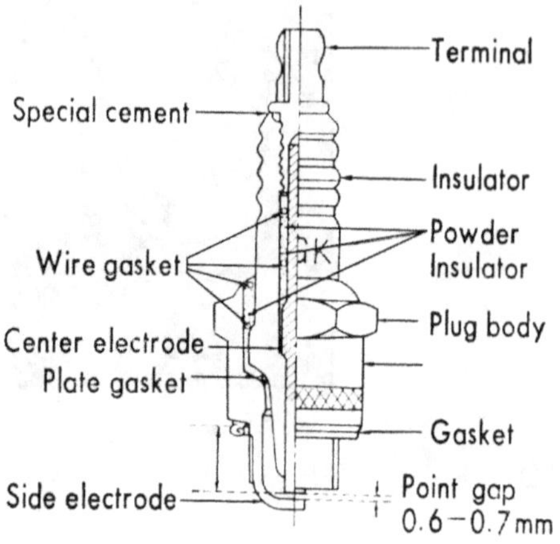

Inspection and Adjustment:

Check the spark plug every 3,000 km. (2.000 miles). The electrode wears and becomes coated with carbon or oil. A worn or dirty plug produces weak sparks or none and causes hard starting, low output, irregular rpm and damages the ignition coil, etc.

Wash the plug with gasoline to remove dirt.

(1) When Too Cold a plug is used.
Oil on the electrode or heavy carbon deposit.
Change to a hotter plug (lower number.)
Check the fuel supply (feed) and clean air cleaner.

(2) When Correct a plug is used.
Nearly white or light brown, sometimes greyish deposit.

(3) When Too Hot a plug is used.
Absence of deposit, bleached appearance of insulator, sometimes blistered.
Change to a colder plug (higher number).
Check the fuel supply and increase feed.

(4) See chart below for plug recommendation.

BRAND	STANDARD	IF PLUG FOULS EASILY (Slow speed)	IF PLUG BURNS EASILY (High speed)
NGK	B-7 H	B-6 H	B-7 HC B-8 H
CHAMPION	L-5	L-7 L-85	LA-10
BOSCH	W 240 T$_1$	W 225 T$_1$	W 290 T$_{16}$
LODGE	3 HN	2 HN	R 49
AC	43 F 42 L-Com.	44 F	

D. Flywheel Magneto:

The flywheel magneto is mounted on the left side of the crank shaft and the permanent magnet fitted to the flywheel rotates around the steel-cored coil.

E. Testing Ignition Coil:

Disconnect plug, and connect the wire with the lead wire of the electro tester. If the spark jumps 6 m/m or over, the coil is in good condition. Lesser spark means unsatisfactory ignition coil or decrease in the magnet.

Normally, the fault lies in the coil.

(When charging efficiency of the lighting coil has dropped, it may be also due to weakened magnet.)

12.2: Charging System:

The charging system consists of the lighting coil of the magneto, silicon rectifier and battery. The current generated by the magneto is transmitted to the headlight, taillight, speedometer light and also to the battery.

The alternating current is rectified to Direct Current by a rectifier for charging.

A. Coil for Charging:

The coils are classified into coil for battery charging and coil for lighting the headlight, taillight and speedometer light at night.

To check whether the coils are satisfactory, link an ampere meter in a series (about 2 Amp. reading) to the battery fuse, as shown in Fig. 94.

Start engine and measure electric current responding to different crank rotations.

Measure with the main switch on separately in day time and at night and if the excess or shortage is within 10-20 % of the standard charging rate, the condition is satisfactory. But if it is below or above the standard, the lighting coil should be replaced.

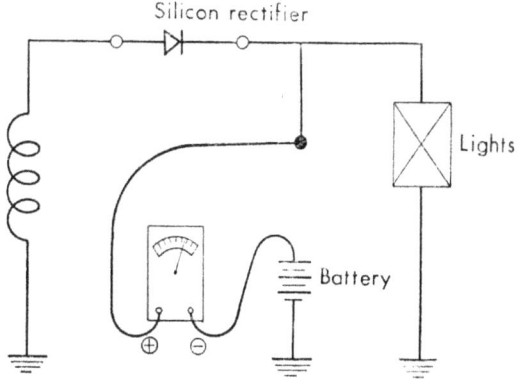

Fig. 94. Check charging rate.

CRANKSHAFT R.P.M.		2500	8000
DAYTIME	Current charged (A)	Start charging	Less than 2.5 A
AT NIGHT	Current charged (A)	Over 0.1 A	Less than 9 V.
	Light voltage (V)	Over 6 V	

The Normal Electric Current Raised by Each Rotation.

B. Silicon Rectifier:

The silicon rectifier performs the funtion of rectifying the A.C. current originating from coil into direct current and charging the battery.

Running the machine in the daytime without the battery or fuse will damage the rectifier and burn out the bulbs.

The battery should be checked periodically without fail.

C. Battery:

The horn, winker light, neutral lamp, stoplight, etc. work on the direct current supplied by the battery. The 6V-4 AH battery for BRIDGESTONE-90 is connected to the rectifier by a fuse and also serves as an earth for the machine.

A periodic check should be conducted by the user and the dealer.
The main item of check and maintenance is the liquid and its specific gravity.

The specific gravity of 1.260 at 20° is full charge.

SERVICE MEMO :

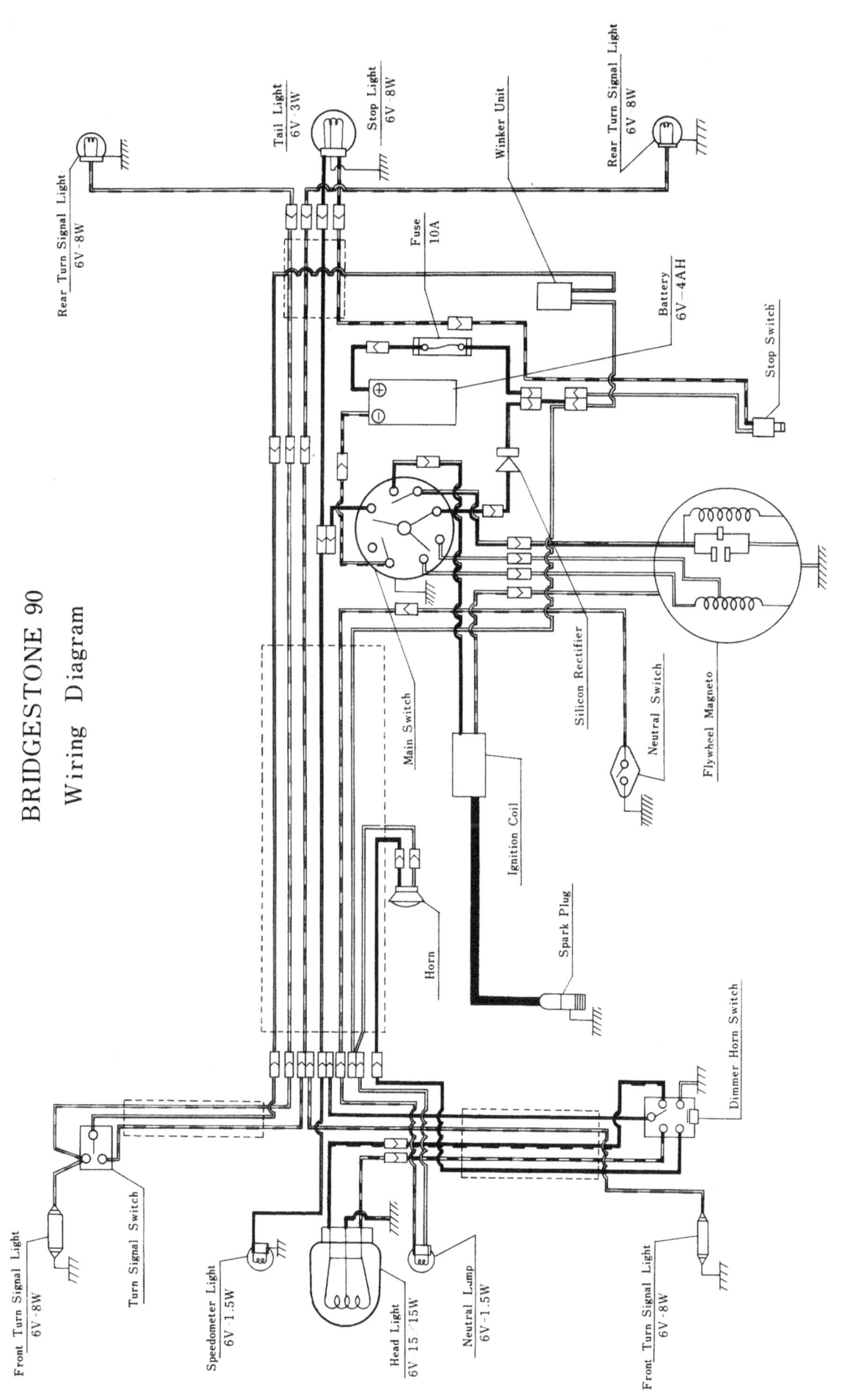

SERVICE MEMO :

13. INSPECTION AND MAINTENANCE

A. Daily Check Procedure

Tire Air Pressure	Front 1.6 kg/cm^2 (22.8 lbs./in^2) Rear 2.0 kg/cm^2 (28.4 lbs./in^2)
Front Brake	Proper adjustment
Rear Brake	Proper adjustment
Fuel	Is it sufficient ?
Horn	Does it work well ?
Lights	Proper operation.
Transmission Oil	Check level.
Battery	Check liquid level.
Carburetor	Adjust idling.

B. Periodic Checking

400 Km (250 miles)   3,000 Km (2,000 miles)   6,000 Km (3500 miles)

ITEM	PROCEDURE	AFTER BRAKE-IN (400 Km)	ONCE EVERY 3,000 Km. (2,000 mile)	ONCE EVERY 6,000 Km. (3,500 mile)
Front & Rear Brake Play	Check	X	X	X
Chain Play	Check	X	X	X
Muffler & Exhaust Carbon	Clean		O	O
Clutch Play	Check	X	X	X
Carburetor Operation	Check		O	O
Battery Liquid	Check	X	X	X
Spark Plug	Clean		X	X
Contact Points Gap	Check	O	O	O
Air Cleaner	Clean		O	O
Cylinder Head Carbon	Clean		X	X
Bolts and Nuts	Tightness	O	O	O
Fuel Cock Filter	Clean		O	O

Items marked "O" Should be checked frequently.

C. Periodic Greasing:

Periodic greasing with a grease gun and lubrication.

	ITEM	1 ST GREASING	2 ND GREASING MILEAGE INTERVAL	PROCEDURE
1.	Front Brake Cam Shaft	400 Km. (250 miles)	3,000 Km. (2,000 miles)	Grease
2.	Rear Brake Cam Shaft	400 Km. (250 miles)	3,000 Km. (2,000 miles)	Grease
3.	Throttle Grip Tube	400 Km. (250 miles)	3,000 Km. (2,000 miles)	Grease
4.	Speedometer Gear Box	6,000 Km. (3,500 miles)	4,000 Km. (2,500 miles)	Grease
5.	Front & Rear Wheel Bearings	3,000 Km. (2,000 miles)	3,000 Km. (2,000 miles)	Grease
6.	Steering Bearings	6,000 Km. (3,500 miles)	6,000 Km. (3,500 miles)	Grease
7.	Oil Felt (Magneto)	6,000 Km. (3,500 miles)	6,000 Km. (3,500 miles)	Grease
8.	Cables	1,500 Km. (1,000 miles)	3,000 Km. (2,000 miles)	Grease
9.	Chain	400 Km. (250 miles)	1,000 Km. (6,00 miles)	Motor Oil
10.	Stand Tube	3,000 Km. (2,000 miles)	3,000 Km. (2,000 miles)	Motor Oil
11.	Front Fork	10,000 Km. (6,000 miles)	10,000 Km. (6,000 miles)	135 cc. of Hydraulic fork oil (or mixture of 70 parts of Spindle oil No. 60 to 3 parts of No. 30 motor oil).

D. Inspection and Maintenance During Storage

As new motorcycles are placed in the warehouse pending sale and delivery, the Distributor/Dealer should carry out certain inspections and certain measures for protection of the machines to avoid trouble after delivery due to rust and other causes resulting from long storage.

Safeguard against such a possibility will save much labour and time.

I. BATTERY :

1. Inspection of specific gravity of electrolyte fluid.
2. Storage of dry charged battery.
3. Initial charging rate.

II. CARBURETOR :

1. Draining off fuel mixture in float chamber.
2. Adjusting for slow running.

III. CONTACT BREAKER IGNITION POINTS :

1. Cleaning of points.
2. Adjustment of point gap.

IV. TRANSMISSION OIL :

1. Quantity of transmission oil.
2. Quality of oil.

V. FUEL TANK :

1. Draining off.

I. BATTERY:

1. Inspection of Specific Gravity:

The condition of the battery can be determined by measuring the specific gravity of the electrolyte solution.

If the gravity is below 1.220, the battery should be charged without delay.

Specific Gravity (At 20°C. (68°F.) Solution Temperature)	Amount of Charge
1.280 (for electric starter)	100%
1.260 (for kick starter)	
1.220	75
1.160	50
1.105	25
1.050	None

(Caution)　Take care of the following points when checking the specific gravity.

(1)　Do not let the hydrometer float touch the side of the wall.

(2)　Read the hydrometer at A (high point of contact) instead of B (low level) as shown in Figure.

(3)　A specific gravity varies according to the temperature of the solution, apply the following conversion table based on standard 20°C. (or 68°F.) for the different temperatures.

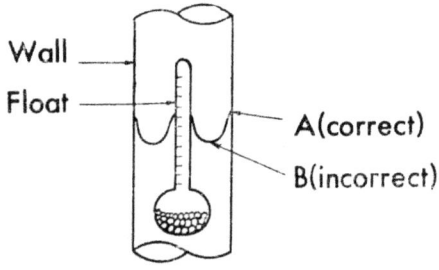

Relation between Specific Gravity and Temperature of Solution.

0°C 32°F	5°C 42°F	10°C 50°F	25°C 59°F	20°C 68°F	25°C 77°F	30°C 86°F	35°C 95°F	40°C 104°F	45°C 113°F
1,218	1,215	1,212	1,208	1,205	1,202	1,198	1,195	1,191	1,188
1,223	1,220	1,217	1,213	1,210	1,207	1,203	1,200	1,196	1,193
1,228	1,225	1,222	1,218	1,220	1,212	1,208	1,205	1,202	1,198
1,233	1,230	1,227	1,223	1,225	1,217	1,213	1,210	1,206	1,203
1,238	1,235	1,232	1,228	1,225	1,222	1,218	1,215	1,211	1,208
1,244	1,241	1,237	1,234	1,230	1,226	1,223	1,219	1,216	1,212
1,249	1,246	1,242	1,239	1,235	1,231	1,228	1,224	1,221	1,217
1,254	1,251	1,247	1,244	1,240	1,236	1,233	1,229	1,226	1,222
1,259	1,256	1,252	1,249	1,245	1,241	1,238	1,234	1,231	1,227
1,264	1,261	1,257	1,254	1,250	1,246	1,243	1,239	1,236	1,232
1,269	1,266	1,262	1,259	1,255	1,251	1,248	1,244	1,240	1,237
1,274	1,271	1,267	1,264	**1,260**	1,256	1,253	1,249	1,245	1,242
1,276	1,276	1,272	1,269	1,265	1,261	1,258	1,254	1,250	1,247
1,284	1,281	1,277	1,274	1,270	1,266	1,263	1,259	1,255	1,252
1,289	1,286	1,282	1,279	1,275	1,270	1,268	1,264	1,260	1,257
1,294	1,260	1,287	1,284	1,280	1,276	1,273	1,269	1,265	1,261

2. Storage of Dry Charged Battery :

Dry charged battery, if stored in a relatively dry place, will remain in good condition for a considerable period, but if the cells absorb moisture during storage, the negative plates will discharge slowly and the charging rate will be longer as shown in the following table.

Storage Period	Decreased Capacity	Capacity
One Month	0 %	100 %
Three month	15 %	85 %
Six month	30 %	70 %
One year	50 %	50 %

3. Initial Charging Rate :

(2) Leave battery from 2 to 12 hours after filling before charging. If the level of electrolyte has dropped, add more electrolyte until the proper level is reached.

(2) Charge at the proper rate as given in table below until all cells are gassing freely and cell voltage and specific gravity stop rising and remain constant.

The total charging time will be about 10 hours. During charging, battery temperature should be kept below 45°C (113°F.) Should the temperature exceed 45°C., stop charging for a time until the temperature falls below 45°C.

Model	Proper Charging	Quick Charging
BRIDGESTONE 7		
Deluxe	0.6 Ampere × 12 hour	3 Ampere × 1 hour
Standard	0.2 ″ × 12 ″	1 ″ × 1 ″
BRIDGESTONE 50		
HOMER (Standard)	0.2 ″ × 12 ″	1 ″ × 1 ″
BRIDGESTONE 90	0.4 ″ × 12 ″	2 ″ × 1 ″

II. CARBURETOR

1. Drain off Remaining Fuel Mixture in Float Chamber:

(**Reason**)

Over three months' storage of motorcycle will cause the fuel mixture in carburetor float chamber to become too rich, due to evaporation of gasoline, which will make starting difficult.

(**Maintenance**)

(2) Disassemble float chamber, and clean it with gasoline.

(2) Clean hole in main jet, and needle jet with an air-pump.

2. Adjusting for Slow Running:

(**Note**) Warm up the engine for 2 or 3 minutes before adjusting.

(**Adjusting**)

(2) Screw in the air screw to the limit and then unscrew.

    2 full turns for model BRIDGESTONE 50 HOMER
    1-1/2 turns for model BRIDGESTONE 90
    2 turns for model BRIDGESTONE 7

(2) Adjust the engine with the throttle stop screw to the lowest revolution it will run.

(3) Turning the air screw back and forward about 1/2 turn each way, find the position where the engine fires best.

(4) Re-adjust the idling speed with the throttle stop screw.

III. CONTACT BREAKER IGNITION POINTS:

1. Cleaning of Points:

After three months storage, polish the points with a point file before starting up the machine.

(**Reason**) After long storage, the points will be coated with a thin oxidized film.

Do not use emery paper, as residue emery powder will cause rapid wear of the points.

2. Adjustment of Point Gap:

Keep the point gap between 0.3-0.4 mm (0.012-0.016 inch)

IV. TRANSMISSION OIL:

Do not overlook to fill up before taking machine out on the road.
Fill with high grade motor oil.

1. Quantity of Transmission Oil:

1 litre (0.26 U.S. Gal.) for model BRIDGESTONE 50 HOMER and 7.

0.6 litre (0.158 U.S. Gal.) for model BRIDGESTONE 90.

2. Quality Oil:

SAE No. 30 in summer.

SAE No. 20 in winter.

or

SAE No. 20 W/30 all season oil.

V. FUEL TANK:

Fuel tank should first be completely drained and all deposits and grit cleaned out.

Then refill with mixture of 1-pint of 2 cycle enging oil (SAE No. 30) and 1.8 gallons of recognized brand of "Regular grade gasoline".

14. TROUBLE SHOOTING

(1) Engine is hard to start.

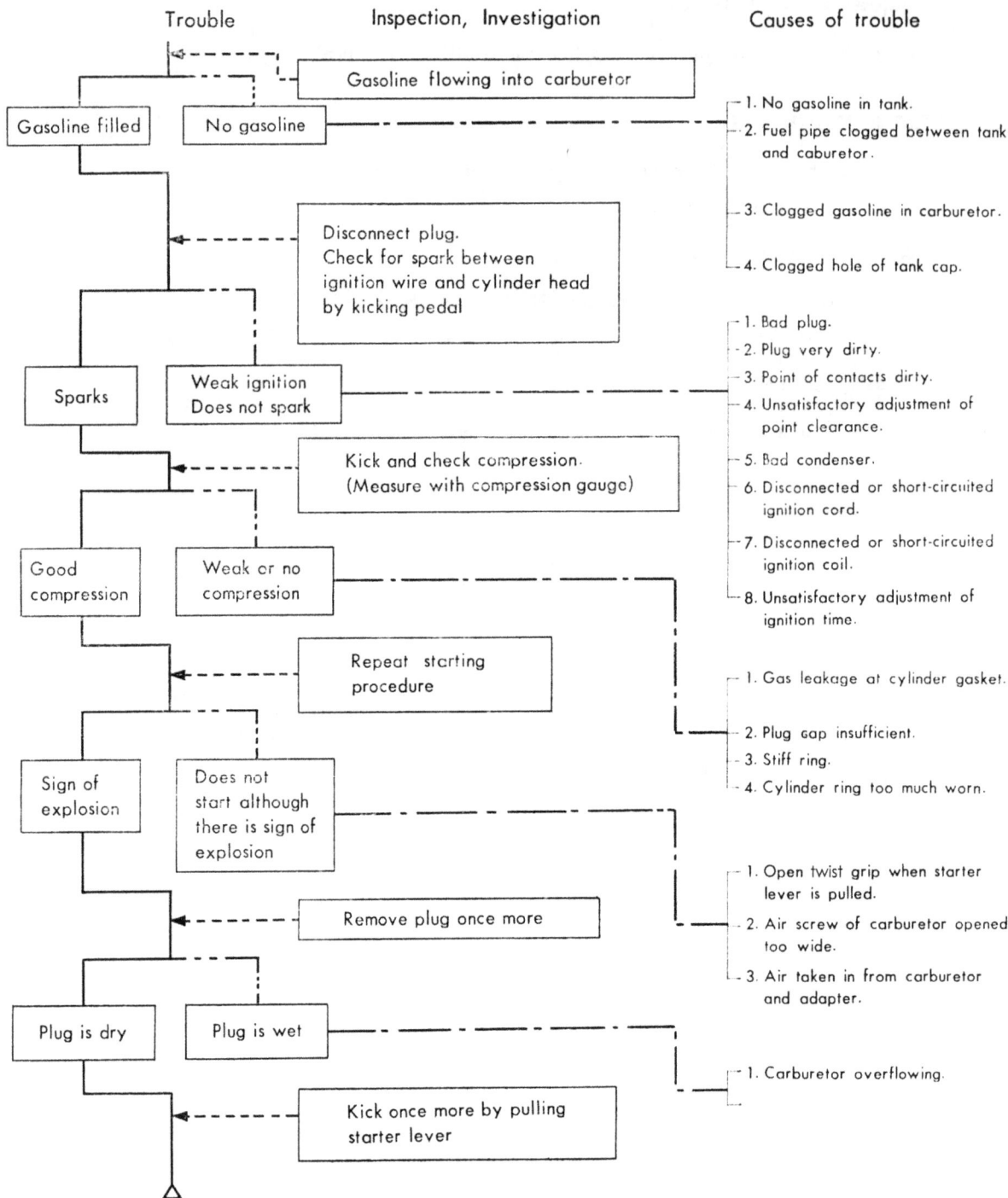

Fuel, spark and compression-are basic points for engine operation. To locate engine trouble first check these points.

(2) High engine revolution cannot be obtained. Insufficient power.

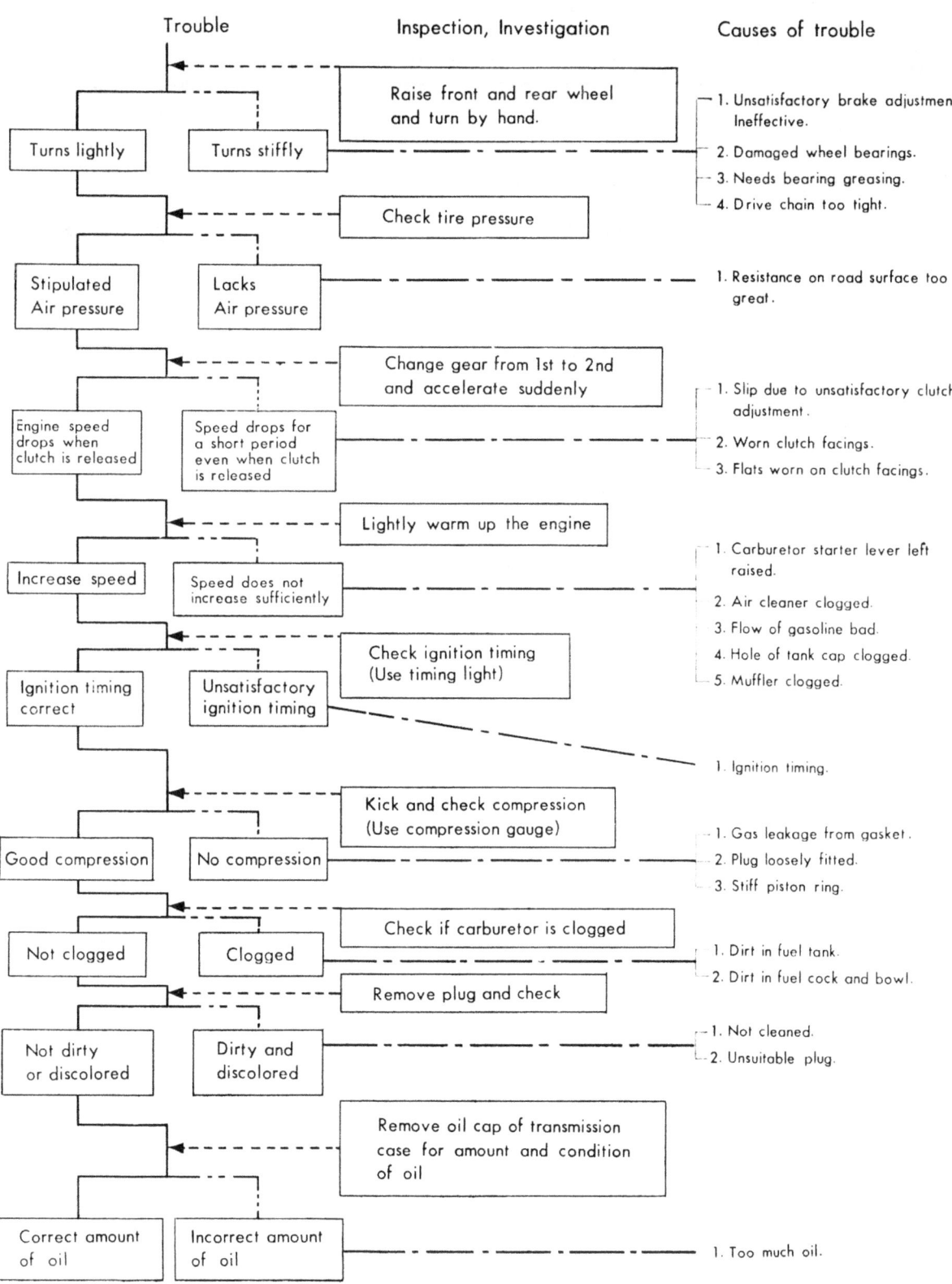

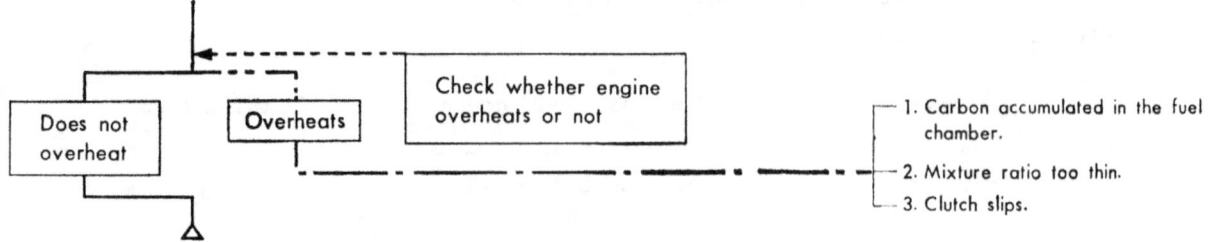

Does not overheat
Overheats
Check whether engine overheats or not
1. Carbon accumulated in the fuel chamber.
2. Mixture ratio too thin.
3. Clutch slips.

(3) Unsatisfactory R.P.M.(Chiefly at low speed and idling)

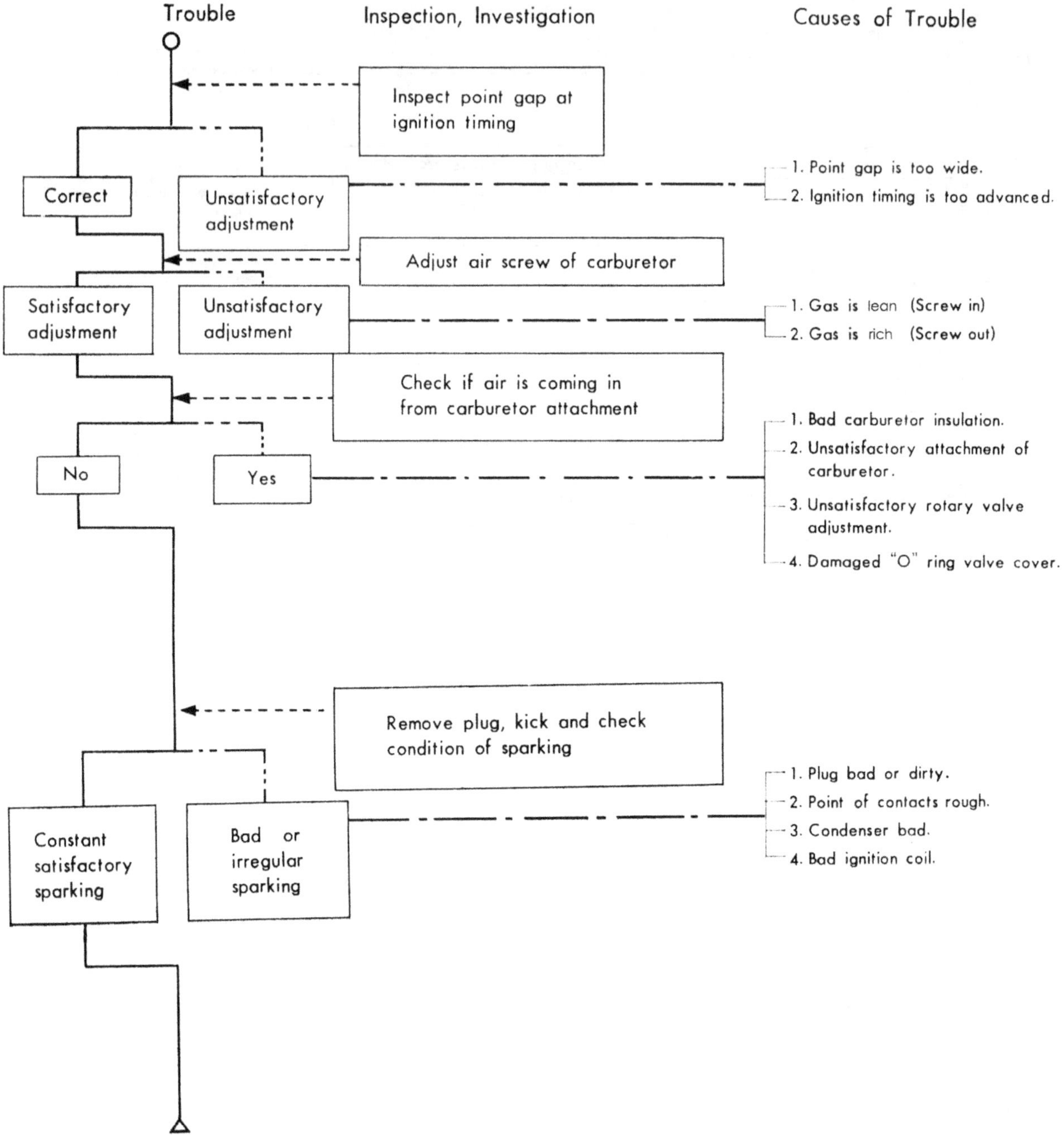

Trouble
Inspection, Investigation
Causes of Trouble
Inspect point gap at ignition timing
Correct
Unsatisfactory adjustment
1. Point gap is too wide.
2. Ignition timing is too advanced.
Adjust air screw of carburetor
Satisfactory adjustment
Unsatisfactory adjustment
1. Gas is lean (Screw in)
2. Gas is rich (Screw out)
Check if air is coming in from carburetor attachment
No
Yes
1. Bad carburetor insulation.
2. Unsatisfactory attachment of carburetor.
3. Unsatisfactory rotary valve adjustment.
4. Damaged "O" ring valve cover.
Remove plug, kick and check condition of sparking
Constant satisfactory sparking
Bad or irregular sparking
1. Plug bad or dirty.
2. Point of contacts rough.
3. Condenser bad.
4. Bad ignition coil.

(4) Irregular Revolutions (At Medium and High speeds)

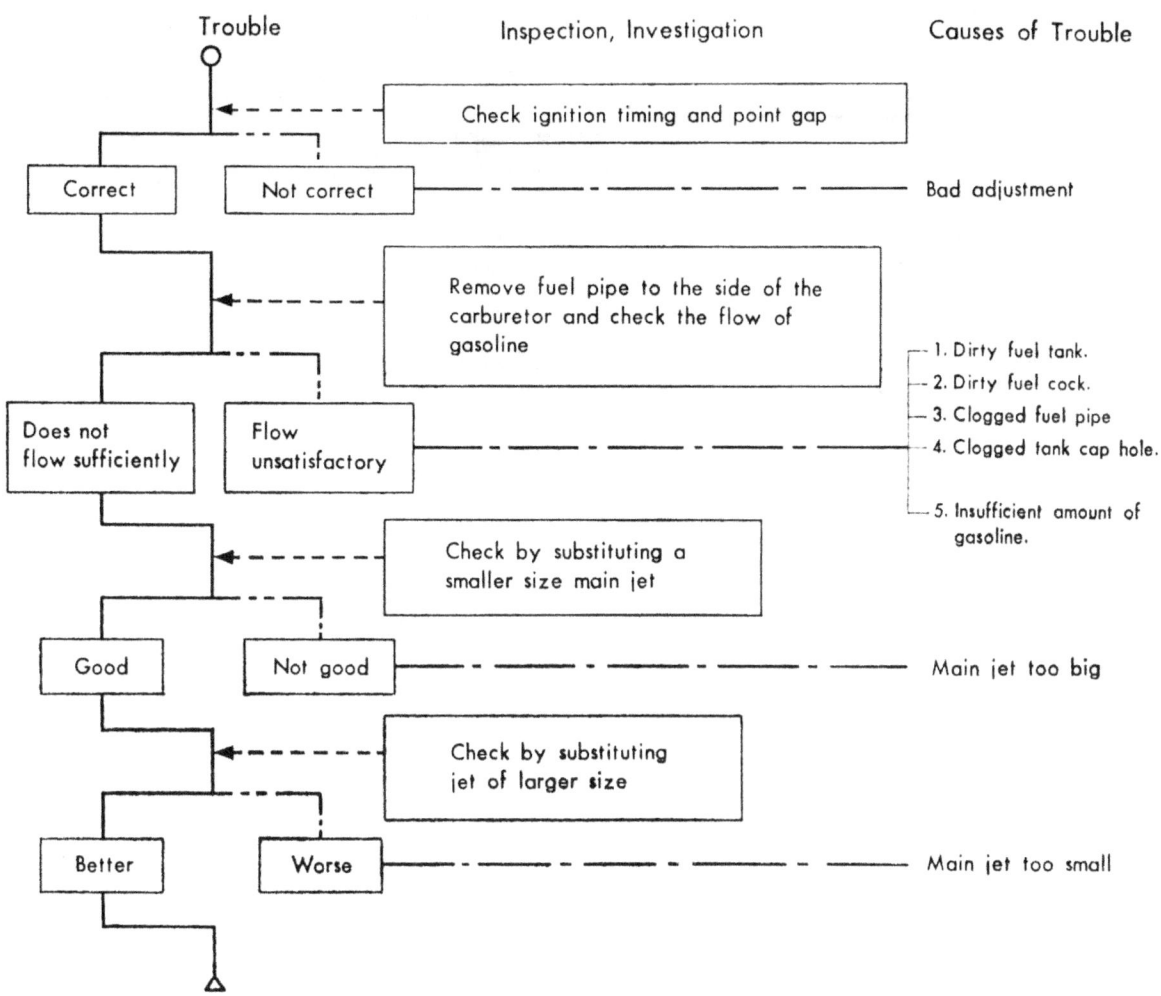

(5) Unsatisfactory Gear Shifting

Trouble	Causes of Trouble
Gears cannot be shifted smoothly	1. Improper working gear shift drum. 2. Bent shift fork. 3. Improper working clutch. 4. Worn claws of drum shifter.
Change pedal does not return smoothly	1. Broken change return spring. 2. Drum shifter touching some part. 3. Bent change shaft.
Gears disengage	1. Bent and worn out shift fork. 2. Worn out claws of drum shifter. 3. Worn out drum stopper.

BRIDGESTONE 90 SERIES

PARTS CATALOGUE

BRIDGESTONE TIRE CO., LTD.

TOKYO, JAPAN

INSTRUCTIONS FOR USING THE PARTS CATALOGUE

1. This catalogue covers all the items of genuine parts and tools of BRIDGESTONE 90 cc motorcycles

2. Please note the following when Placing orders.

    a. Be sure to state accurately the Index No., Part No., and Name of each part.

    b. All the items recessed (set-back) under individual "assembly items" represent a group of parts comprising the "assembly".

    c. The numbers shown in the column "No. Req'd" represent the quantities required for one unit.

    d. The numbers shown in the column "Min. lot" represent the quantities to be ordered in one lot, and in the event of larger quantities, order in multiple quantities of the minimum specified.

    e. "Old Part No." indicates the Part Number which was in force until 1966.

    f. "Serial No. from (MFG date)" means effective Serial No. and effective date of modification.

    g. Symbols CUR, CBK, MB, FAR, MS and XC1 indicate Red, Black, Metallic blue, Metallic silver and Chrome plating finish respectively.

    h. Dimensions of the parts listed in this catalogue in millimeters.

CONTENTS

Index No.	Description	Page
	Engine Group	
1	Cylinder · Cylinder head	4~5
2	Crankshaft · Piston · Rotary valve	6~7
3	Carburetor	8~9
4	Flywheel magneto · Neutral switch	10~11
5	Left crank case · Neutral switch	12~13
6	Right crank case	14~15
7	Crank case cover	16~17
8	Left crank case cover	18~19
9	Clutch	20~21
10	Transmission gears	22~23
11	Change arm · Shift drum · Gear change pedal	24~25
12	Kick shaft · Kick pedal	26~27
	Body Group	
13	Frame	28~31
14	Front fork assy	32~33
15	Front fender · Head lamp body · Handle bar	34~35
16	Rear fork · chain case · Rear cushions	36~37
17	Fuel tank · Fuel cock	38~39
18	Clutch grip	40~41
19	Throttle grip	42~43
20	Front turn signal · Tail lamp	44~45
21	Speedometer · Wires	46~47
22	Brake pedal · Stand · Foot rest	48~49
23	Air cleaner	50~51
24	Muffler · Exhaust pipe	52~53
25	Dual seat · Covers · Carrier	54~55
26	Front wheel	56~57
27	Rear wheel	58~61
28	Head lamp · Main switch · Wire harness · Battery	62~63
29	Service tool · Special tool	64~65
30	Exclusive parts for U.S.A.	66~67
31	Exclusive parts for Trail model	68~69
32~36	Exclusive parts for model BS 90 M	70~78
37~39	Exclusive parts for model BS 90 SP	79~81
40~44	Exclusive parts for models 90D/OI, 90T/OI & 90M/OI	82~91
45~46	Exclusive parts for 90SP/OI	92
47	Exclusive parts for U.S.A	92

1) CYLINDER · CYLINDER HEAD

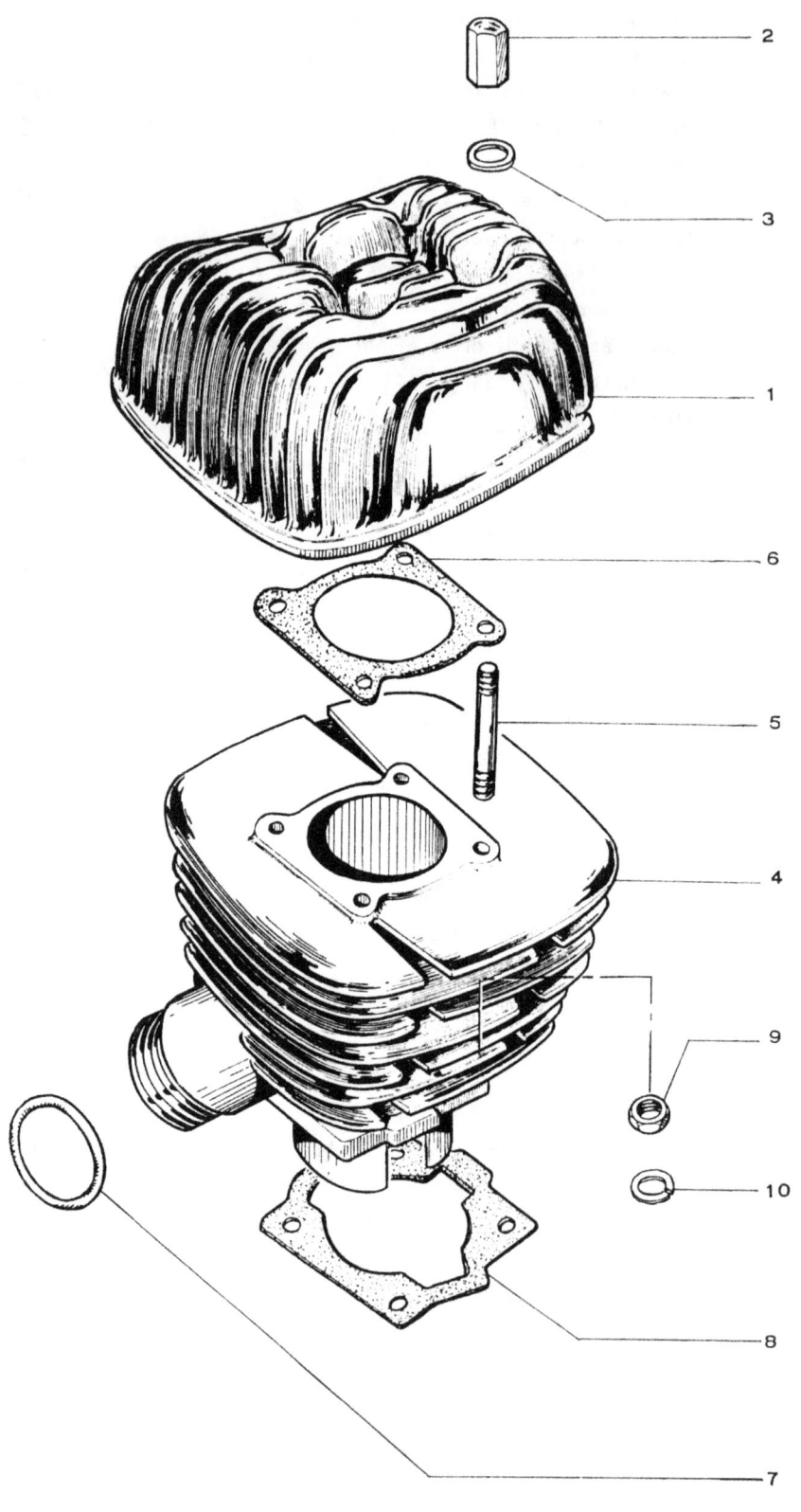

1) CYLINDER · CYLINDER HEAD

Index No.	Part No.	Part Name	No. Req'd	Unit Price US $	Serial No. From (MFG date)	Old Part No.	Min. Lot	N. B.
1- 1	1111-5000	Cylinder head	1			EA1 11111		
1- 2	1115-5000	Cylinedr head nut	4			EA1 11112		
1- 3	0411-0613	Plane washer A	4			HW 6	50	
1- 4	1121-5030	Cylinder	1		12H060061 (Aug. '66)			
1- 4	1121-5010	Cylinder	1		12N036925 (Feb. '65)	EAE 11211		
1- 4	1121-5000	Cylinder	1			EA1 11211		
1- 5	1126-5000	Cylinder head stud	4			EA1 11212		
1- 6	1141-5000	Cylinder head gasket	1			EA1 11411	10	
1- 7	1142-5000	Exhaust pipe gasket	1			EA1 11412	10	
1- 8	1143-5000	Cylinder base gasket	1			EA1 11413	10	
1- 9	0211-0600	Hexagon nut A	4			6N1 6	50	
1-10	0431-0615	Spring washer	4			SW 6	50	

MEMO

2) CRANKSHAFT · PISTON · ROTARY VALVE

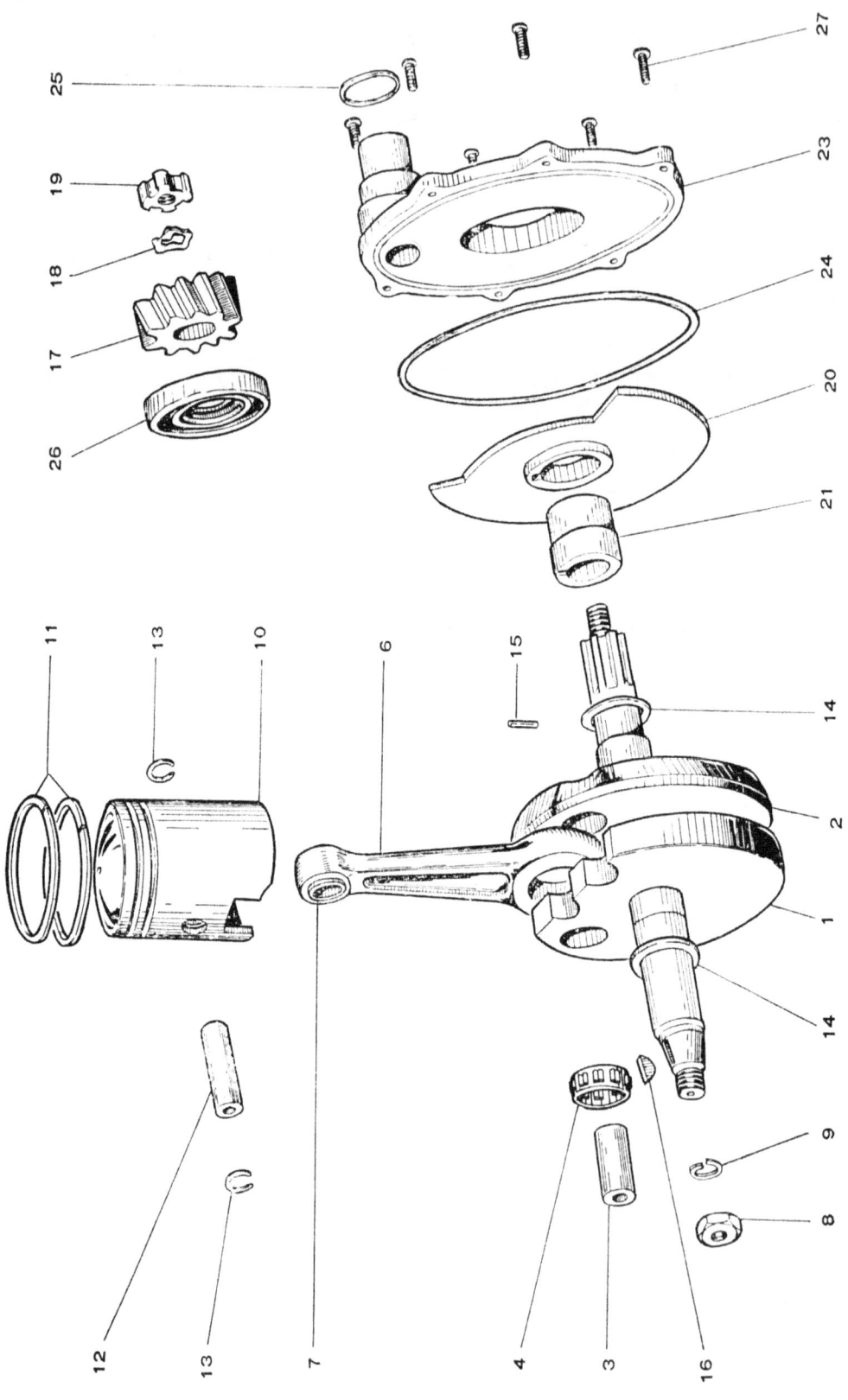

— 6 —

Index No.	Part No.	Part Name	No. Req'd	Unit Price US $	Serial No. From (MFG date)	Old Part No.	Min. Lot	N. B.
2- 0	1301-5010	Crank shaft comp	1			EA2 13100		
2- 1	1311-5010	Left crank shaft	1		12M036326 (Dec. '64)	EA2 13111		
2- 1	1311-5000	Left crank shaft	1		Old type	EA1 13111		
2- 2	1312-5010	Right crank shaft	1		12M036326 (Dec. '64)	EA2 13121		
2- 2	1312-5000	Right crank shaft	1		Old type	EA1 13121		
2- 3	1321-5000	Crank pin	1			EA1 13151		
2- 4	1325-5010	Needle bearing	1					
2- 6	1331-5010	Connecting rod	1		12M036326 (Dec. '64)	EA2 13211		
2- 7	1333-5010	Needle bearing	1		12M036326 (Dec. '64)	EA2 13212		
2- 7	1334-5000	Connecting rod bushing	1			EA1 13212		
2- 8	09021-103	12 Hexagon nut	1			EA1 13221	10	
2- 9	0432-1230	Spring washer	1			SW 12	50	
2-10	1341-5000	Piston S.T.D.	1			EA1 13310		
2-10	1349-5000	Piston S.T.D. 0.03 o/s	1		As optional			
2-10	1342-5000	Piston 0.25 o/s	1			EA1 13310 -25		
2-10	1343-5000	Piston 0.50 o/s	1			EA1 13310 -50		
2-11	1305-5000	Piston ring assy S.T.D.	1			EA1 13320		
2-11	1306-5000	Piston ring assy 0.25 o/s	1			EA1 13320 -25		
2-11	1307-5000	Piston ring assy 0.50 o/s	1			EA1 13320 -50		
2-12	1381-5000	Piston pin	1			EA1 13331		
2-13	1382-5000	Piston pin circlip	2			EA1 13332		
2-14	09049-106	20×0.3 shim	2~4			EA1 13411	50	
2-15	09063-104	3×10 dowel	1		12P039777 (April '65)	GB2 13413	50	
2-15	09062-103	3×15 dowel	1		Old type	EA1 13413	50	
2-16	09067-101	3×15 woodruff key	1			EO 3314	50	
2-17	1385-5000	Drive pinion	1			EA1 13421		
2-18	09046-101	10 wave washer	1			EA1 13422	50	
2-19	09029-103	10mm left turn thread nut	1			EA1 13423	10	
2-20	1412-5010	Rotary valve comp	1		12N036925 (Feb. '65)	EA2 14112		
2-20	1412-5000	Rotary valve comp	1		Old type	EA1 14112		
2-22	1451-3210	Crank shaft collar	1		12P039777 (April '65)	GB2 14121		
2-21	1451-5000	Crank shaft collar	1		Old type	EA1 14121		
2-23	1431-5000	Rotary valve cover	1			EA1 14131		
2-24	09066-103	100 O ring	1			EA1 14132	50	
2-25	09066-104	23 O ring	1			EA1 14133	50	
2-26	09090-108	25 oil seal	1			EA1 14141	10	
2-27	0311-0620	Cross recd pan head screw	6			PNK 6×20	50	

3) CARBURETOR

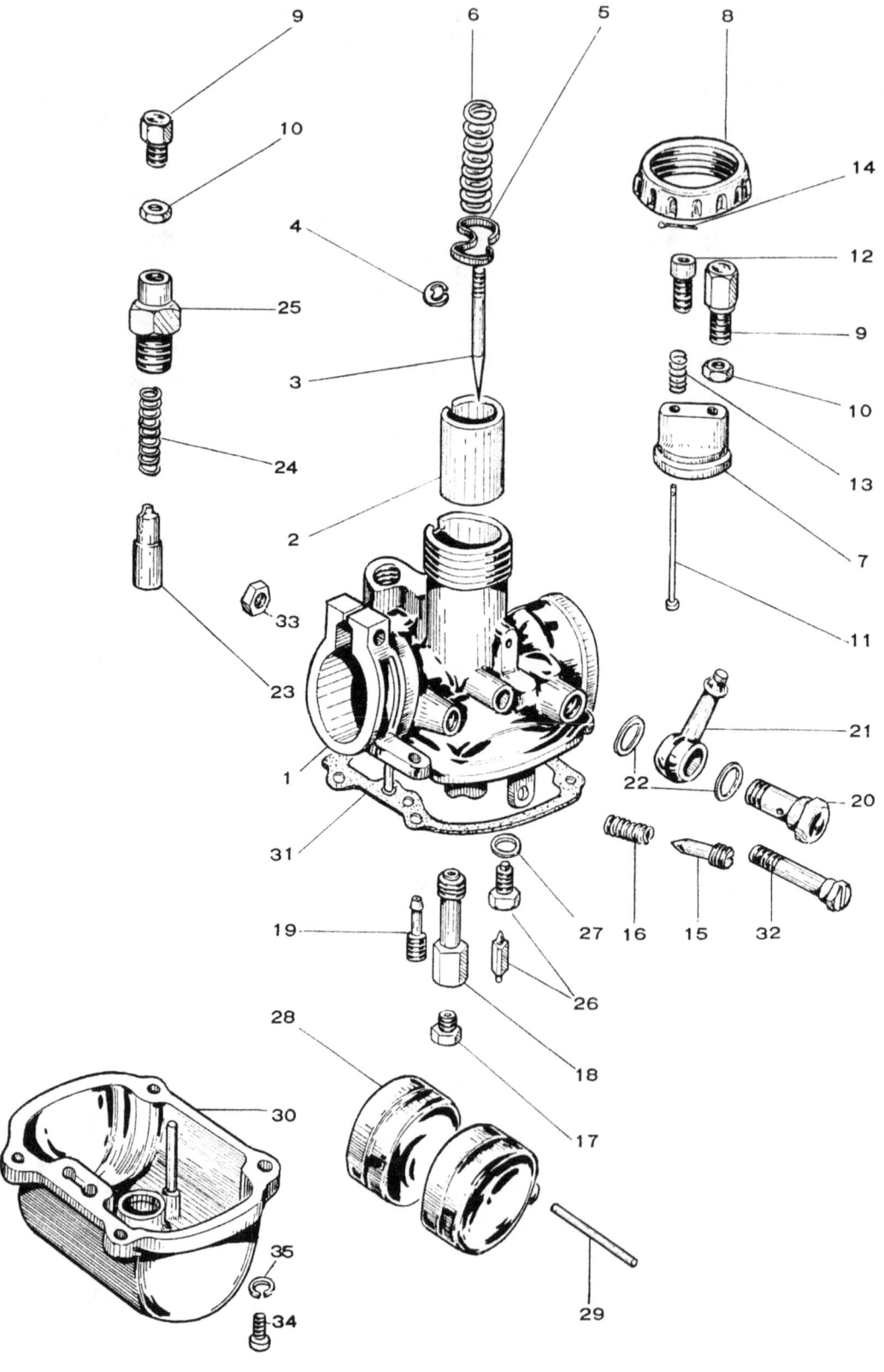

Index No.	Part No.	Part Name	No. Req'd	Unit Price US $	Serial No. From (MFG date)	Old Part No.	Min. Lot	N. B.
3- 0	1600-5000	Carburetor assy	1		M.J No. 100	EA1 16100		
3- 0	1600-5030	Carburetor assy	1		M.J No. 130	EA13 16100		
3- 1	1611-5000	Mixing chamber body	1			EA1 16111		
3- 2	1614-5000	Throttle valve	1			EA1 16121		
3- 3	1615-3021	Jet needle	1			E2 8122-1		
3- 4	1616-3021	Needle clip	1			E2 8123-1		
3- 5	1617-3021	Spring seat	1			E2 8124-1		
3- 6	1618-5000	Throttle valve spring	1			EA1 16125		
3- 7	1619-5000	Mixing chamber top	1			EA1 16126		
3- 8	1621-5000	Mixing chamber cap	1			EA1 16127		
3- 9	1622-5000	Cable adjuster	2			EA1 16128		
3-10	1623-5000	Adjuster lock nut	2			EA1 16129		
3-11	1626-5000	Throttle stop rod	1			EA1 16131		
3-12	1627-5000	Throttle stop screw	1			EA1 16132		
3-13	1628-5000	Stop screw spring	1			EA1 16133		
3-14	0551-1010	Split pin	1			WP 1×10	50	
3-15	1631-5000	Pilot air screw	1			EA1 16135		
3-16	1632-3010	Air screw spring	1			E2 8135		
3-17	1635-5000 100	100 main jet	1			EA1 16141-100		
3-17	1635-5000 110	110 main jet	1			EAE 16141-110		
3-17	1635-5000 130	130 main jet	1			EA13 16141-130		
3-18	1633-3100	Needle jet	1			GA1 16145		
3-19	1634-3110	Pilot jet	1		12R044929 (June, '65)	GA3 16146		
3-19	1634-5000	Pilot jet	1		Old type	EA1 16143		
3-20	1651-5000	Union bolt	1			EA1 16151		
3-21	1652-3100	Connecting union	1			GA1 16193		
3-22	1654-3100	Union gasket	2			GA1 16196		
3-23	1645-5000	Starter pluger	1			EA1 16161		
3-24	1646-5000	Plunger spring	1			EA1 16162		
3-25	1647-5000	Plunger cap	1			EA1 16163		
3-26	1660-3100	Float valve assy	1			GA1 16170		
3-27	1665-3100	Valve seat gasket	1			GA1 16173		
3-28	1666-3100	Float	1			GA1 16181		
3-29	1667-3100	Float pin	1			GA1 16182		
3-30	1656-5000	Float chamber body	1			EA1 16183		
3-31	1657-3100	Float chamber gasket	1			GA1 16184		
3-32	1613-3020	Clamp screw	1			E2 8191		
3-33	0211-0500	Hexagon nut A	1			6N1 5	50	
3-34	0311-0414	Cross recd pan head screw	4			PNK 4×14	50	
3-35	0431-0410	Spring washer	4			SW 4	50	

4) FLYWHEEL MAGNETO · IGNITION COIL

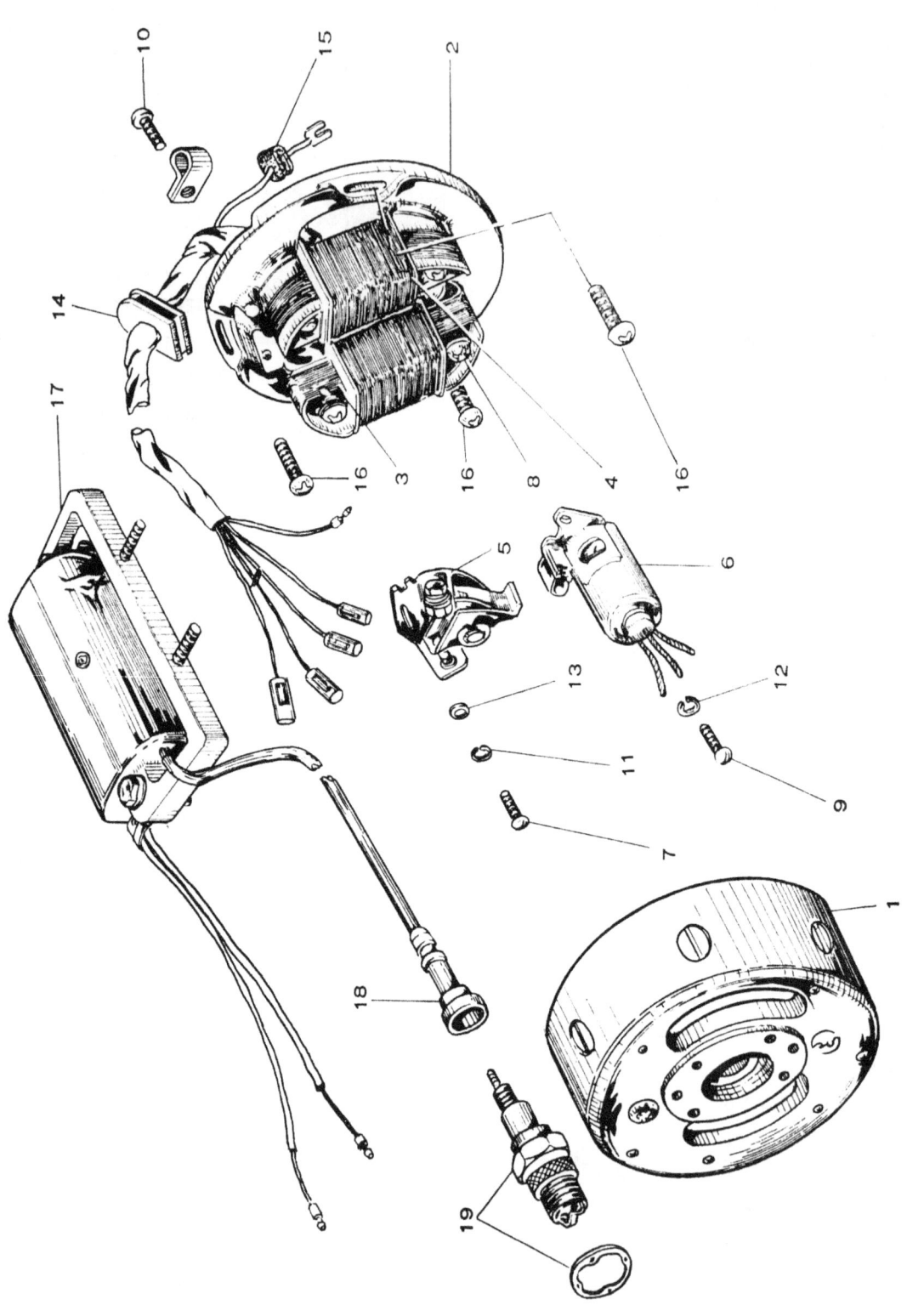

4) FLYWHEEL MAGNETO · IGNITION COIL

Index No.	Part No.	Part Name	No. Req'd	Unit Price US $	Serial No. From (MFG date)	Old Part No.	Min. Lot	N. B.
4- 0	1701-5000	Flywheel magneto assy	1			EA1 17100		
4- 1	1718-5000	Magneto flywheel	1			EA1 17111		
4- 2	1710-5000	Magnet stator assy	1			EA1 17210		
4- 3	1713-5000	Magneto primary coil	1			EA1 17212		
4- 4	1714-5000	Magneto lighting coil	1			EA1 17213		
4- 5	1752-5000	Contact breaker assy	1			EA1 17230		
4- 6	1753-5000	Condenser	1			EA1 17241		
4- 7	0361-0412	Pan head screw	1			NK 4×12	50	
4- 8	0361-0424	Pan head screw	4			NK 4×24	50	
4- 9	0861-0510	Pan head screw	1			NK 5×10	50	
4-10	0361-0407	Pan head screw	1			NK 4× 7	50	
4-11	0431-0410	Spring washer	6			SW 4	50	
4-12	0431-0513	Spring washer	1			SW 5	50	
4-13	0411-0410	Plane washer A	1			HW 4	50	
4-14	1755-5000	Wire harness grommet	1			EA1 17251		
4-15	1764-5000	Neutral switch wire grommet	1			EA1 17252		
4-16	0311-0512	Cross recd pan head screw	3			PNK 5×12	50	
4-17	8501-5001	Ignition coil assy	1			EA1 89310		
4-18	8520-5000	Plug cap comp	1			EA1 89320		
4-19	1781-5010	Spark plug	1			EA2 17410		NGK B-7H
		Exclusive parts for 6V-25/25W						
4-	6101-5010	Clutch grip assy	1			EA11 61100		
4-	6104-5010	Throttle grip assy	1			EA11 61200		
4-	8102-5010	Head lamp assy	1			EA2 81200		
4-	8150-5010	Head lamp lens comp	1			EA2 81220		
4-	8160-5010	Socket assy	1			EA2 81230		
4-	8171-5010	Head lamp bulb	1			EA2 81242		
4-	1701-5010	Flywheel magneto assy	1			EA2 17100		
4-	1718-5010	Magnet flywheel	1			EA2 17111		
4-	1713-5010	Magneto primary coil	1			EA2 17211		
4-	1714-5010	Magneto lighting coil	1			EA2 17213		
4-	8803-5010	Resistor assy	1					
4-	8825-5010	Connecting wire	1					

5) LEFT CRANK CASE · NEUTRAL SWITCH

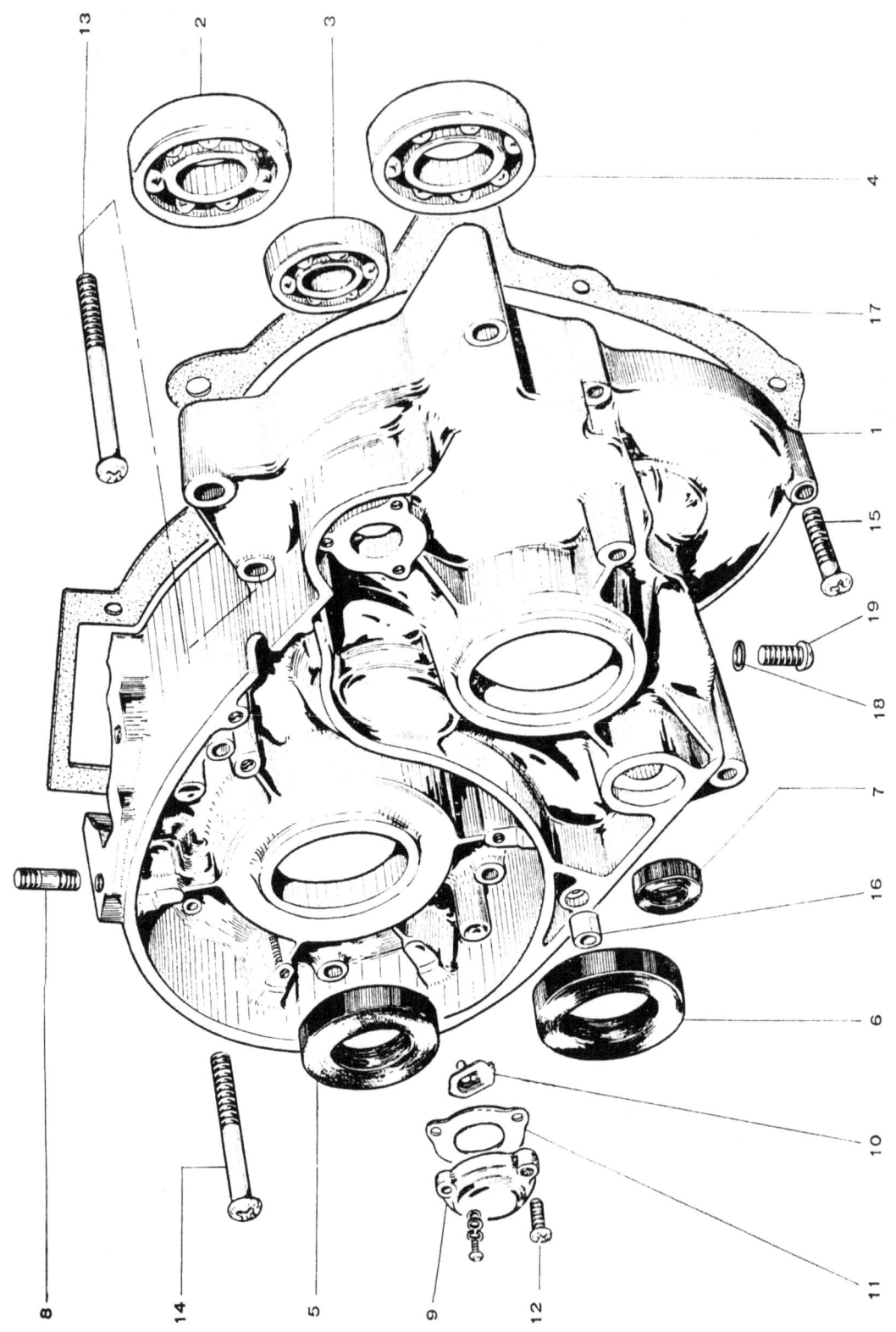

5) LEFT CRANK CASE · NEUTRAL SWITCH

Index No.	Part No.	Part Name	No. Req'd	Unit Price US $	Serial No. From (MFG dete)	Old Part No.	Min. Lot	N. B.
5- 1	2110-5010	Left crank case comp	1					
5- 2	07-6304-01	Ball bearing	1			EA1 21121	10	
5- 3	07-6201-01	Ball bearing	1			EA1 21122	10	
5- 4	07-6303-01	Ball bearing	1			E0 3311	10	
5- 5	09090-106	20 oil seal	1			EA1 21124	10	
5- 6	09090-107	21 oil seal	1			GA1 21261	10	
5- 7	09090-101	12 oil seal	1			E0 2614	10	
5- 8	2121-5000	Cylinder mounting stud	2			EA1 21127		
5- 9	1761-5000	Neutral switch case	1			EA1 17311		
5-10	1762-5000	Neutral switch contact plate	1			EA1 17312		
5-11	1763-5000	Neutral switch gasket	1			EA1 17313		
5-12	0311-0516	Cross recd pan head screw	3			PNK 5×16	50	
5-13	0313-0655	Cross recd pan head screw	4			PNK 6×55	50	
5-14	0313-0645	Cross recd pan head screw	4			PNK 6×45	50	
5-15	0311-0625	Cross recd pan head screw	1			PNK 6×25	50	
5-16	09057-101	6×10×10B dowel	1			E0 2516	50	
5-17	2181-5000	Crank case gasket	1			EA1 21511	10	
5-18	09064-102	6 Fiber gasket	1			E0 2632	50	
5-19	0111-0608	Hexagon bolt A	2			6B 6×8	50	

MEMO

6) RIGHT CRANK CASE

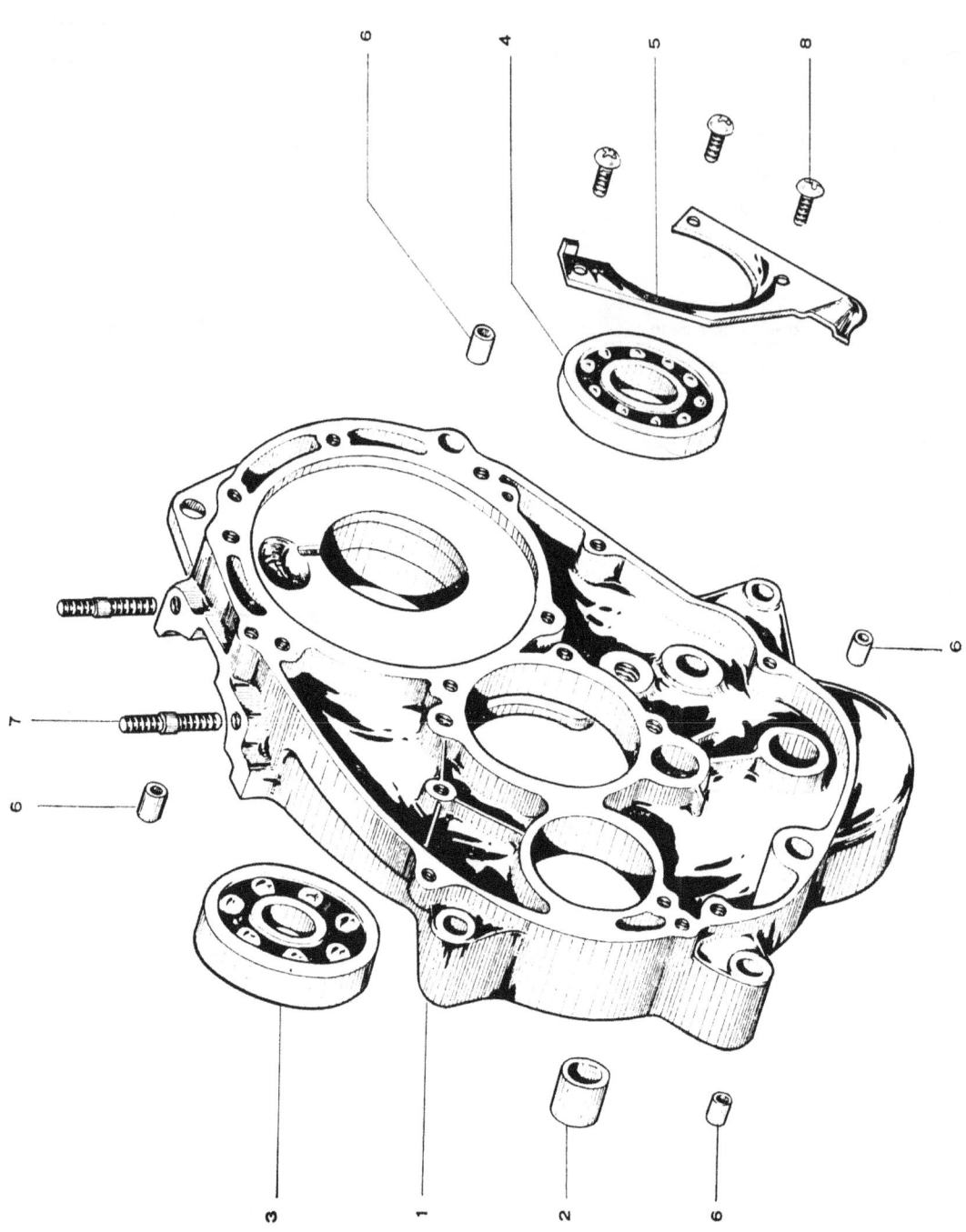

6) RIGHT CRANK CASE

Index No.	Part No.	Part Name	No. Req'd	Unit Price US $	Remarks			N. B.
					Serial No. From (MFG date)	Old Part No.	Min. Lot	
6- 1	2130-5001	Right crank case comp	1			EA1 21210 -1		
6- 2	2133-5000	Driving shaft bush	1			EA1 21213		
6- 3	07-6304-01	Ball bearing	1			EA1 21121	10	
6- 4	07-6006-01	Ball bearing	1			EA1 21222	10	
6- 5	2145-5000	Counter shaft bearing holder	1			EA1 21224		
6- 6	09057-101	6×10×10B Dowel	4			E0 2516	50	
6- 7	2121-5000	Cylinder mounting stud	2			EA1 21127		
6- 8	0311-0614	Cross recd pan head screw	3			PNK 6×14	50	
6-	2135-5000	Breather vinyl tube	1					

MEMO

7) CRANK CASE COVER

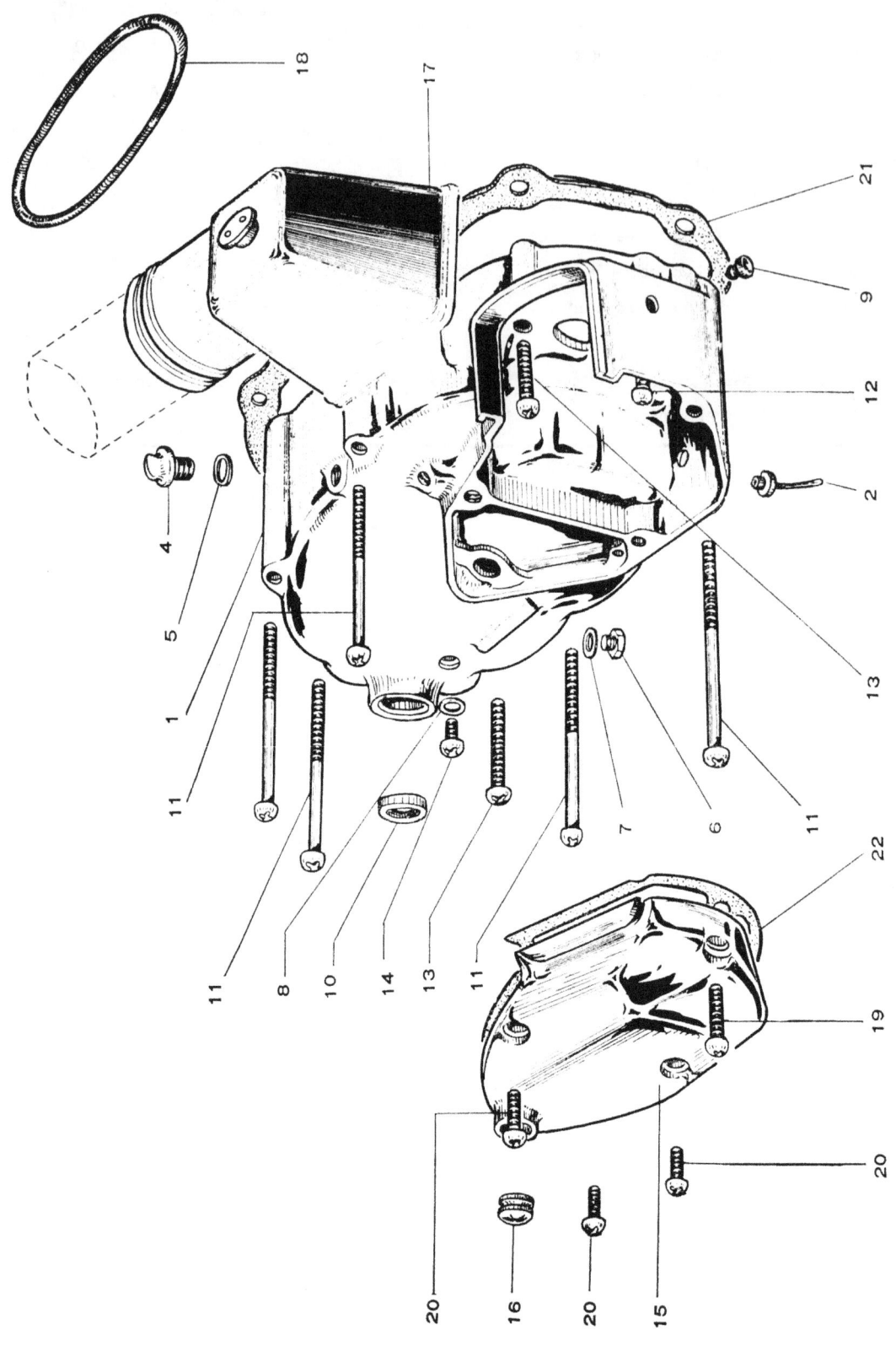

7) CRANK CASE COVER

Index No.	Part No.	Part Name	No. Req'd	Unit Price US $	Serial No. From (MFG date)	Old Part No.	Min. Lot	N. B.
7- 1	2160-5000	Crank case cover comp	1			EA1 21310		
7- 2	2162-5002	Drain pipe	1		12T051145 (Aug. '65)			
7- 4	2165-5000	Oil filler plug	1			EA1 21332		
7- 5	09066-105	14 O ring	1			EA1 21333	50	
7- 6	09058-102	16 drain plug	1			EA1 21334	50	
7- 7	09065-102	16 aluminum gasket	1			EA1 21335	50	
7- 8	09064-102	6 fiber gasket	1			EO 2632	50	
7- 9	2168-5000	12 rubber plug	1			EA1 21337	50	
7-10	09090-103	15 oil seal	1			EO 2613	10	
7-11	0313-0665	Cross recd pan head screw	5			PNK 6×65	50	
7-12	0313-0645	Cross recd pan head screw	1			PNK 6×45	50	
7-13	0313-0635	Cross recd pan head screw	2			PNK 6×35	50	
7-14	0111-0608	Hexagon bolt A	1			6B 6× 8	50	
7-15	2176-5000	Carburetor cover	1			EA1 21351		
7-16	2179-5000	Release screw cap	1			EA1 21352		
7-17	2177-5000	Carburetor cap	1			EA1 21353		
7-18	2178-5000	Carburetor cap ring	1			EA1 21355		
7-19	0311-0625	Cross recd pan head screw	1			PNK 6×25	50	
7-20	0311-0620	Cross recd pan head screw	3			PNK 6×20	50	
7-21	2183-5000	Crank case cover gasket	1			EA1 21512	10	
7-22	2185-5000	Carburetor cover gasket	1			EA1 21513	10	
7-	09066-102	17 O ring	1			EA1 14122	50	

MEMO

8) LEFT CRANK CASE COVER

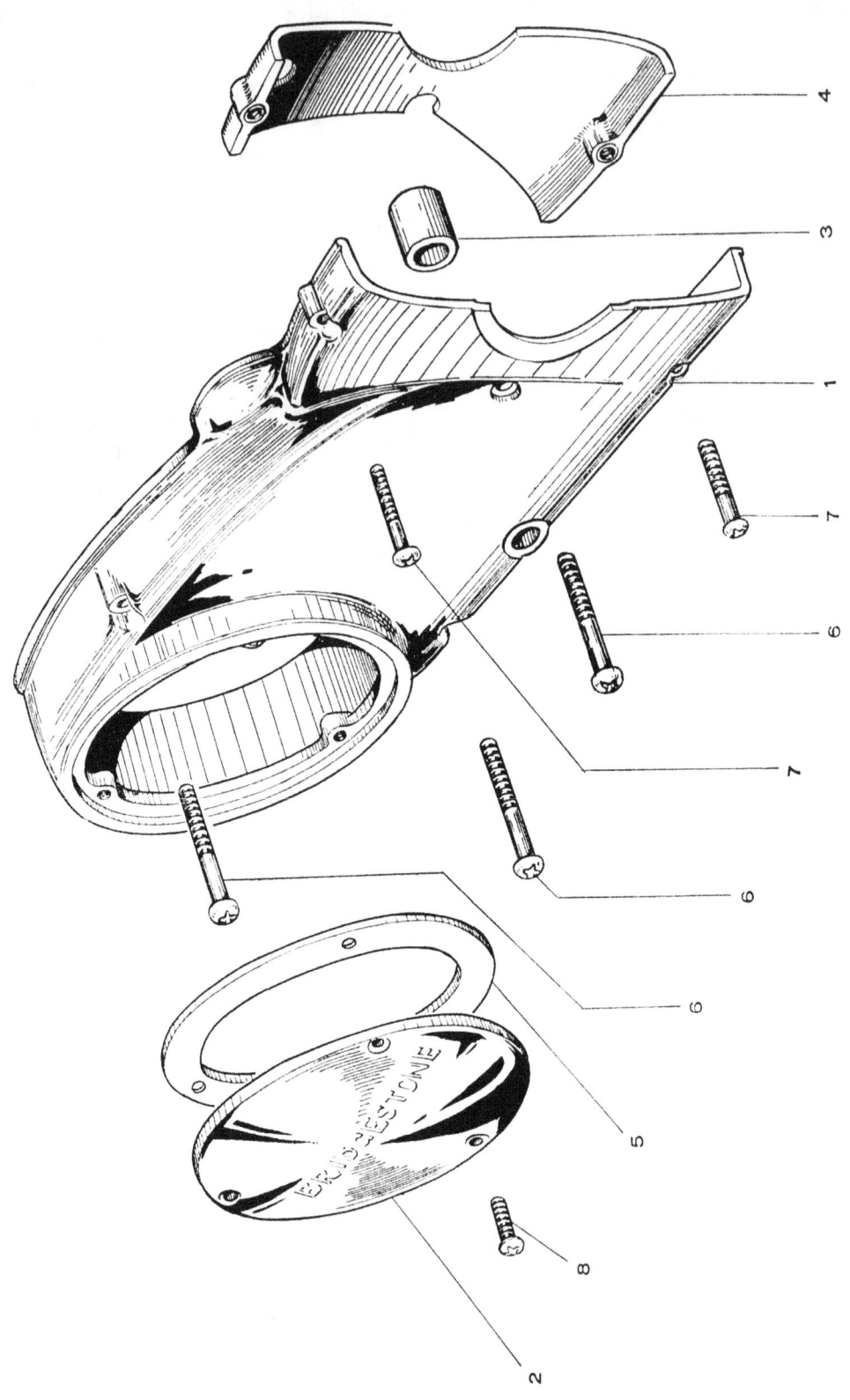

8) LEFT CRANK CASE COVER

Index No.	Part No.	Part Name	No. Req'd	Unit Price US $	Serial No. From (MFG date)	Old Part No.	Min. Lot	N. B.
8- 1	2151-5020	Left crank case cover	1					
8- 2	2152-5001	Contact breaker cover	1			EA1 21412 -1		
8- 3	2156-5000	Gear change shaft rubber	1			EA1 21422		
8- 4	2153-5001	Dust cover A	1			EA1 21431 -1		
8- 5	2184-5000	Contact breaker cover gasket	1			EA1 21514		
8- 6	0313-0635	Cross recd pan head screw	3			PNK 6×35	50	
8- 7	0311-0620	Cross recd pan head screw	2			PNK 6×20	50	
8- 8	0311-0510	Cross recd pan head serew	3			PNK 5×10	50	

MEMO

9) CLUTCH

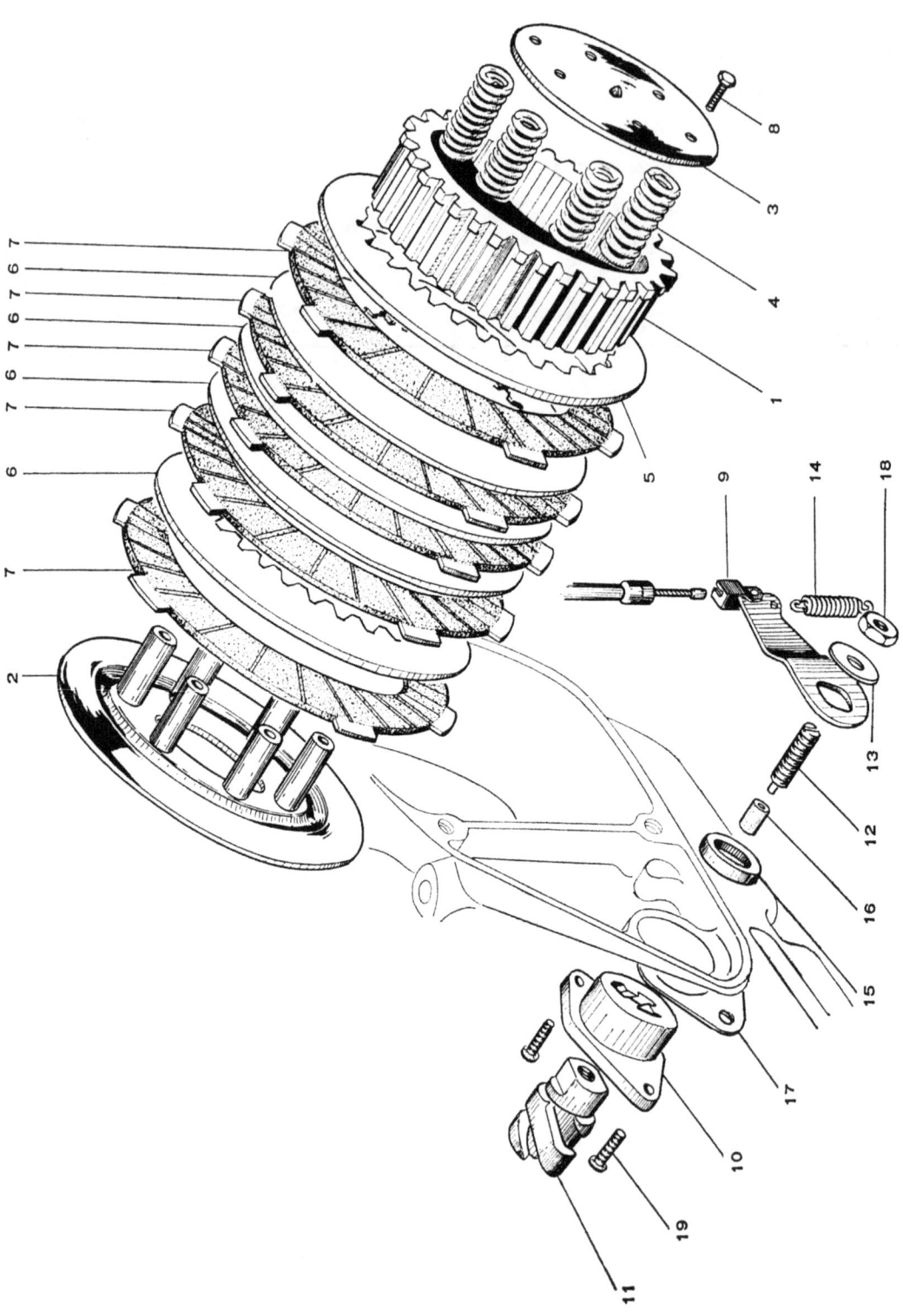

9) CLUTCH

Index No.	Part No.	Part Name	No. Req'd	Unit Price US $	Serial No. From (MFG date)	Old Part No.	Min Lot	N. B.
9- 1	2221-5000	Clutch hub	1			EA1 22111		
9- 2	2210-5000	Pressure plate comp	1			EA1 22112		
9- 3	2227-5000	Set plate comp	1			EA1 22115		
9- 4	2218-5000	Clutch spring	6			EA1 22118		
9- 5	2216-5000	Outer plate	1			EA1 22119		
9- 6	2215-5000	Inner plate	4			EA1 22120		
9- 7	2214-5000	Friction plate	5			EA1 22121		
9- 8	0113-0512	Hexagon bolt A	6			6B 5×12	50	
9- 9	2260-5000	Release arm comp	1			EA1 22221		
9-10	2264-5000	Release screw	1			EA1 22225		
9-11	2265-5000	Release push screw	1			EA1 22226		
9-12	2267-5000	Release adjust screw	1			EA1 22227		
9-13	2268-5000	Release adjust screw washer	1			EA1 22228		
9-14	2271-5000	Release arm return spring	1			EA1 22229		
9-15	09090-102	15 oil seal	1			EA1 22230	10	
9-16	09056-105	6×10 A dowel	1			EA1 22231	50	
9-17	2186-5000	Release screw gasket	1			EA1 21515		
9-18	0211-0600	Hexagon nut A	1			6N1 6	50	
9-19	0331-0614	Cross round head screw	2			RSK 6×14	50	
9-	2272-5000	Release guide washer	1			EA1 22232		

MEMO

10) TRANSMISSION GEARS

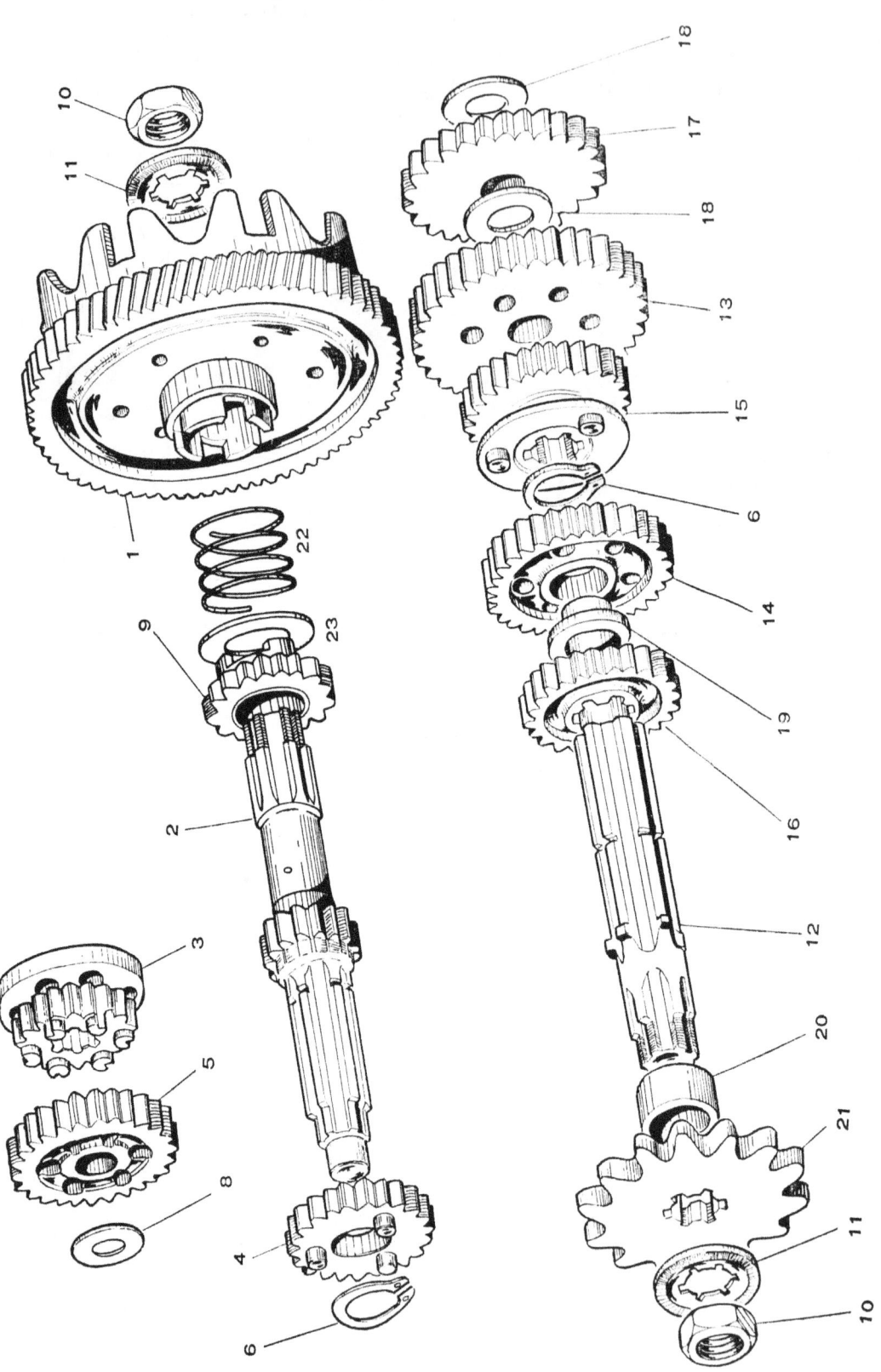

— 22 —

10) TRANSMISSION GEARS

Index No.	Part No.	Part Name	No. Req'd	Unit Price US $	Remarks Serial No. From (MFG date)	Old Part No.	Min. Lot	N. B.
10- 1	2410-5001	Driven gear comp	1			EA1 23211		
10- 2	2421-5001	Counter shaft	1		12T052885 (Aug. '66)	EA1 23211 -1		
10- 3	2426-5000	2nd gear A	1			EA1 23212		
10- 4	2431-5000	3rd gear A	1			EA1 23213		
10- 5	2436-5000	4th gear A	1			EA1 23214		
10- 6	09002-103	17B snap ring	2			EA1 23215		
10- 7	2478-5000	Driven gear bush	1		12T052885 Abolished	EA1 23216		
10- 8	09048-101	12 thrust washer	1			EA1 23217	10	
10- 9	2610-5000	Kick gear A comp	1			EA1 23220		
10-10	09021-102	16 hexagon nut	2			EA1 23231	10	
10-11	09047-103	17 lock washer	2			EA1 23232	10	
10-12	2446-5001	Drive shaft	1			EA1 23311 -1		
10-13	2451-5000	1st gear B	1			EA1 23312		
10-14	2456-5000	2nd Gear B	1			EA1 23313		
10-15	2461-5000	3rd Gear B	1			EA1 23314		
10-16	2466-5000	4th Gear B	1			EA1 23315		
10-17	2616-5000	Kick starter gear B	1			EA1 23316		
10-18	09048-102	13 thrust washer	2			EA1 23317	10	
10-19	2481-5000	Driving shaft spacer	1			EA1 23318		
10-20	2483-5000	Driving sprocket spacer	1			EA1 23321		
10-21	2484-5000	Driving sprocket	1		13 teeth	EA1 23322		
10-22	2424-5000	Driving gear spring	1		12V054760 (Oct. '65)			Newly adopted
10-23	09048-106	17 thrust washer	1		″		10	″ ″

MEMO

11) CHANGE ARM · SHIFT DRUM · GEAR CHANGE PEDAL

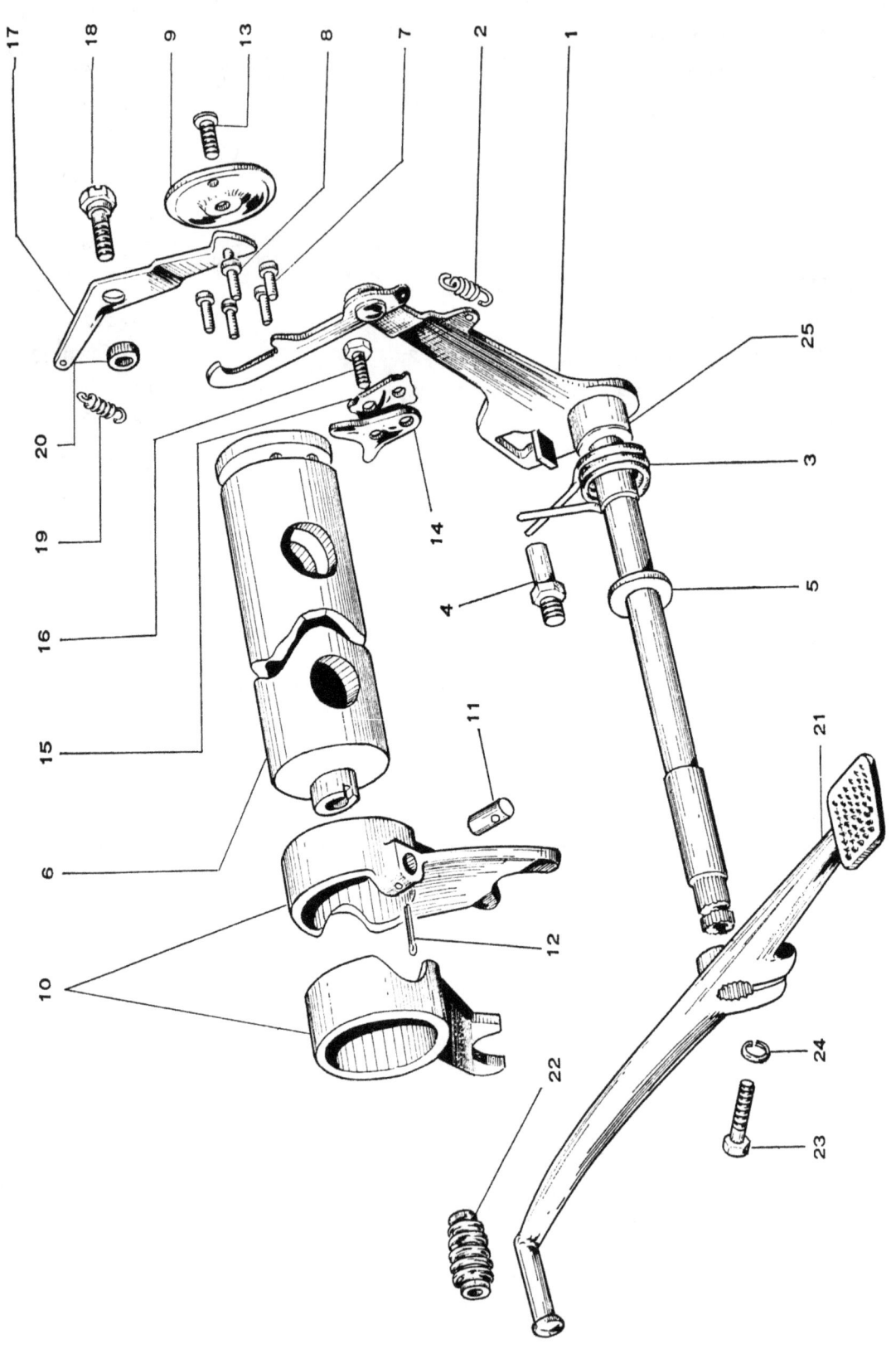

Index No.	Part No.	Part Name	No. Req'd	Unit Price US $	Serial No. From (MFG date)	Old Part No.	Min. Lot	N. B.
11- 1	2510-5002	Change arm comp	1		12B037034 (Feb. '66)	EA1 24110 -1		
11- 1	2510-5000	Change arm comp	1		Old type	EA1 24110		
11- 2	2517-5000	Drum shifter spring	1			EA1 24115		
11- 3	2551-5000	Change shaft return spring	1			EA1 24117		
11- 4	2553-5000	Change arm stopper pin	1			EA1 24118		
11- 5	2552-3002	Change shaft spring seat	1			EO 6114 -2		
11- 6	2502-5001	Shift drum assy	1		12Q042257 (May. '66)	EA1 24210 -1		
11- 6	2505-5000	Shift drum assy	1		Old type	EA1 24210		
11- 7	2522-3200	Shift pin	4		12J030755 (Oct. '64)	GB1 24212		
11- 7	2522-5000	Shift pin	4		Old type	EA1 24212		
11- 8	2523-3200	Holder stopper pin	1		12J030755 (Oct. '64)	GB1 23213		
11- 8	2523-5000	Holder stopper pin	1		Old type	EA1 24213		
11- 9	2524-3200	Shift pin holder	1		12J030755 (Oct. '64)	GB1 24214		
11- 9	2554-5000	Shift pin holder	1		Old type	EA1 24214		
11-10	2541-5001	Shift fork	2			EA1 24215 -1		
11-11	2544-3200	Fork guide	2		12S002364 (July. '65)	GB1 24216		
11-11	2544-5000	Fork guide	2		Old type	EA1 24216		
11-12	0551-2525	Split pin	2			WP 25×25	50	
11-13	0311-0512	Cross recd pan head screw	1			PNK 5×12	50	
11-14	2549-5001	Drum guide plate	1		12O037850 (Mar. '65)	EA1 24221 -1		
11-14	2549-5000	Drum guide plate	1		Old type	EA1 24221		
11-15	0461-0611	Internal toothed washer	2			TW 6S	50	
11-16	0311-0614	Cross recd pan head screw	2			PNK 6×14	50	
11-17	2531-5001	Drum stopper arm	1			EA1 24236		
11-18	2536-5000	Drum stopper bolt	1			EA1 24235		
11-19	2538-5000	Drum stopper spring	1			EA1 24237		
11-20	2537-5000	Drum stopper spacer	1					
11-21	2581-5000	Gear change pedal	1			EA1 24311		
11-22	2582-5000	Change pedal rubber	1			EA1 24312		
11-23	0113-0620	Hexagon bolt A	1			6B 6×20	50	
11-24	0431-0615	Spring washer	1			SW 6	50	
11-25	2557-8000	Change shaft spacer	1		12B037034 (Feb. '66) Newly adopted			
		Exclusive parts for return-change						
11-	2502-5010	Shift drum assy	1					
11-	2524-5010	Shift pin holder	1					
11-	2526-5010	Shift pin B	2					
11-	2531-5010	Drum stopper arm	1					
11-	2535-5010	Stopper plate	1					
11-	2539-5010	Guide plate stopper	1					

12) KICK SHAFT · KICK PEDAL

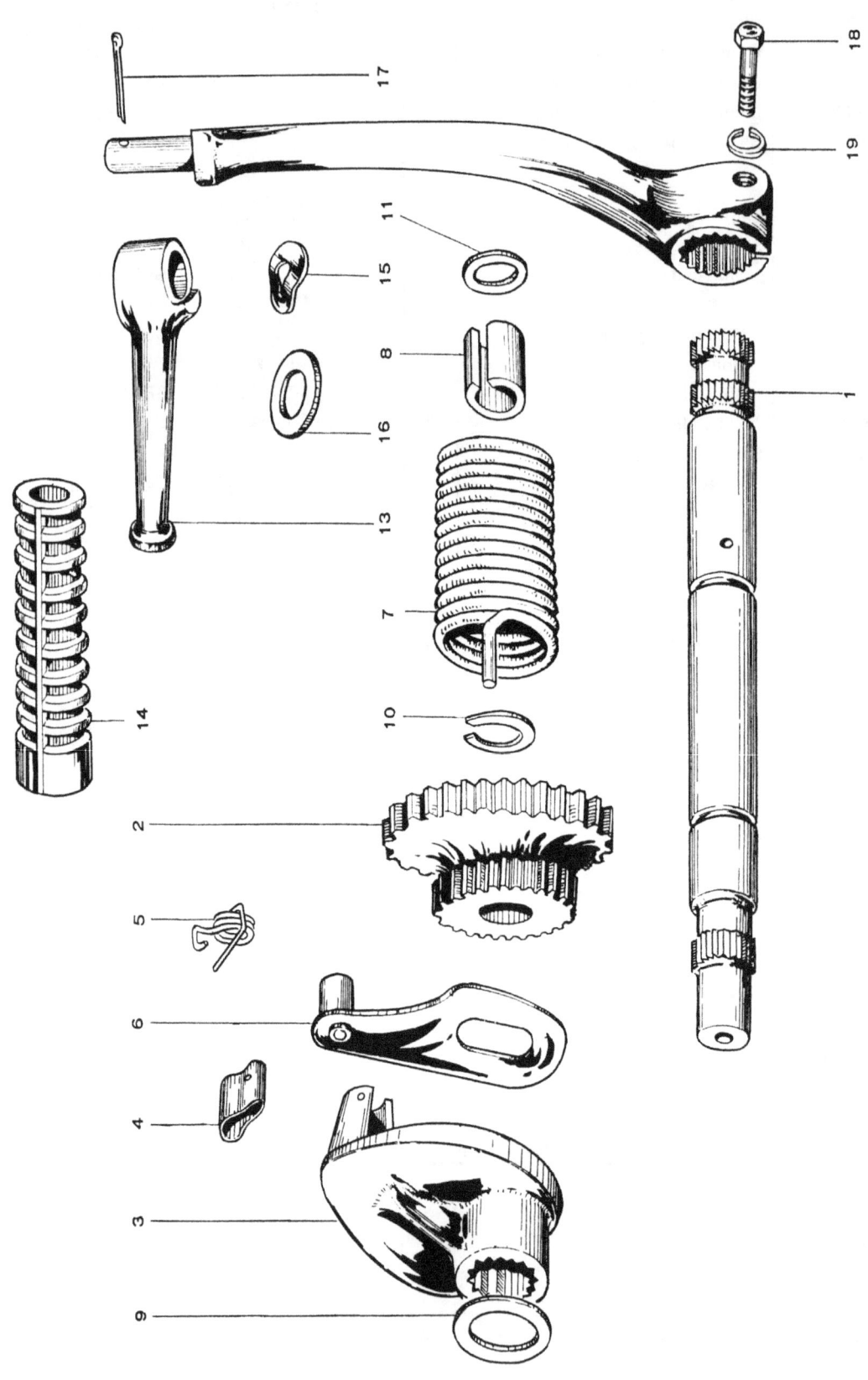

12) KICK SHAFT · KICK PEDAL

Index No.	Part No.	Part Name	No. Req'd	Unit Price US $	Serial No. From (MFG date)	Old Part No.	Min. Lot	N. B.
12- 1	2621-5002	Kickstarter shaft	1			EA1 25111-2		
12- 2	2631-5000	Kickstarter gear C	1			EA1 25112		
12- 3	2632-5000	Kickstarter ratchet arm	1			EA1 25113		
12- 4	2633-5000	Kickstarter ratchet	1			EA1 25114		
12- 5	2634-5000	Kickstarter ratchet spring	1			EA1 25115		
12- 6	2635-5000	Kickstarter ratchet stopper	1			EA1 25120		
12- 7	2636-5001	Kickstarter return spring	1			EA1 25131-1		
12- 8	2638-5000	Return spring spacer	1			EA1 25132		
12- 9	09048-101	12 thrust washer	1			EA1 23217	10	
12-10	09006-101	15F snap ring	1			EO 5215-1	10	
12-11	09041-106	15 plane washer	1			EO 7213	10	
12-12	2680-5000	Kickstater arm assy	1			EA1 25200		
12-13	2690-3010	Kickstarter pedal	1			E2 8512-1		
12-14	2683-3010	Kickstater pedal rubber	1			E1 8513		
12-15	2684-5000	Kickstarter pedal spring	1			EA1 25214		
12-16	09041-107	10 plane washer	1			E1 8515	10	
12-17	0551-3018	Split pin	1			WP 3×18	50	
12-18	0113-0625	Hexagon bolt A	1			6B 6×25	50	
12-19	0431-0615	Spring washer	1			SW 6	50	

MEMO

13) FRAME

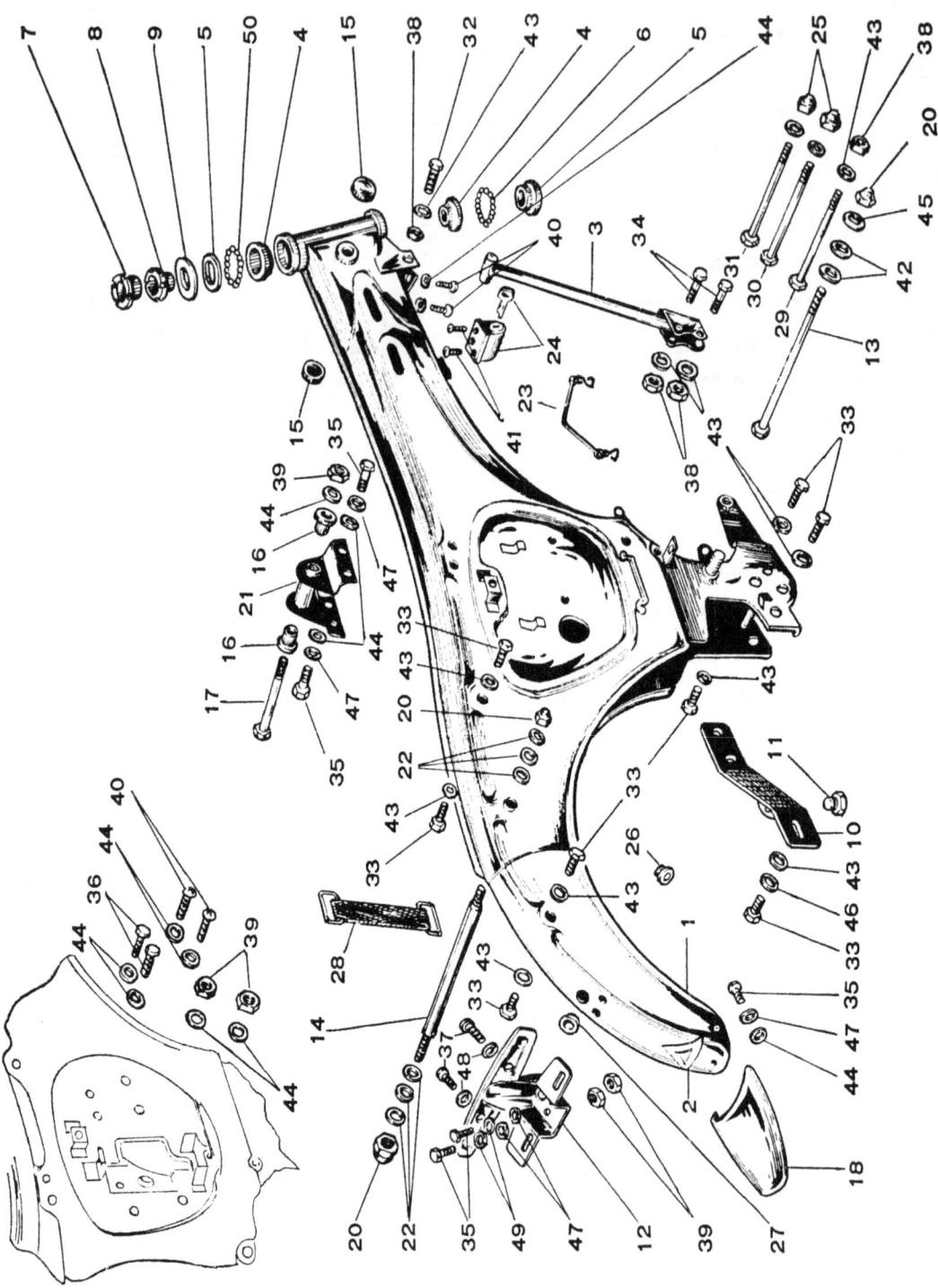

− 28 −

13) FRAME

Index No.	Part No.	Part Name	No. Req'd	Unit Price US $	Serial No. From/MFG date	Old part No.	Min. Lot	N. B.
13- 1	3110-5001 CUR	Frame comp	1			EA1 31100 -CUR		
13- 1	3110-5001 MB	Frame comp	1			EA1 31100 -MB		
13- 1	3110-5001 CBK	Frame comp	1			EA1 31100 -CBK		
13- 3	3331-5000	Down tube	1			EA1 31320		
13- 4	3313-5000	Inner race	2			EA1 31411		
13- 5	3311-5000	Outer race	2			EA1 31412		
13- 6	0611-0316	Ball	22			M0 1815	50	
13- 7	3321-5000	Race lock unt	1			EA1 31414		
13- 8	3322-5000	Race adjuster	1			EA1 31415		
13- 9	3319-5000	Race cap	1			EA1 31416		
13-10	3334-5000	Muffler bracket	1			EA1 31417		
13-11	3335-3000	Stand rubber stopper	1			M0 1829		
13-12	3266-5000 CUR	License number plate bracket	1			EA1 31419 -CUR		
13-12	3266-5000 MB	License number plate bracket	1			EA1 31419 -MB		
13-12	3266-5000 CBK	License number plate bracket	1			EA1 31419 -CBK		
13-13	3414-5000	Pivot shaft	1			EA1 31421		
13-14	3415-5000	Rear cushion shaft	1			EA1 31422		
13-15	3416-5000	Front tank cushion rubber	2			EA1 31423		
13-16	3417-5000	Rear tank cushion rubber	2			EA1 31424		
13-17	3419-5000	Tank mounting bolt	1			EA1 31425		
13-18	3422-5000-MS	Rear mud guard	1			EA1 31426 -MS		
13-20	09525-105	10 cap nut	3			EA1 31428	10	
13-21	3418-5000	Rear tank bracket	1			EA1 31429		
13-22	09541-107	10 plane washer	6			EA1 31432	10	
13-23	3354-5001	Tool band	1					
13-24	3433-5000	Handle lock	1			EA1 31450		
13-25	09525-102	8 cap nut	2			M0 1839	10	
13-26	3412-3000	Rear fender grommet	1			M0 1831		
11-27	3412-3000	Rear fender grommet	1			M0 1831		
13-28	3353-3001	Battery band	1			M0 1833 -1		
13-29	09511-113	8×114 hexagon bolt	1			6B 8×114	10	
13-30	09511-133	8×98 hexagon bolt	1					
13-30	09500-114	8×106 hexagon bolt	1		Old type	6B 8×106	10	
13-31	09511-115	8×102 hexagon bolt	1			6B 8×102	10	
13-32	0111-0862	Hexagon bolt A	1			6B 8× 62	10	
13-33	0111-0816	Hexagon bolt A	8			6B 8× 16	50	
13-34	0111-0832	8×32 hexagon bolt	2			6B 8× 32	50	

13) FRAME

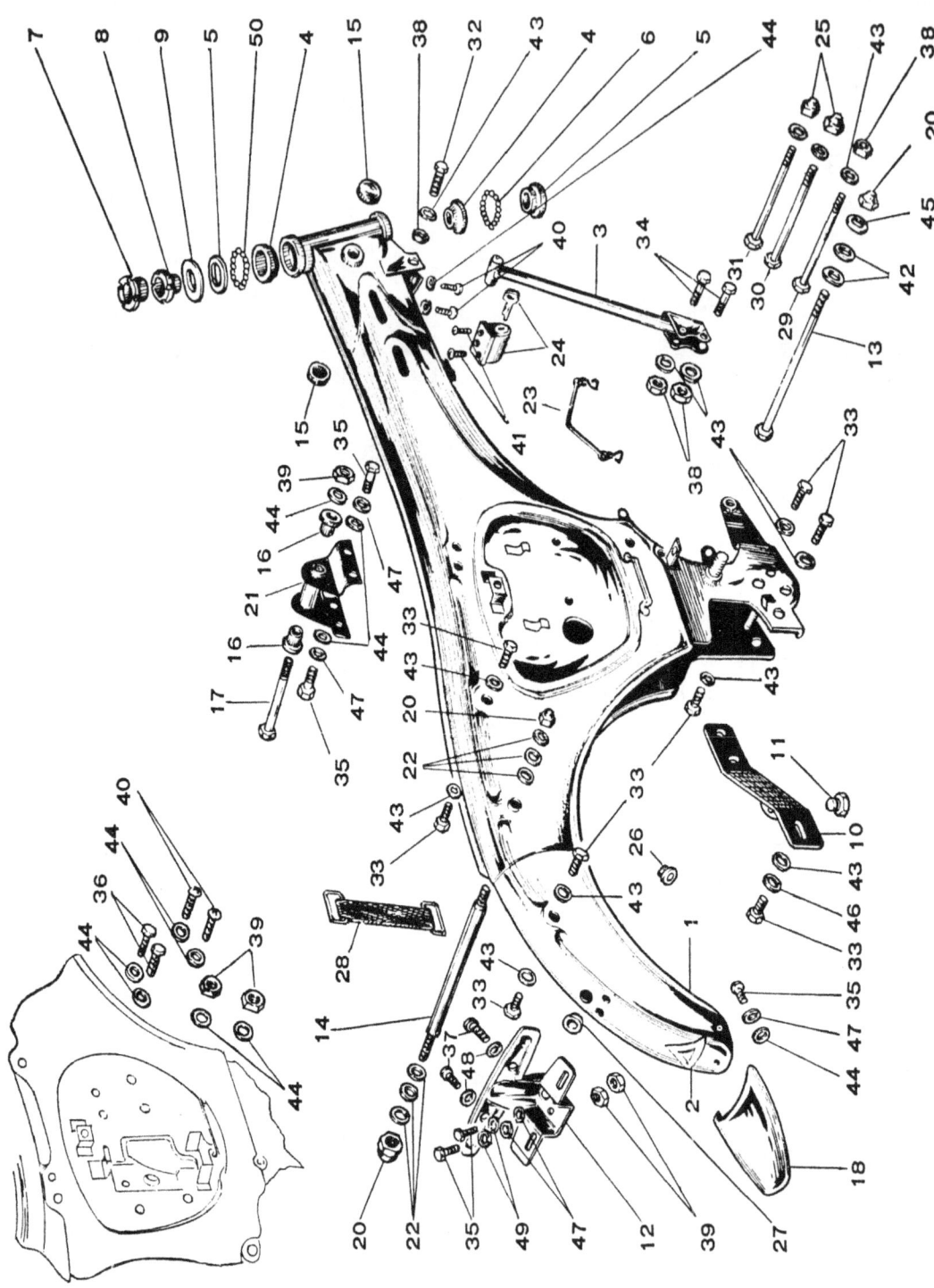

— 30 —

13) FRAME

Index No.	Part No.	Part Name	No. Req'd	Unit Price US $	Serial No. From (MFG date)	Old Part No.	Min. Lot	N. B.
13-35	0111-0614	Hexagon bolt A	6			6B 6× 14	50	
13-36	0111-0610	Hexagon bolt A	5			6B 6× 10	50	
13-37	0121-0510	Hexagon bolt B	2			6B 5×10	50	
13-38	0211-0800	Hexagon nut A	4			6N1 8	50	
13-39	0211-0600	Hexagon nut A	8			6N1 6	50	
13-40	0311-0610	Cross recd pan head screw	4			PNK 6×10	50	
13-41	0381-0610	Flat head screw	2			SK 6×10	50	
13-42	0411-1025	Plane washer A	2			HW 10	50	
13-43	0411-0818	Plane washer A	14			HW 8	50	
13-44	0411-0613	Plane washer A	16			HW 6	50	
13-45	0431-1025	Spring washer	1			SW 10	50	
13-46	0431-0820	Spring washer	1			SW 8	50	
13-47	0431-0615	Spring washer	9			SW 6	50	
13-48	0431-0513	Spring washer	2			SW 5	50	
13-49	0451-0611	External toothed washer	4			B 6S	50	
13-50	3318-5000	Ball cage	1			EA1 31410		

MEMO

14) FRONT FORK ASSY

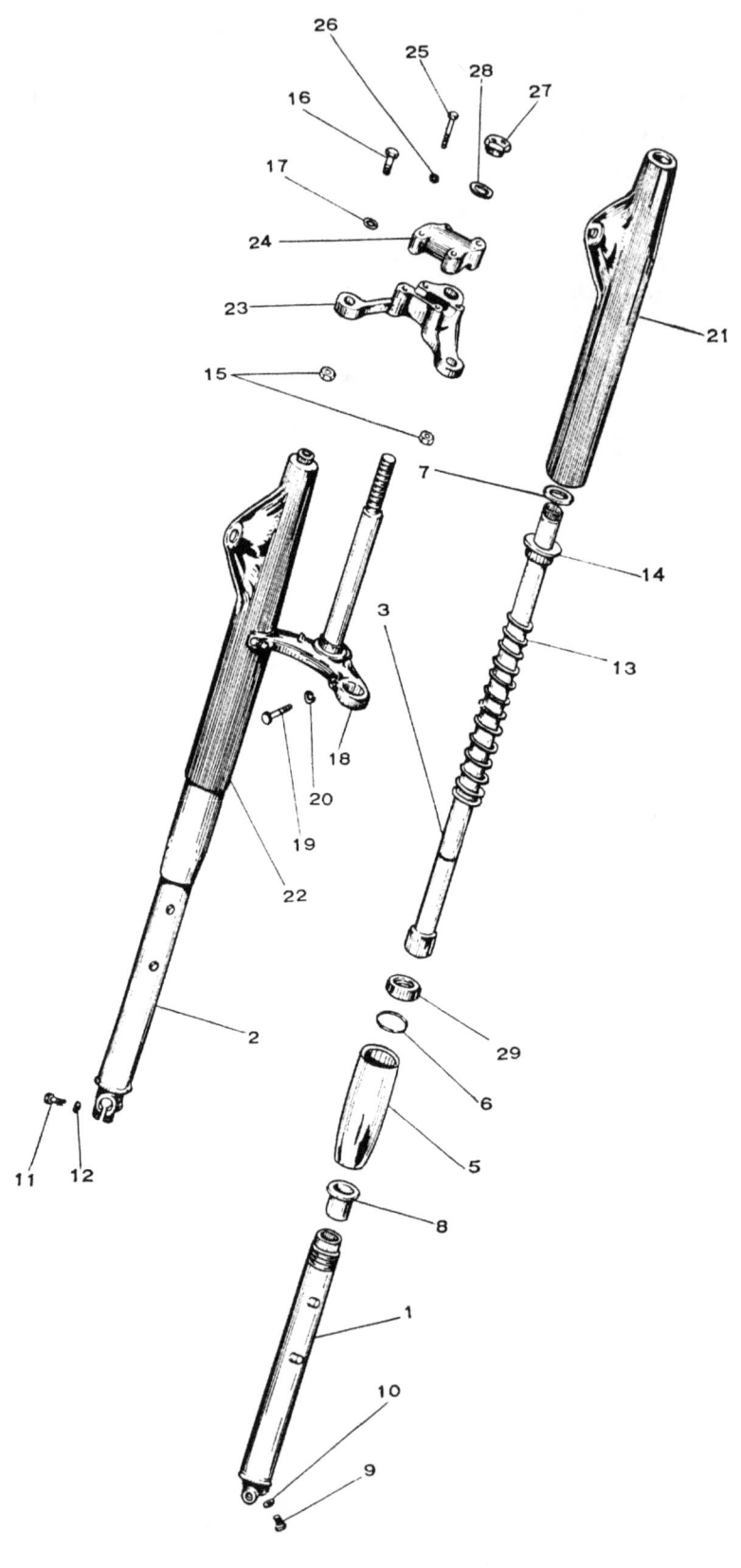

14) FRONT FORK ASSY

Index No.	Part No.	Part Name	No. Req'd	Unit Price US $	Serial No. From (MFG date)	Old Part No.	Min. Lot	N. B.
14- 0	4100-5000 CUR	Front fork assy	1			EA1 41000 -CUR		
14- 0	4100-5000 MB	Front fork assy	1			EA1 41000 -MB		
14- 0	4100-5000 CBK	Front fork Assy	1			EA1 41000 -CBK		
14- 1	4111-5001 MS	Outer tube A	1			EA1 41110 -1MS		
14- 2	4131-5001 MS	Outer tube B	1			EA1 41210 -1MS		
14- 3	4113-5001	Inner tube A	2			EA1 41120 -1		
14- 5	4114-5000	Outer tube nut	2			EA1 41131		
41- 6	09566-102	33 O ring	2			EA1 41132	10	
14- 7	4115-5000	Main spring seat	2			EA1 41134		
14- 8	4116-5000	Cushion slide metal	2			EA1 41141		
14- 9	09531-101	4×7 Cross recd pan head screw	2			EA1 41161	50	
14-10	4118-5000	Drain plug gasket	2			EA1 41162		
14-11	09511-116	8×25 hexagon bolt	1			EA1 41251	10	
14-12	0431-0820	Spring washer	1			SW 8	50	
14-13	4121-5000	Front main cushion	2			EA1 41171		
14-14	4122-5000	Main spring guide	2			EA1 41172		
14-15	4123-5000	Inner tube packing	2			EA1 41181		
14-16	4124-5000	Upper bridge bolt	2			EA1 41182		
14-17	09541-111	Plane washer A	2			EA1 41183	50	
14-18	4151-5000 CBK	Lower bridge	1			EA1 41310 -CBK		
14-19	09511-137	10×25 hexagon bolt	2			EA1 41321	10	
14-20	0431-1025	Spring washer	2			SW 10	50	
14-21	4171-5000 CUR	Left fork cover	1			EA1 41410 -CUR		
14-21	4171-5000 MB	Left fork cover	1			EA1 41410 -MB		
14-21	4171-5000 CBK	Left fork cover	1			EA1 41410 -CBK		
14-22	4181-5000 CUR	Right fork cover	1			EA1 41420 -CUR		
14-22	4181-5000 MB	Right fork cover	1			EA1 41420 -MB		
14-22	4181-5000 CBK	Right fork cover	1			EA1 41420 -CBK		
14-23	4161-5000	Upper bridge	1			EA1 41511		
14-24	4162-5000	Handle holder	1			EA1 41521		
14-25	0142-0836	Hexagon bolt D	4			EA1 41541	50	
14-26	0411-0818	Plane washer A	4			HW 8	50	
14-27	4164-5000	Steering head nut	1			EA1 41551		
14-28	4165-5000	Steering head washer	1			EA1 41552		
14-29	09590-108	27 oil seal	2			EA1 41133	10	

15) FRONT FENDER · HEAD LAMP BODY · HANDLE BAR

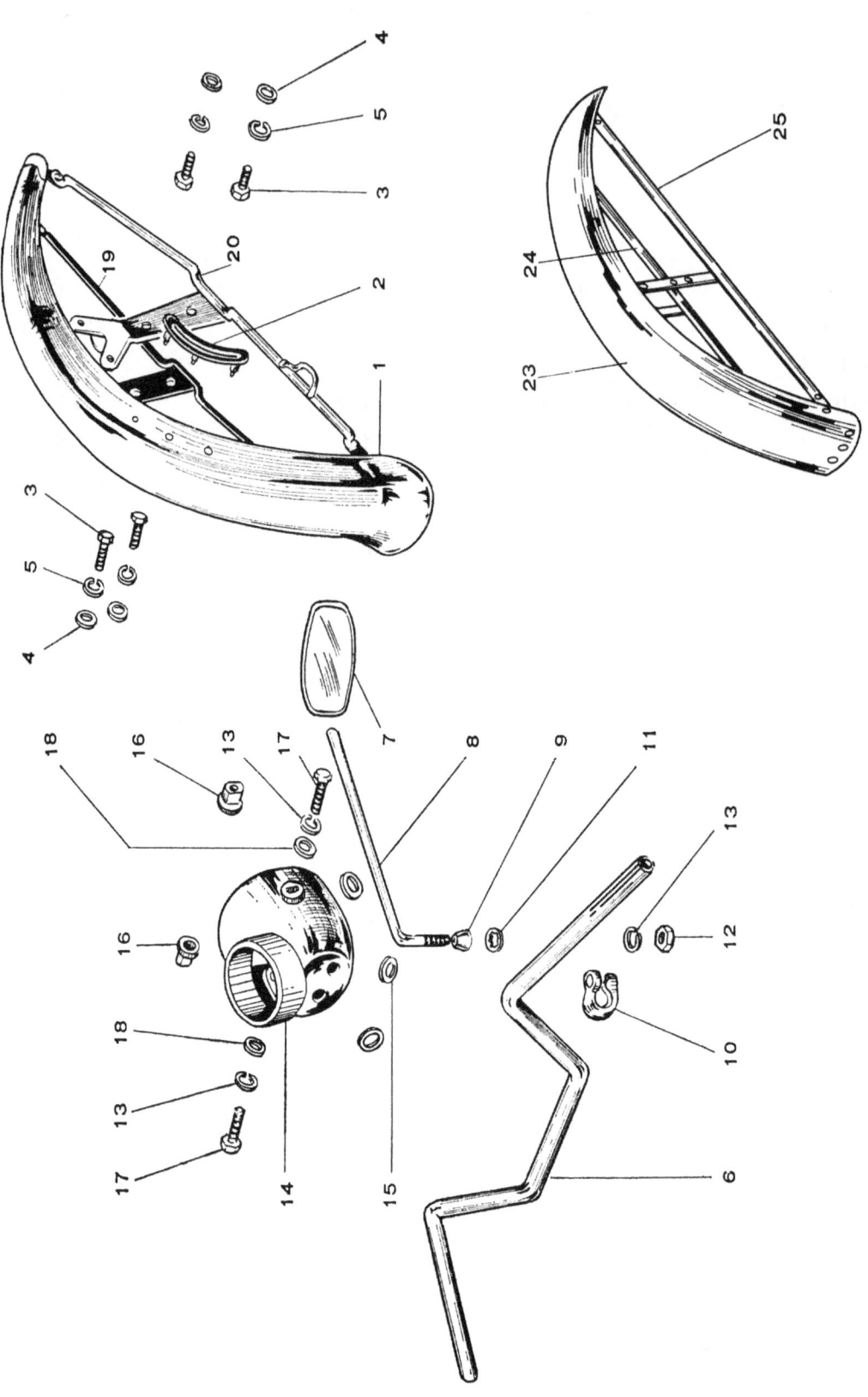

15) FRONT FENDER · HEAD LAMP BODY · HANDLE BAR

Index No.	Part No.	Part Name	No. Req'd	Unit Price US $	Serial No. From (MFG date)	Old Part No.	Min. Lot	N. B.
15- 1	4410-5002 CUR	Front fender comp	1			EAE 42100 -CUR		
15- 1	4410-5002 MB	Front fender comp	1			EAE 42100 -MB		
15- 1	4410-5002 CBK	Front fender comp	1			EAE 42100 -CBK		
15- 2	4432-5000	Front fender protector	1			EA1 42221		
15- 3	0111-0608	Hexagon bolt A	4			6B 6×8	50	
15- 4	0411-0613	Plane washer A	4			HW 6	50	
15- 5	0431-0615	Spring washer	4			SW 6	50	
15- 6	4511-5000	Handle bar	1			EA1 43111		
15-	4601-3101	Back mirror assy	1			GA1 44100 -1		
15- 7	4610-3100	Back mirror comp	1			GA1 44110		
15- 8	4621-3101	Back mirror stay	1			GA1 44121 -1		
15-10	4622-3102	Back mirror clamp	1			GA1 44140 -1		
15-12	0211-0800	Hexagon nut A	1			6N1 8	50	
15-13	0421-0816	Plane washer B	1			KHW 8	50	
15-14	8111-5000 CUR	Head lamp body	1			EA1 81110 -CUR		
15-14	8111-5000 MB	Head lamp body	1			EA1 81110 -MB		
15-14	8111-5000 CBK	Head lamp body	1			EA1 81110 -CBK		
15-16	8126-5000	Lamp setting nut	2			EA1 81113		
15-17	0111-0822	8×22 Hexagon bolt	2			6B 8×22	50	
15-18	0411-0818	Plane washer A	2			HW 8	50	
15-13	0431-0820	Spring washer	2			SW 8	50	
15-19	4421-5000 CUR	Left fender stay	1			EA1 42120 -CUR		
15-19	4421-5000 MB	Left fender stay	1			EA1 42120 -MB		
15-19	4421-5000 CBK	Left fender stay	1			EA1 42120 -CBK		
15-20	4422-5000 CUR	Left fender stay	1			EA1 42130 -CUR		
15-20	4422-5000 MB	Left fender stay	1			EA1 42130 -MB		
15-20	4422-5000 CBK	Left fender stay	1			EA1 42130 -CBK		
15-21	0311-0610	Cross recd pan head screw	8			PNK 6×10	50	
15-22	0461-0611	Internal toothed washer	8			TW 6S	50	
		New fenders and stays						
15-23	4410-5012 XCl	Front fender comp	1		Stainless	EAE 91710 -XC1		
15-23	4410-5041 MS	Front fender comp	1		Metallic silver	EAE 91710 -MS		
15-24	4421-5010	Left fender stay	1		Stainless	EA1 91720		
15-24	4421-5010 MS	Left fender stay	1		Metallic silver	EA1 91720 -MS		
15-25	4422-5010	Right fender stay	1		Stainless	EA1 91730		
15-25	4422-5010 MS	Right fender stay	1		Metallic silver	EA1 91730 -MS		
15-	4435-5010	Front fender plug	1			EA1 91741		

16) REAR FORK · CHAIN CASE · REAR CUSHION

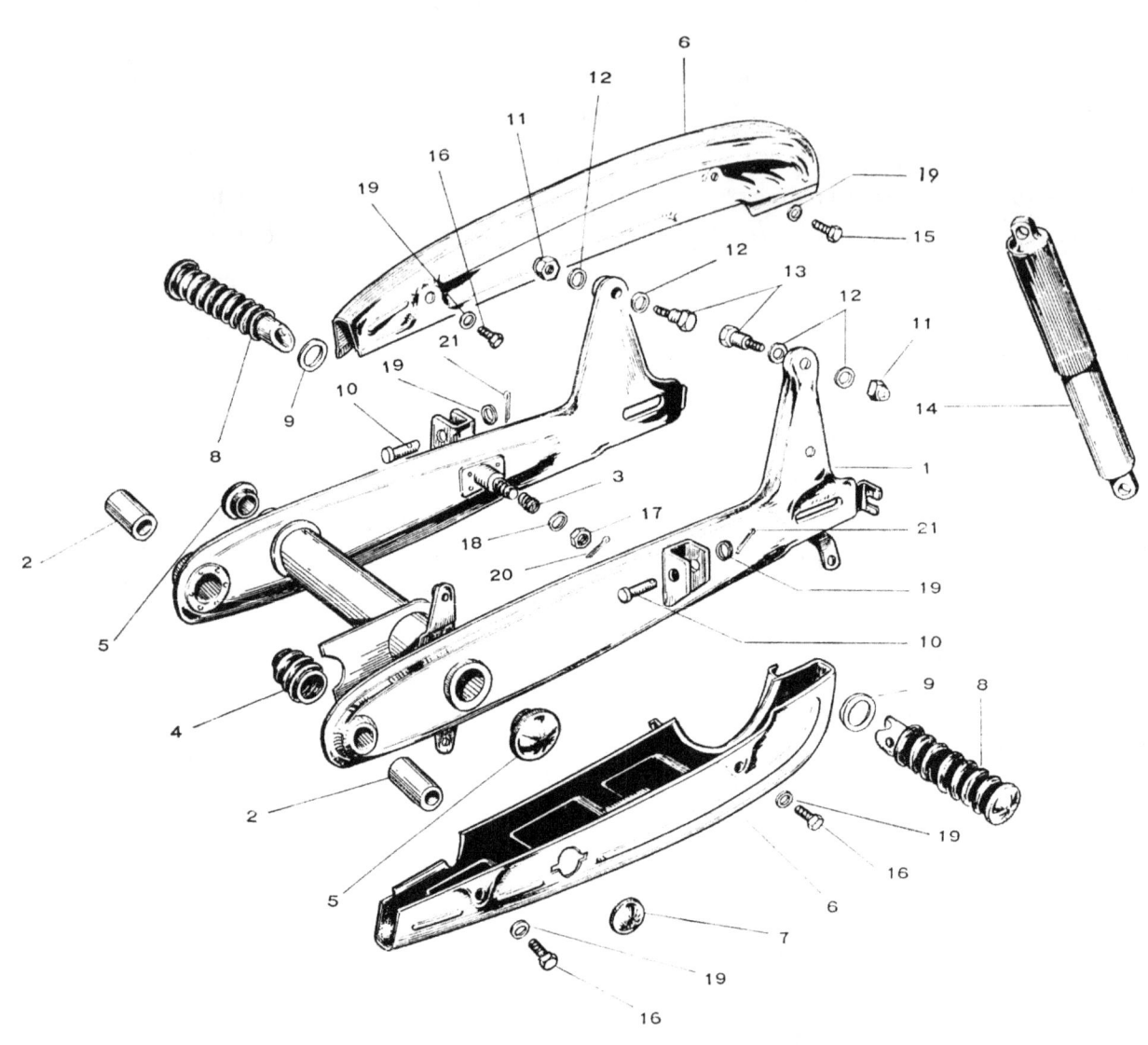

16) REAR FORK · CHAIN CASE · REAR CUSHION

Index No.	Part No'	Part Name	No. Req'd	Unit Price US $	Serial No. From (MFG date)	Old Part No	Min. Lot	N. B.
16- 1	4810-5000 CUR	Rear fork comp	1			EA1 47100 -CUR		
16- 1	4810-5000 MB	Rear fork comp	1			EA1 47100 -MB		
16- 1	4810-5000 CBK	Rear fork comp	1			EA1 47100 -CBK		
16- 2	4851-5000	Rear fork bush	2			EA1 47211		
16- 3	4854-5000	Torque rod spring	1			EA1 47212		
16- 4	4853-3001	Chain protector	1			MO 3172 -1		
16- 5	4852-5000	Rear fork cap	2			EA1 47213		
16- 6	4701-5000 MS	Chain case assy	1			EA1 45100 -MS		
16- 6	4751-5010	Half chain case	1			EA1 91800		
16- 7	4731-3000	CHain inspection cap	1			MO 3361		
16- 8	3702-5000	Rear footrest assy	2			EA1 67300		
16- 9	3762-5000	Rear footrest washer	2			EA1 67322		
16-10	3763-5000	Rear footrest pin	2			EA1 67323		
16-11	09525-105	10 cap nut	2			EA1 31428	10	
16-12	09541-107	10 Plane washer	4			EA1 31432	10	
16-13	0123-1040	Hexagon bolt B	2			6B 10×40	10	
16-14	4901-5000 CUR	Rear cushion assy	2			EA1 48100 -CUR		
16-14	4901-5000 MB	Rear cushion assy	2			EA1 48100 -MB		
16-14	4901-5000 CBK	Rear cushion assy	2			EA1 48100 -CBK		
16-15	0111-0618	Hexagon bolt A	1			6B 6×18	50	
16-16	0111-0608	Hexagon bolt A	3			6B 6× 8	50	
16-17	0211-0800	Hexagon nut A	1			6N1 8	50	
16-18	0411-0818	Plane washer A	1			HW 8	50	
16-19	0411-0613	Plane washer A	6			HW 6	50	
16-20	0551-2020	Split pin	1			WP 20×20	50	
16-21	0551-1612	Split pin	2			WP 16×12	50	

MEMO

17) FUEL TANK · FUEL COCK

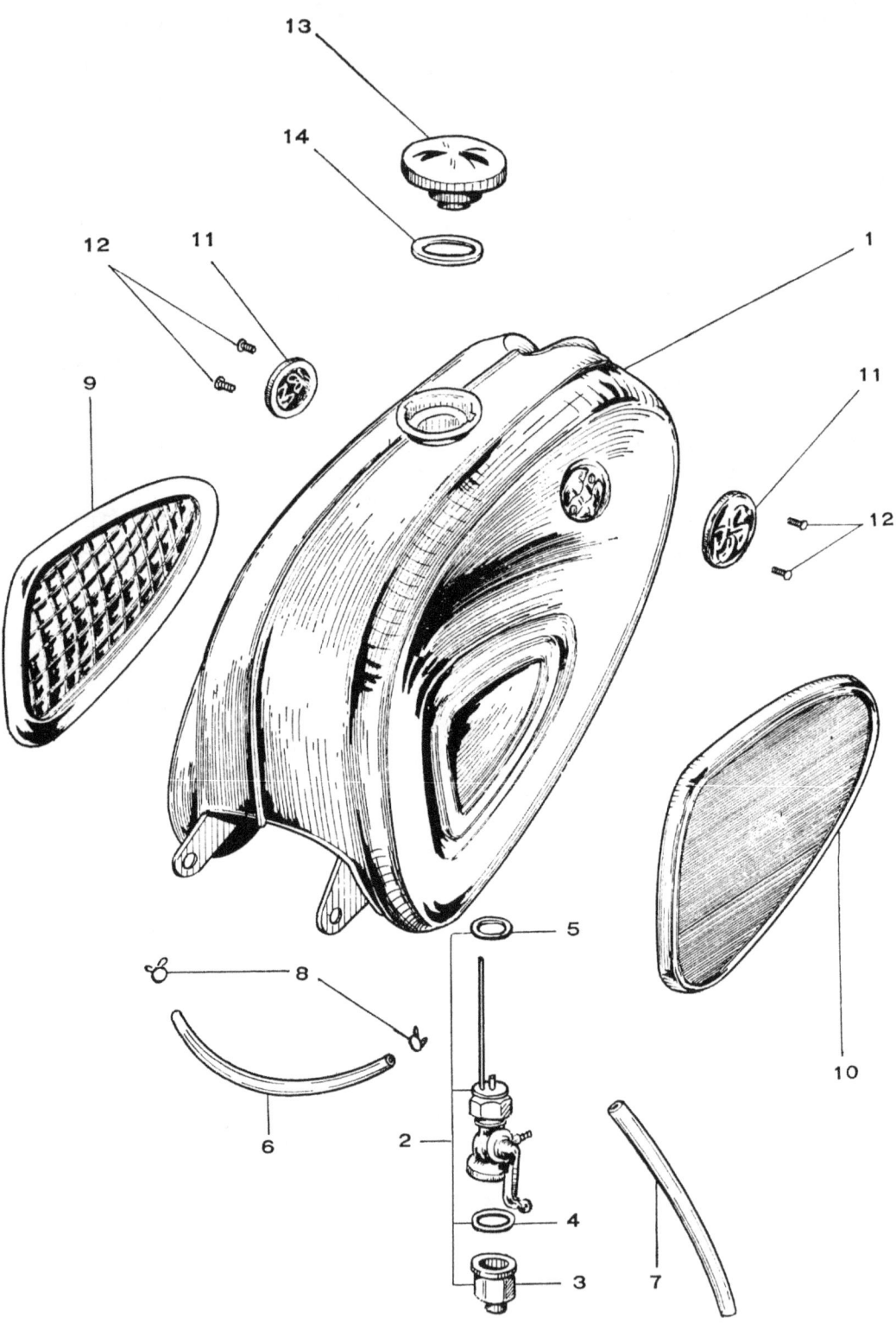

17) FUEL TANK · FUEL COCK

Index No.	Part No.	Part Name	No. Req'd	Unit Price US $	Remarks		Min. Lot	N. B.
					Serial No. From (MFG date)	Old Part No.		
17- 1	5110-3200 CUR	Fuel tank comp	1		12Z056391 (Dec. '65)	GB1 51110 -CUR		
17- 1	5110-3200 MB	Fuel tank comp	1		〃	GB1 51110 -MB		
17- 1	5110-3200 CBK	Fuel tank comp	1		〃	GB1 51110 -CBK		
17- 1	5110-5001 CUR	Fuel tank comp	1		Old type	EA1 51110 -1CUR		
17- 1	5110-5001 MB	Fuel tank comp	1		〃 〃	EA1 51110 -1MB		
17- 1	5110-5001 CBK	Fuel tank comp	1		〃 〃	EA1 51110 -1CBK		
17- 2	5103-5000	Fuel cock assy	1			EA1 52100		
17- 3	5182-5000	Fuel strainer cup	1			EA1 52113		
17- 4	5183-3000	Strainer cup gasket	1			MO 7163		
17- 5	5184-3000	Fuel cock gasket	1			MO 7166		
17- 6	5186-5000	Tank connecting tube	1			EA1 52121		
17- 7	5172-5000	Fuel tube	1			EA1 52122		
17- 8	5187-3004	Fuel tube clip	2			MO 7183 -4		
17- 9	5141-3200	Left knee grip	1		12Z056391 (Dec. '65)	GB1 51211		
17- 9	5141-5000	Left knee grip	1		Old type	EA1 51211		
17-10	5142-3200	Right knee grip	1		12Z056391 (Dec. '65)	GB1 51212		
17-10	5142-5000	Right knee grip	1		Old type	EA1 51212		
17-11	5143-5000	Fuel tank emblem	2			EA1 51213		
17-12	0311-0306	Cross reca pan head screw	4			PNK 3× 6	50	
17-13	5102-3200	Tank cap assy	1		12P048261 (April '65)	GB1 51300		
17-13	5160-3002	Tank cap comp	1		Old type	MO 7105 -2		

MEMO

18) CLUTCH GRIP

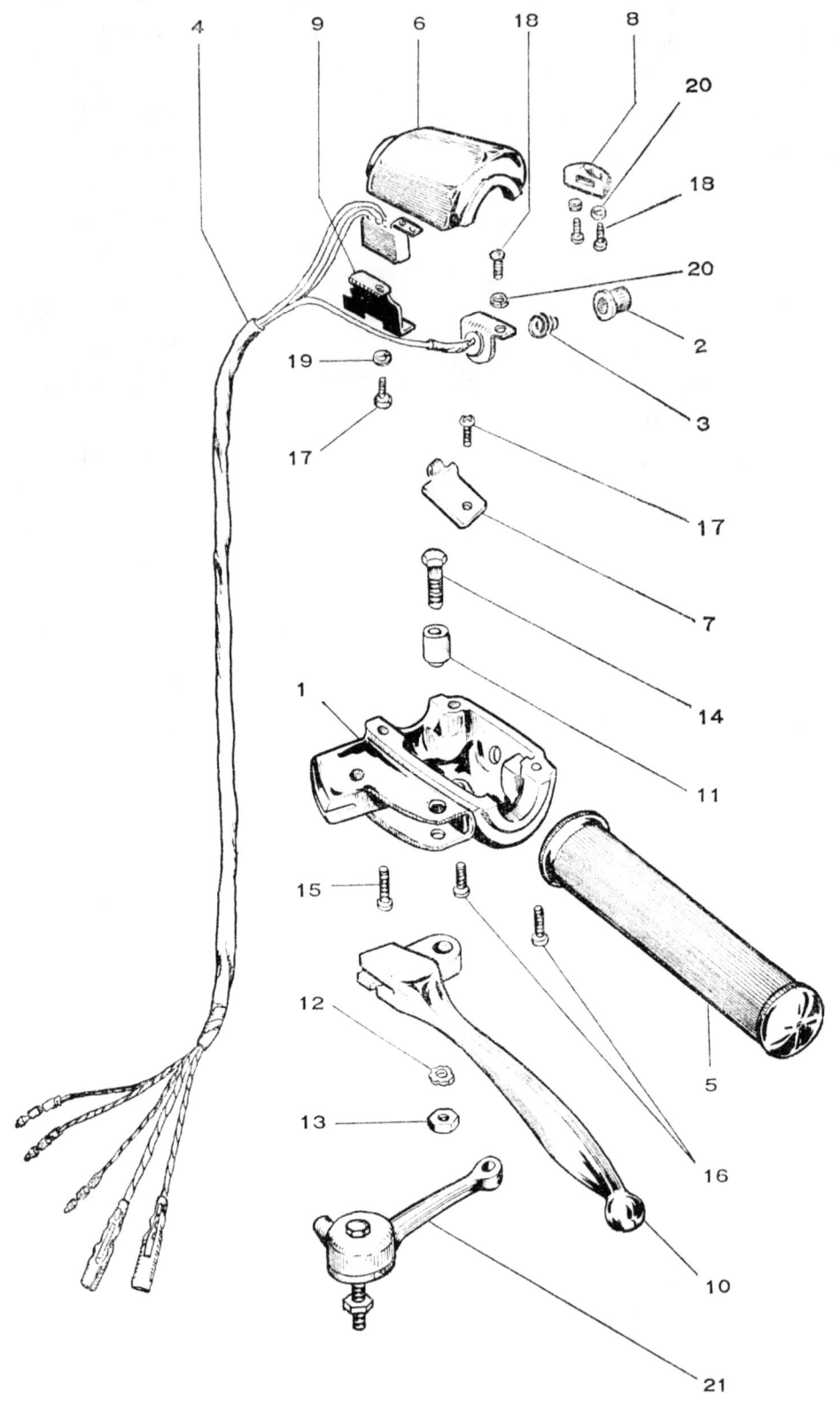

18) CLUTCH GRIP

Index No.	Part No.	Part Name	No. Req'd	Unit Price US $	Serial No. From (MFG date)	Old Part No.	Min. Lot	N. B.
18-	6101-5000	Clutch grip assy	1			EA1 61100		
18- 1	6111-5000	Left switch case	1			EA1 61111		
18- 2	6113-3100	Horn switch button	1			GA1 61113		
18- 3	6114-3100	Horn switch spring	1			GA1 61114		
18- 4	6115-5000	Left handle wire	1			EA1 61120		
18- 5	6123-3100	Left handle grip	1			GA1 61130		
18- 6	6121-5000	Left switch case cover	1			EA1 61141		
18- 7	6116-3100	Left wire clamp	1			GA1 61142		
18- 8	6119-3100	Handle switch knob	1			GA1 61143		
18- 9	6117-3100	Dimmer switch clamp	1			GA1 61144		
18-10	6122-3011	Clutch lever	1			M4 5212-1		
18-11	6124-3100	Lever pivot collar	1			GA1 61261		
11-12	0451-0510	External toothed washer	1			GA1 61262	50	
18-13	0211-0500	Hexagon nut A	1			6N1 5	50	
18-14	0111-0518	Hexagon bolt A	1			6B 5×18	50	
18-15	0311-0518	Cross recd pan head screw	1			PNK 5×18	50	
18-16	0311-0514	Cross recd pan head screw	2			PNK 5×14	50	
18-17	0311-0306	Cross recd pan head screw	2			PNK 3× 6	50	
18-18	0361-0206	Pan head screw	3			NK 2× 6	50	
18-19	0431-0307	Spring washer	1			SW 3	50	
18-20	0431-0205	Spring washer	3			SW 2	50	
18-21	6103-5000	Starter lever assy	1			EA1 61170		

MEMO

19) THROTTLE GRIP

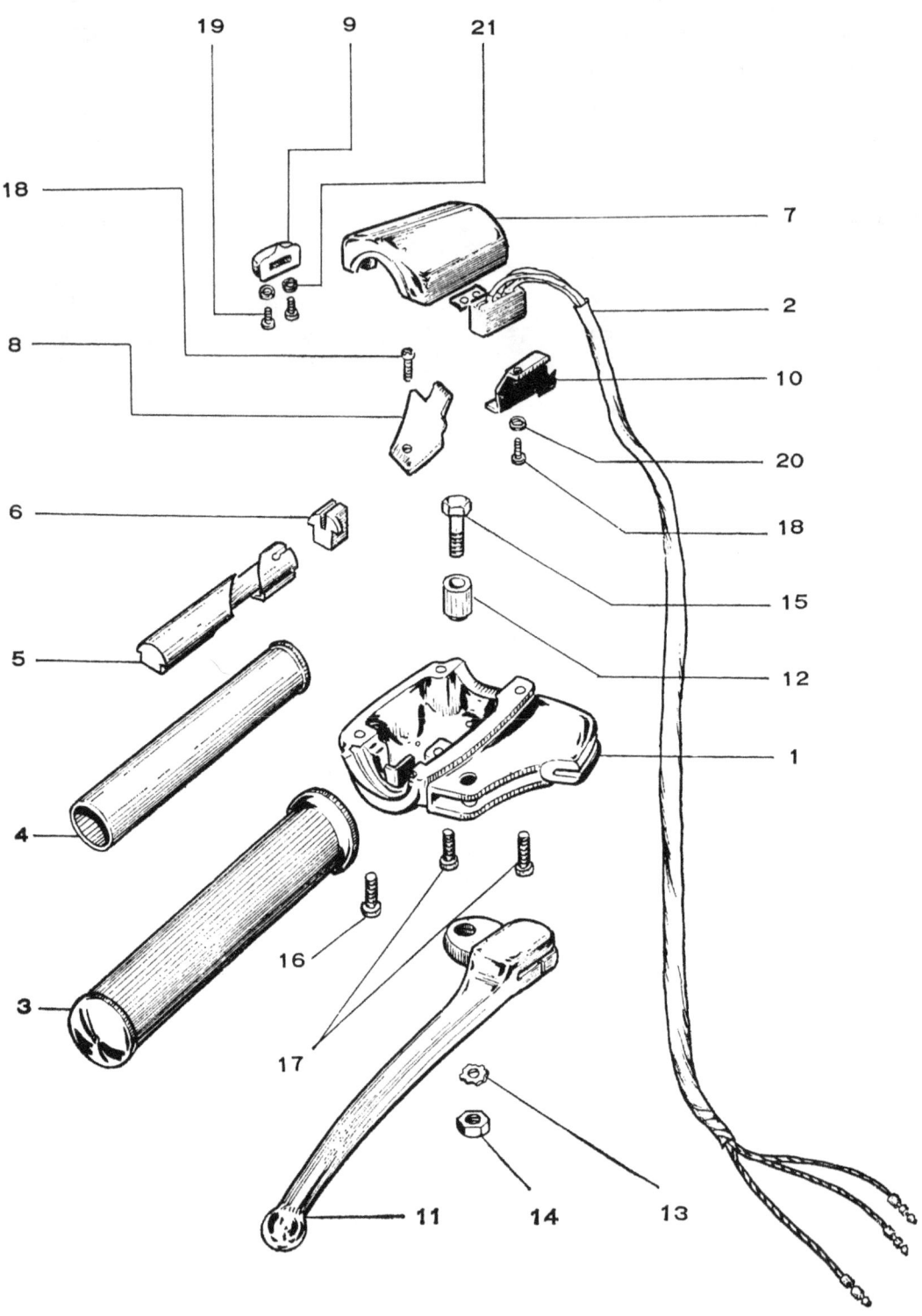

19) THROTTLE GRIP

Index No.	Part No.	Part Name	No. Req'd	Unit Price US $	Serial No. From (MFG date)	Old Part No.	Min. Lot	N. B.
19- 0	6104-5000	Throttle grip assy	1			EA1 61200		
19- 1	6141-3101	Right switch case	1			GA1 61211 -1		
19- 2	6145-5000	Right handle wire	1			EA1 61220		
19- 3	6153-3100	Right handle grip	1			GA1 61230		
19- 4	6154-3100	Throttle grip pipe	1			GA1 61231		
19- 5	6155-3100	Throttle sliding shoe	1			GA1 61232		
19- 6	6156-3100	Throttle cable stopper	1			GA1 61233		
19- 7	6151-5000	Right switch case cover	1			EA1 61241		
19- 8	6146-3100	Right wire clamp	1			GA1 61242		
19- 9	6119-5000	Handle switch knob	1			EA1 61243		
19-10	6147-3100	Turn signal switch clamp	1			GA1 61244		
19-11	6152-3100	Front brake lever	1			GA1 61260		
19-12	6124-3100	Lever pivot collar	1			GA1 61261		
19-13	0451-0510	External toothed washer	1			GA1 61262	50	
19-14	0211-0500	Hexagon nut A	1			6N1 5	50	
19-15	0111-0518	Hexagon bolt A	1			6B 5×18	50	
19-16	0311-0518	Cross recd pan head screw	1			PNK 5×18	50	
19-17	0311-0514	Cross recd pan head screw	2			PNK 5×14	50	
19-18	0311-0306	Cross recd pan head screw	2			PNK 3× 6	50	
19-19	0361-0206	Pan head screw	2			NK 2× 6	50	
19-20	0431-0307	Spring washer	1			SW 3	50	
19-21	0431-0205	Spring washer	2			SW 2	50	

MEMO

20) FRONT TURN SIGNAL · TAIL LAMP

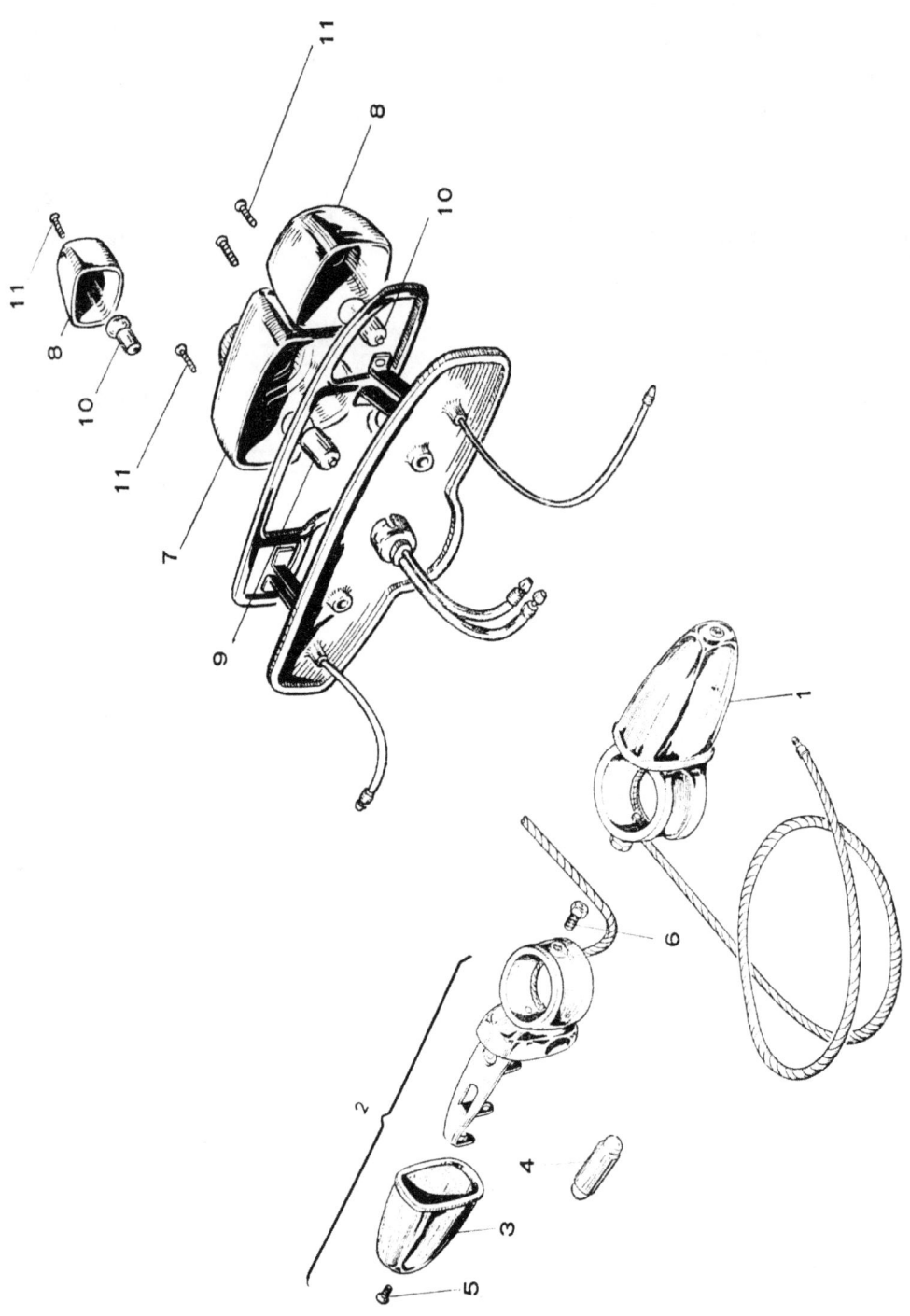

20) FRONT TURN SIGNAL · TAIL LAMP

Index No.	Part No.	Part Name	No. Req'd	Unit Price US $	Serial No. From (MFG date)	Old Part No.	Min. Lot	N. B.
20- 1	8301-5000	Front left turn signal assy	1			EA1 61700		
20- 2	8302-5000	Front right turn signal assy	1			EA1 61800		
20- 3	8331-5000	Front turn signal lens	2			EA1 61715		
20- 4	8332-3010	Winker bulb	2			M2 6233-1		
20- 5	0341-0306	Cross round head screw	2			PRK 3× 6	50	
20- 6	0121-0512	Hexagon bolt B	2			EA1 61717	50	
20-	8201-5001	Tail lamp assy	1					
20- 7	8251-5000	Tail lamp lens	1			EA1 83121		
20- 8	8371-5000	Rear turn signal lens	2			EA1 83122		
20- 9	8252-5000	Tail lamp bulb	1			EA1 83125		
20-10	8332-5000	Rear turn signal bulb	2			EA1 83126		
20-11	0342-0318	Cross oval head screw	4			PRK 3×18	50	

MEMO

21) SPEEDOMETER · WIRES

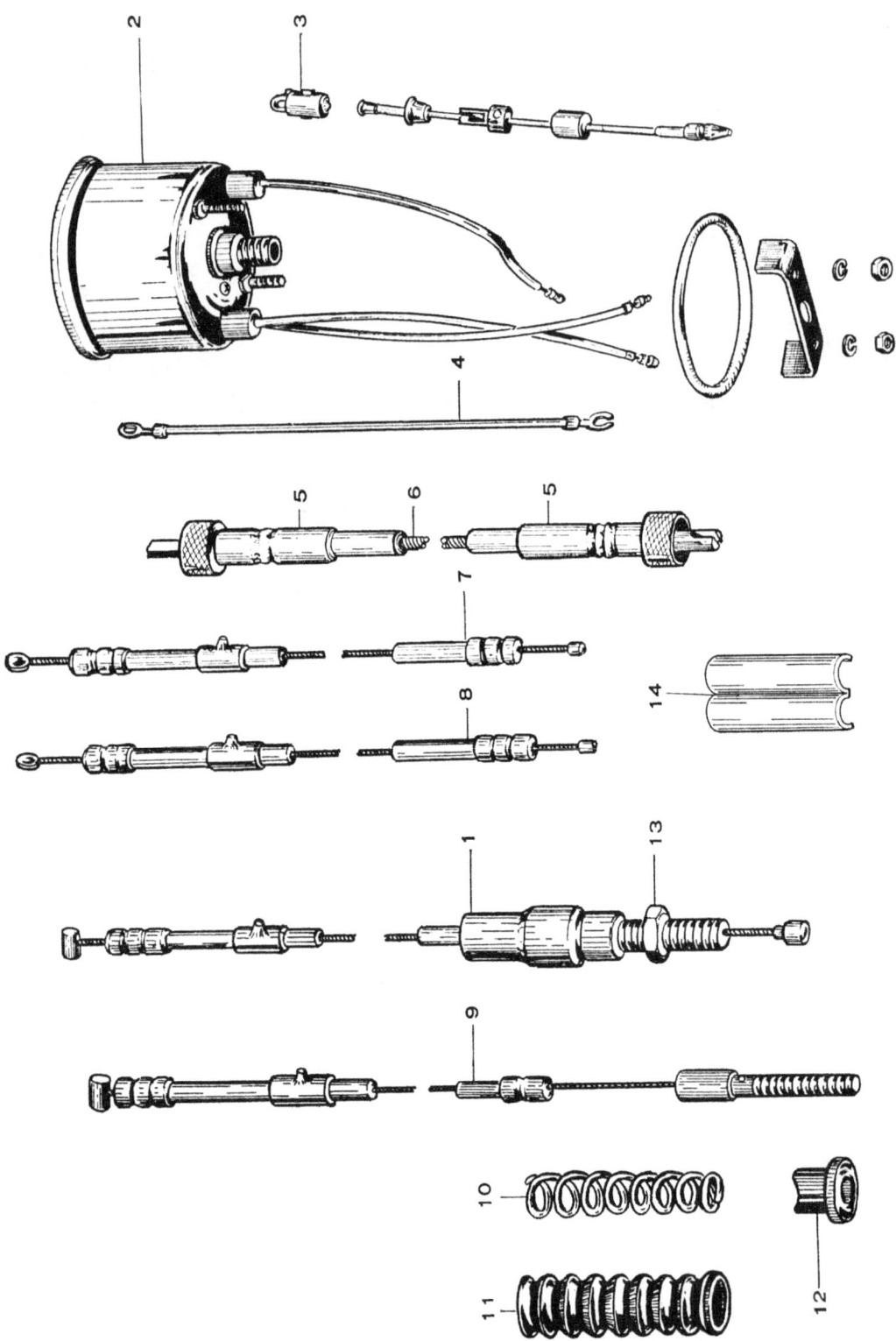

— 46 —

21) SPEEDOMETER · WIRES

Index No.	Part No.	Part Name	No. Req'd	Unit Price US $	Remarks Serial No. From (MFG date)	Old Part No.	Min. Lot	N. B.
21- 1	6186-5000	Clutch wire	1			EA1 22240		
21- 2	8401-5011	Speedometer assy	1		Mile/hour.	EAE 61300-1		
21- 2	8401-5001	Speedometer assy	1		Km/hour.	EA1 61300-1		
21- 3	8424-3010	Speedometer bulb	2			M2 5315		
21- 4	8833-5001	Speedometer earth wire	1		121 025444 Sep. '64	EA1 61321-1		
21- 4	8833-5000	Speedometer earth wire	1		Old type	EA1 61321		
21- 5	6171-5000	Speedometer drive cable assy	1			EA1 61510		
21- 6	9411-5000	Speedometer inner cable	1			EA1 61512		
21- 7	6176-5000	Throttle control wire	1			EA1 61520		
21- 8	6178-5000	Carburetor starter wire	1			EA1 61530		
21- 9	6181-5000	Front brake wire	1			EA1 61541		
21-10	6182-5000	Brake wire spring	1			EA1 61542		
21-11	6183-5000	Brake wire boot	1			EA1 61543		
21-12	3832-3000	Brake rod adjuster	1			MO 4332		
21-13	0211-0800	Hexagon nut A	1			6N1 8	50	
21-14	6189-5000	Cable clamp B	2			EA1 61562		
21-	8824-5010	High beamwire	1		For mile/h.	EAE 88121		
		Exclusive parts for flat handle bar						
21-	4511-5010	Flat handle bar	1			EA1 91611		
21-	6181-5010	Front brake wire	1			EA1 91640		
21-	6186-5010	Clutch wire	1			EA1 91650		
21-	6176-5010	Throttle contact wire	1			EA1 91620		
21-	6178-5010	Carburetor starter wire	1			EA1 91630		

MEMO

22) BRAKE PEDAL · STAND · FOOTREST

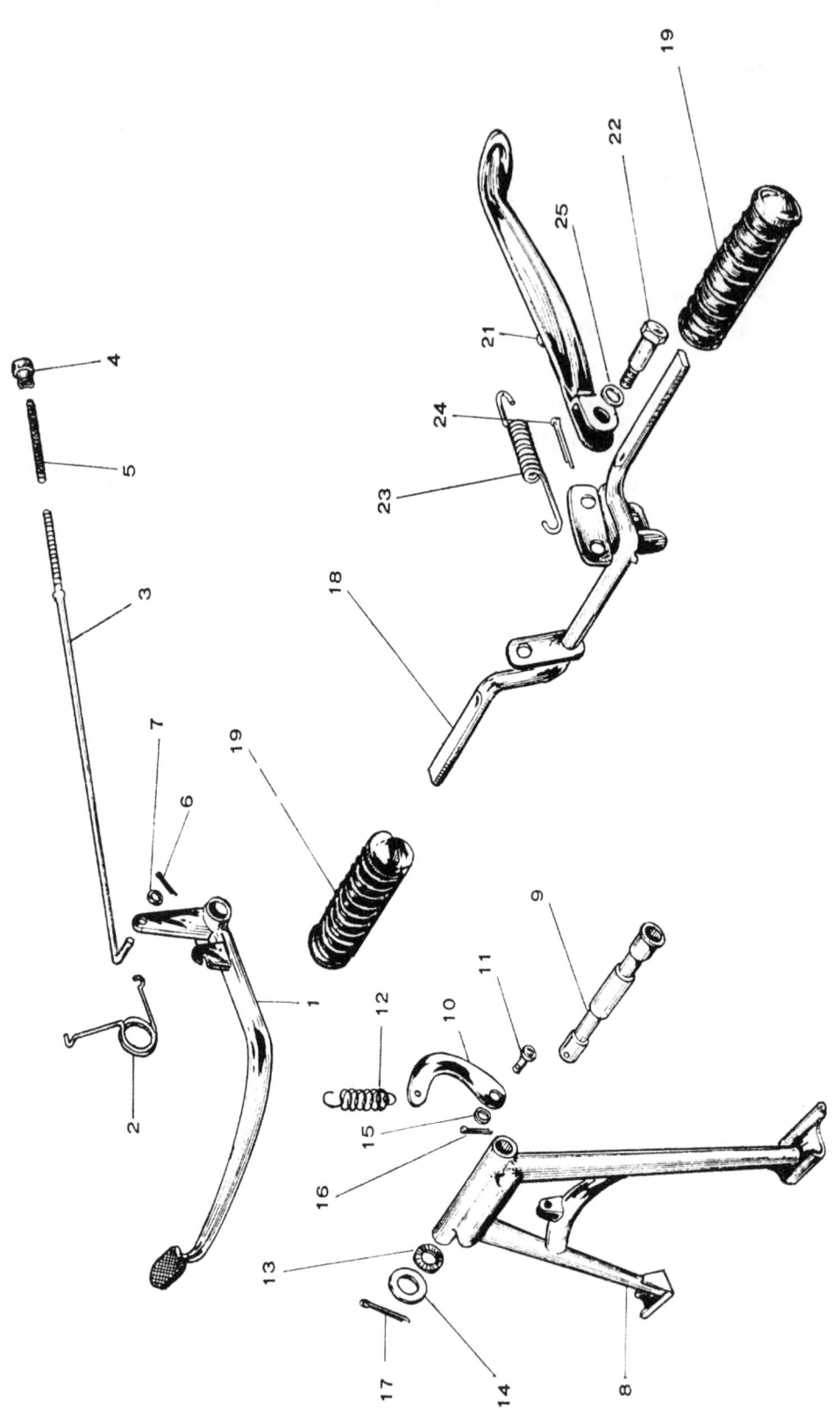

22) BRAKE PEDAL · STAND · FOOTREST

Index No.	Part No.	Part Name	No. Req'd	Unit Price US $	Serial No. From (MFG date)	Old Part No.	Min. Lot	N. B.
22- 1	3810-5030	Brake pedal comp	1					
22- 2	3821-5000	Brake pedal spring	1			EA1 61621		
22- 3	3831-3001	Rear brake rod	1			MO 4331-1		
22- 4	3832-3000	Brake rod adjust	1			MO 4332		
22- 5	3833-3000	Brake rod spring	1			MO 4333		
22- 6	0551-1612	Split pin	1			WP 16×12		
22- 7	0411-0613	Plane washer A	1			HW 6	50	
22- 8	3610-5000 CBK	Main stand comp	1			EA1 66410-CBK		
22- 9	3621-3200	Main stand shaft	1			GB1 66421		
22-10	3622-5000	Spring guide	1			EA1 66422		
22-11	3623-5000	Spring hook pin	1			EA1 66423		
22-12	3624-5000	Main stand spring	1			EA1 66424		
22-13	09546-101	16 Wave washer	1			WW 16	50	
22-14	09541-103	15 Plane washer	1			MO 8332		
22-15	0411-0613	Plane washer A	1			HW 6	50	
22-16	0551-1612	Split pin	1			WP 16×12	50	
22-17	0551-3028	Split pin	1			WP 3×28	50	
22-18	3710-5000 CBK	Foot rest bar comp	1			EA1 67110-CBK		
22-19	3721-3002	Foot rest rubber	2			MO 8421-2		
22-21	3650-5000	Side stand comp	1			EA1 67210		
22-22	3662-5000	Side stand bolt	1			EA1 67211		
22-23	3663-5000	Side stand spring	1			EA1 67212		
22-24	0231-0800	Hexagon nut C	1				50	
22-25	09541-107	10 plane washer	1			EA1 31432	50	

MEMO

23) AIR CLEANER

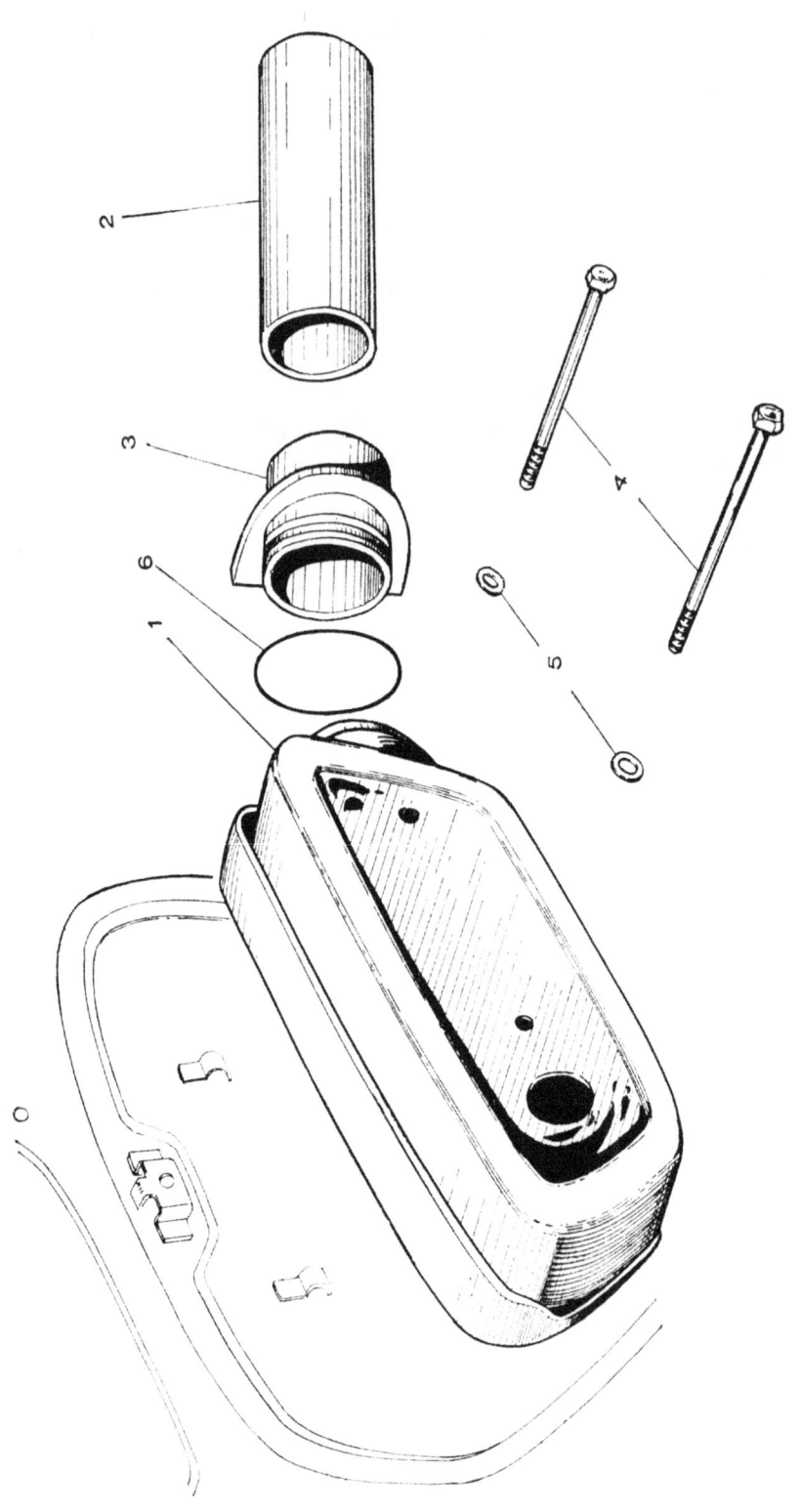

— 50 —

23) AIR CLEANER

Index No.	Part No.	Part Name	No. Req'd	Unit Price US $	Remarks Serial No. From (MFG date)	Remarks Old Part No.	Min. Lot	N. B.
23- 1	6211-5001	Air cleaner element	1			EA1 62110-1		
23- 2	6241-5000	Air pipe	1			EA1 62121		
23- 3	6242-5000	Air pipe joint	1			EA1 62122		
23- 4	0111-0665	Hexagon bolt A	2			6B 6×65		
23- 5	0411-0613	Plane washer A	2			HW 6	50	
23- 6	6243-5000	Cleaner spring ring	1			EA1 62123		

MEMO

24) MUFFLER · EXHAUST PIPE

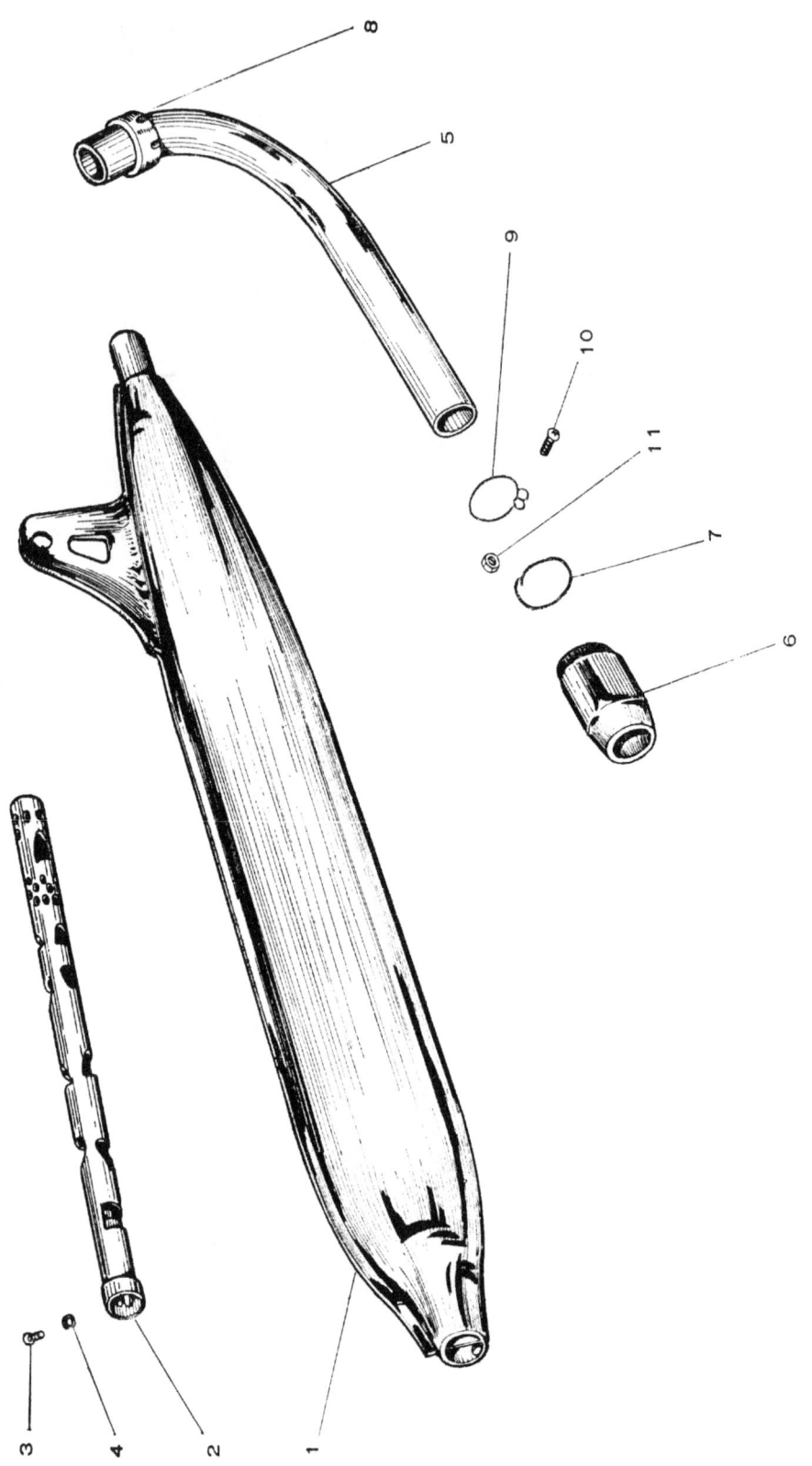

24) MUFFLER · EXHAUST PIPE

Index No.	Part No.	Part Name	No. Req'd	Unit Price US $	Serial No. From (MFG date)	Old Part No.	Min. Lot	N. B.
24- 1	6301-5000	Muffler assy	1			EA1 63300		
24- 2	6320-5000	Diffuser pipe	1			EA1 63313		
24- 3	0121-0506	Hexagon bolt B	1			6B 5× 6	50	
24- 4	0411-0512	Plane washer A	1			HW 5	50	
24- 5	6351-5030	Exhaust pipe	1		12N036928 (Feb. '65)	EAE 63111		
24- 5	6351-5000	Exhaust pipe	1		Old type	EA1 63111		
24- 6	6362-5000	Muffler joint rubber	1			EA1 63121		
24- 7	6364-5000	Muffler joint ring	1			EA1 63122		
24- 8	6361-5000	Exhaust pipe clamp	1			EA1 63123		
24- 9	6363-5000	Muffler joint stopper	1			EA1 63124		
24-10	0311-0412	Cross recd pan head screw	1			PNK 4×12	50	
24-11	0211-0400	Hexagon nut A	1			6N1 4	50	

MEMO

25) DUAL SEAT · COVERS · CARRIER

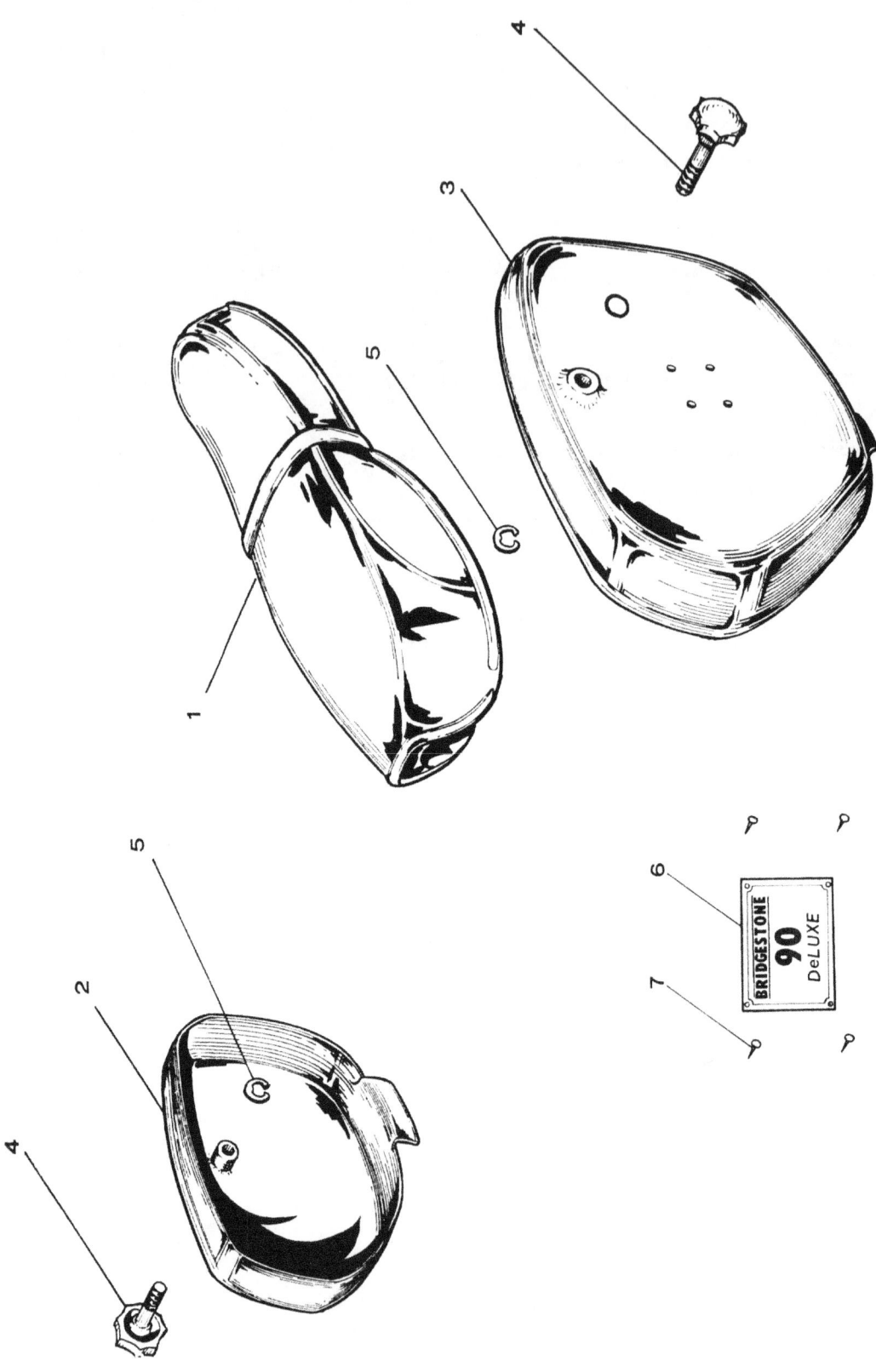

25) DUAL SEAT · COVERS · CARRIER

Index No.	Part No.	Part Name	No. Req'd	Unit Price US $	Serial No. From (MFG date)	Old Part No.	Min. Lot	N. B.
25- 1	6460-5010	Dual seat comp	1			EA1 91100		
25- 2	6821-3220 CUR	Right cover	1					
25- 2	6821-3220 MB	Right cover	1					
25- 2	6821-3210 CBK	Right cover	1					
25- 3	6811-5030 CUR	Left cover	1					
25- 3	6811-5030 MB	Left cover	1					
25- 3	6811-5020 CBK	Left cover	1					
25- 4	6831-5000	Cover knob	2			EA1 68112		
25- 5	6832-3001	Circlip	2			MO 8633 -1		
25- 6	6815-5030	Cover ornament	2		BS 90D			
25- 7	6823-8000	Eyelet	8				50	
		Single seat and Carrier						
25-	6410-4020	Seat comp	1					
25-	0111-0816	Hexagon bolt A	2			6B 8×16	50	
25-	0411-0818	Plane washer A	2			HW 8	50	
25-	6510-5000 CUR	Luggage carrier assy	1			EA1 65100 -CUR		
25-	6510-5000 MB	Luggage carrier assy	1			EA1 65100 -MB		
25-	6510-5000 CBK	Luggage carrier assy	1			EA1 65100 -CBK		

MEMO

26) FRONT WHEEL

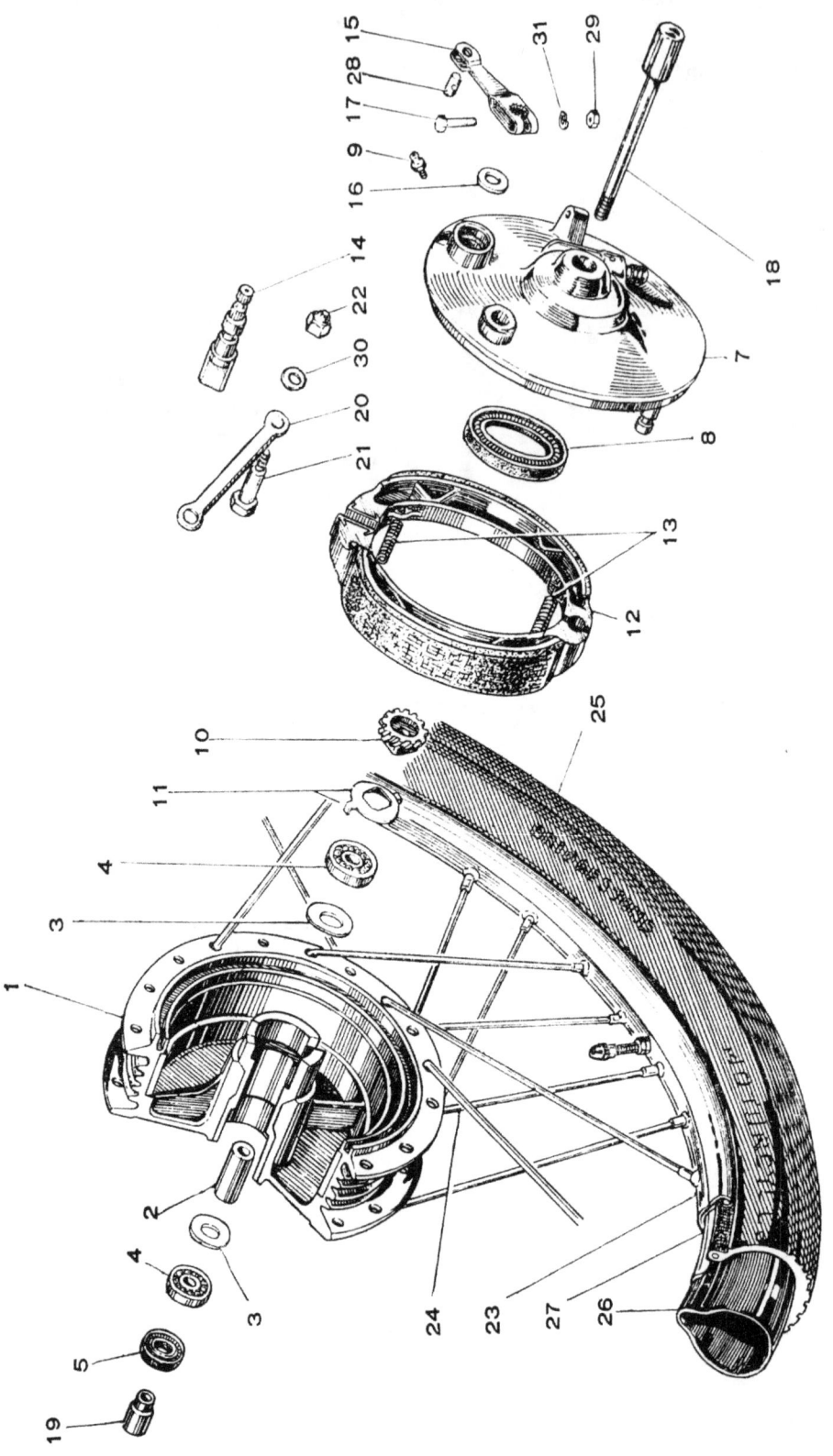

26) FRONT WHEEL

Index No.	Part No.	Part Name	No. Req'd	Unit Price US $	Serial No. From (MFG date)	Old Part No.	Min. Lot	N. B.
26- 1	7111-5002	Front drum	1		12Q041249 (May. '65)	EA1 71110 -2		
26- 2	7114-5000	Front drum collar	1			EA1 71114		
26- 3	7115-3000	Collar supporter	2			MO 4119		
26- 4	07-6201-03	Ball bearing	1			MO 4116 -1	10	
26- 4	07-6201-43	Ball bearing	1		Left side	EA1 71116	10	
26- 5	09590-104	20 Oil seal	1			GA3 71117	10	
26- 7	7130-5002	Front brake panel	1			EA1 71130 -2		
26- 7	7130-5003	Front brake panel	1			EA1 71130 -3		For old type
26- 8	09590-105	40 Oil seal	1			GA3 71134	10	
26- 9	7134-3002	Grease nipple	1			MO 4137A -1		
26-10	7148-5001	Speedmeter gear	1					
21-11	7149-3110	Speedometer gear connetor	1			GA3 71142		
26-12	7140-5000	Brake shoe comp	2			EA1 71150		
26-13	7145-3110	Brake shoe spring	2			GA3 71161		
26-14	7151-3110	Front brake cam	1			GA3 71171		
26-15	7353-3004	Brake arm C	1			MO 4251 -4		
26-16	7152-3001	Cam dust seal	1			MO 4248 -1		
26-17	0121-0628	Hexagon bolt B	1			MO 4249 -2	50	
26-18	7221-5000	Front wheel axle	1			EA1 71181		
26-19	7226-3110	Front axle collar	1			GA3 71182		
26-20	7166-5000	Font torque link	1			EA1 71191		
26-21	7167-5000	Front link bolt	1			EA1 71192		
26-22	09525-102	Cap nut	1			MO 1839	10	
26-23	7241-5000	Wheel rim	1			EA1 71200		
26-24	7108-5000	Front spoke assy	1			EA1 71300		
26-25	7251-5000	Front wheel tire	1			EA1 71410		
26-26	7252-5000	Wheel tube	1			EA1 71420		
26-27	7253-3000	Tire flap	1			MO 4193		
26-28	7361-3003	Brake arm pin	1			MO 4252 -3		
26-29	0211-0600	Hexagon nut A	1			6N1 6	50	
26-30	0431-0820	Spring washer	1			SW 8	50	
26-31	0431-0615	Spring washer	1			SW 6	50	
26-	7228-3110	Cap dust seal	1			GA3 71185		

When placing order of "*" items, please order by separate cover.

27) REAR WHEEL

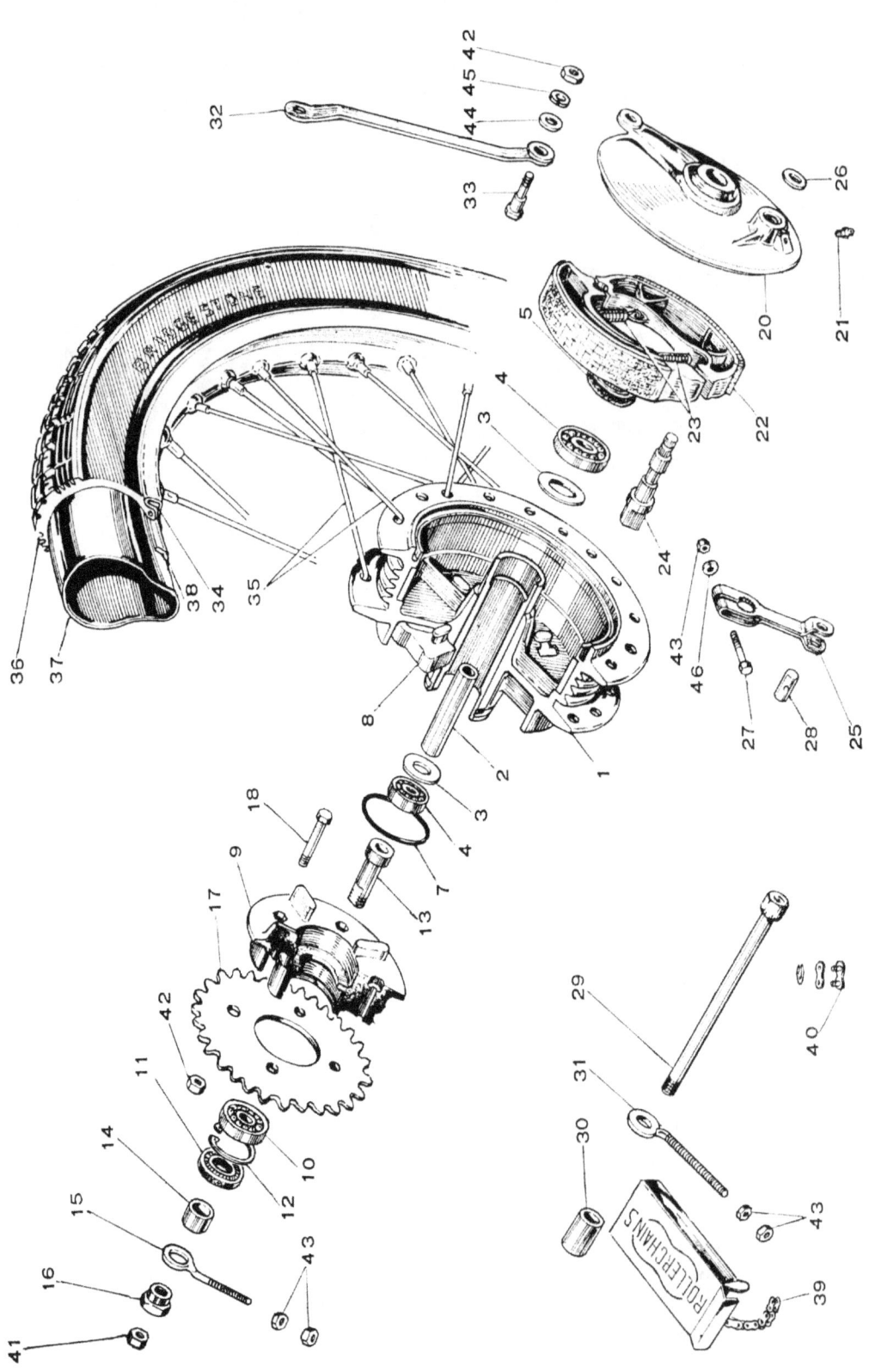

27) REAR WHEEL

Index No.	Part No.	Part Name	No. Req'd	Unit Price US $	Serial No. From (MFG date)	Old Part No.	Min. Lot	N. B.
27- 1	7311-5001	Rear brake drum	1		12Q040982 (May. '65)	EA1 72110 -1		
27- 2	7314-5000	Rear drum collar	1			EA1 72114		
27- 3	7115-3000	Collar supporter	2			MO 4119		
27- 4	07-6201-03	Ball bearing	2			MO 4116 -1	10	
27- 5	09590-106	17 Oil seal	1			GA3 72117	10	
27- 7	09566-101	40 O ring	1			GA3 72118	10	
27- 8	7319-3111	Rear wheel	4		12Q040982 (May. '65)	GA3 72119 -1		
27- 8	7319-3110	Rear wheel	4		Old type	GA3 72119		
27- 9	7371-3110	Driving flange	1			GA3 72131		
27-10	07-6203-03	Ball bearing	1			GA3 72132	10	
27-11	09590-107	23 Oil seal	1			GA3 72133	10	
27-12	09507-101	40 A Circlip	1			GA3 72134	10	
27-13	7376-5001	Driving flange collar	1					
27-14	7377-5000	Oil seal collar	1			EA1 72142		
27-15	4861-3110	Chain adjuster	1			GA3 72143		
27-16	7379-3111	Flange collar nut	1					
27-17	7381-5000	Final driven sprocket	1			EA1 72151		
27-18	09511-112	8×33 Hexagon bolt	4			GA3 72153	10	
27-20	7331-5001	Brake panel	1		12Q040982 (May. '65)	EA1 72160 -1		
27-20	7331-5000	Brake panel	1		Old type	EA1 72160		
27-21	7134-3002	Grease nipple	1			MO 4137A -1		
27-22	7140-5000	Brake shoe comp	2			EA1 71150		
27-23	7145-3110	Brake shoe spring	2			GA3 71161		
27-24	7351-3110	Rear brake cam	1			GA3 72171		
27-25	7353-3004	Brake cam C	1			MO 4251 -4		
27-26	7152-3001	Cam dust seal	1			MO 4248 -1		
27-27	0121-0628	Hexagon bolt B	1			MO 4249 -2	50	
27-28	7361-3003	Brake arm pin	1			MO 4252 -3		
27-29	7421-3110	Rear wheel axle	1			GA3 72181		
27-30	7426-3110	Rear axle collar	1			GA3 72182		
27-31	4861-3002	Chain adjuster	1			MO 3181 -2		
27-32	7366-5000	Rear torque link	1			EA1 72191		
27-33	7367-3001	Rear link bolt	1			MO 4259 -1		
27-34	7241-5000	Wheel rim	1			EA1 71200		
27-35	7308-5000	Rear spoke assy	1			EA1 72300		
27-36	7451-5000	Rear wheel tire	1			EA1 72410		
27-37	7252-5000	Wheel tube	1			EA1 71420		
27-38	7253-3000	Tire flap	1			MO 4193		

27) REAR WHEEL

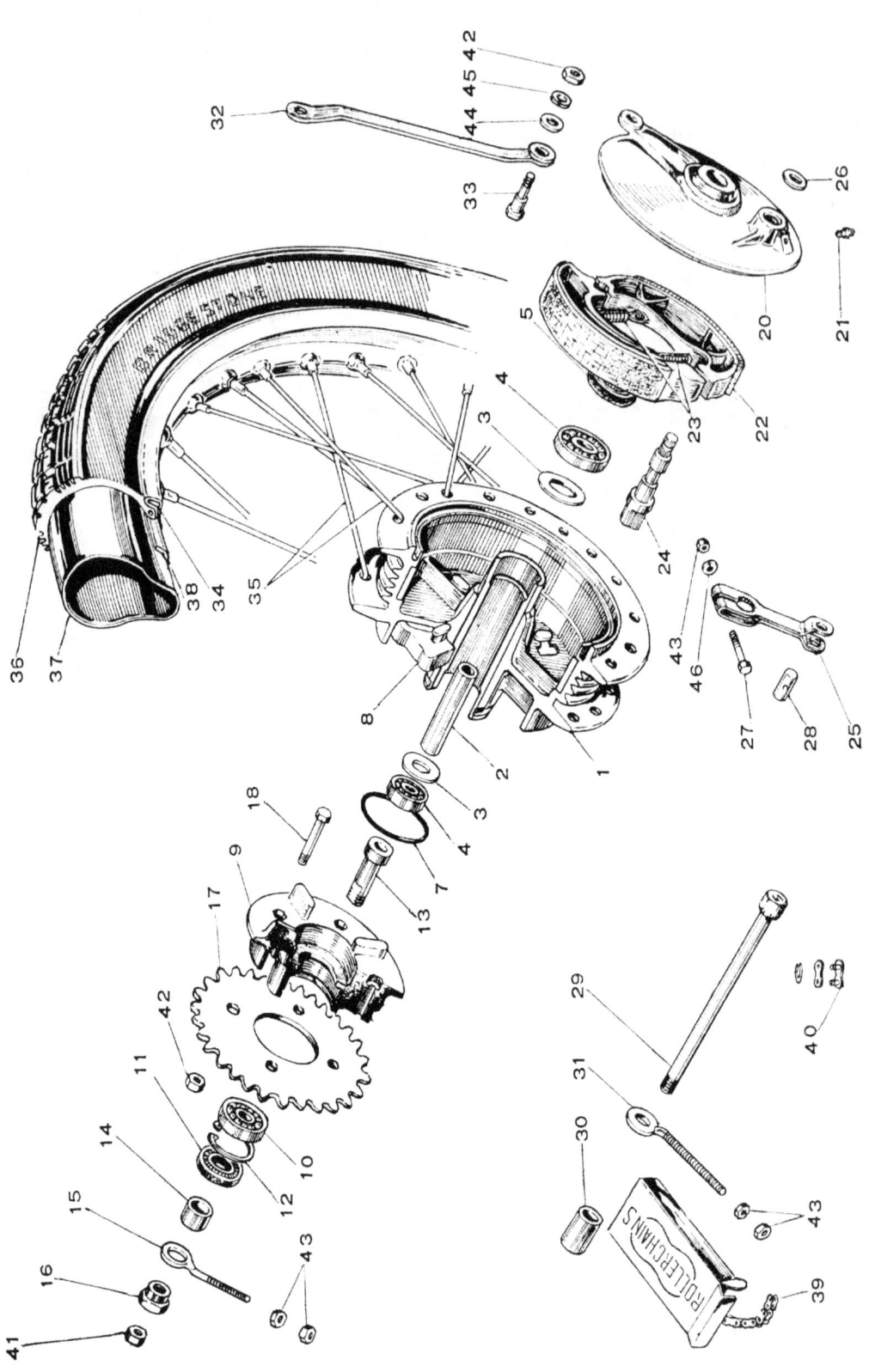

— 60 —

27) REAR WHEEL

Index No.	Part No.	Part Name	No. Req'd	Unit Price US $	Serial No. From (MFG date)	Old Part No.	Min. Lot	N. B.
27-39	7501-5000	Roller chain assy	1			EA1 73000		
27-40	7520-5000	Chain joint comp	1			EA1 73200		
27-41	7422-3110	Axle nut	1			GA3 72184		
27-42	0211-0800	Hexagon nut A	5			6N1 8	50	
27-43	0211-0600	Heaxgon nut A	5			6N1 6	50	
27-44	0411-0818	Plane washer A	1			HW 8	50	
27-45	0431-0820	Spring washer	1			SW 8	50	
27-46	0431-0615	Spring washer	1			SW 6	50	
27-	0411-1025	Plane washer A	1			HW 10	50	

MEMO

28) HEAD LAMP · MAIN SWITCH · WIRE HARNESS · BATTERY

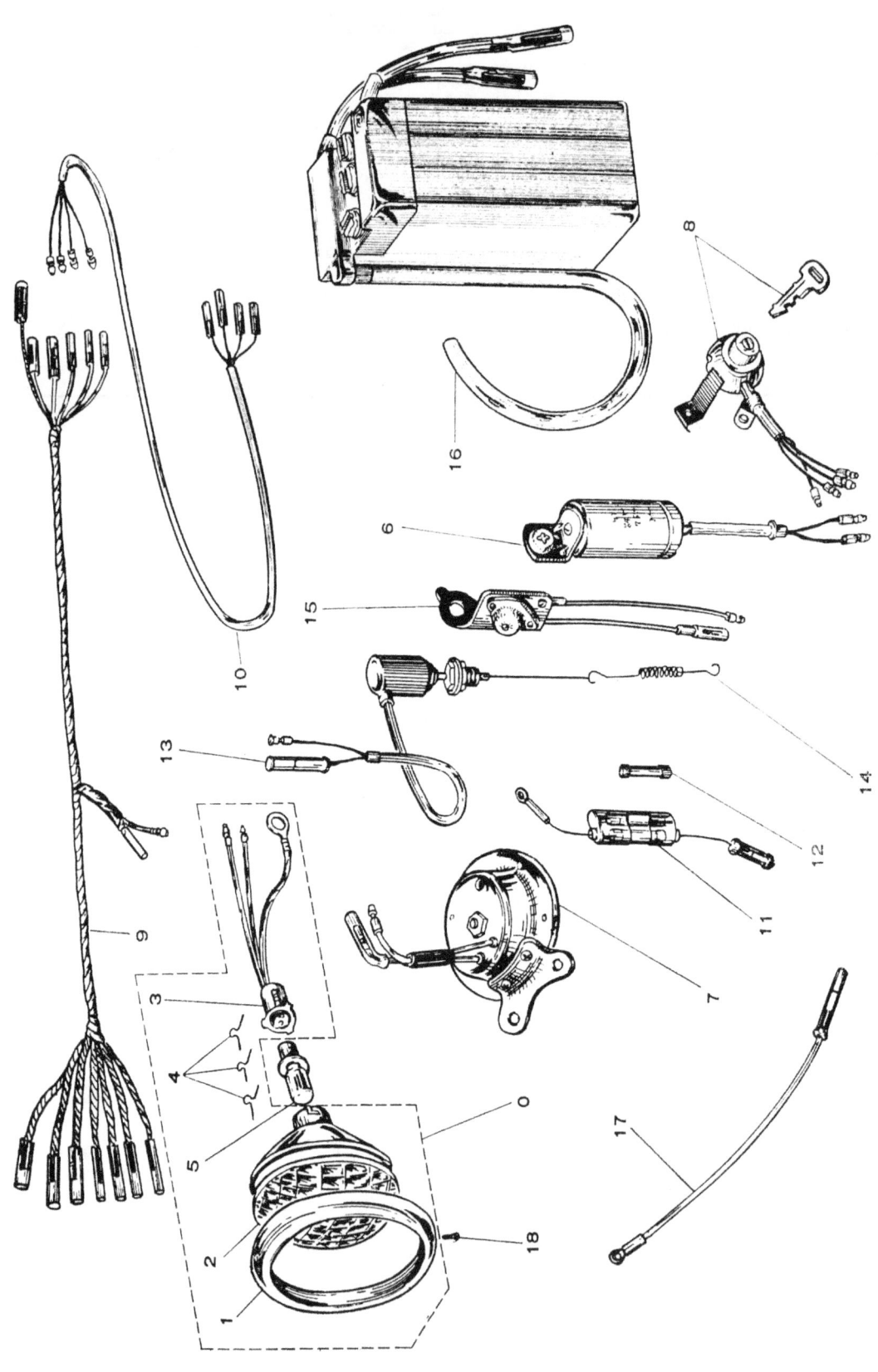

28) HEAD LAMP · MAIN SWITCH · WIRE HARNESS · BATTERY

Index No.	Part No.	Part Name	No. Req'd	Unit Price US $	Serial No. From (MFG date)	Old Part No.	Min. Lot	N. B.
28–	8102-5000	Head lamp assy	1			EA1 81200		
28- 1	8140-5000	Head lamp rim comp	1			EA1 81210		
28- 2	8150-5000	Head lamp lens comp	1			EA1 81220		
28- 3	8160-5000	Socket comp	1			EA1 81230		
28- 4	8172-5000	Rim set pin	3			EA1 81241		
28- 5	8171-5000	Head lamp bulb	1			EA1 81242		
28- 6	8305-5001	Turn signal relay	1			EA1 84100		
28- 7	8402-5000	Horn assy	1			EA1 85110		
28- 8	8601-5000	Main switch assy	1			EA1 86100		
28- 9	8810-3200	Wire harness comp	1			GB1 88110		
28-10	8821-5000	Rear wire harness	1			EA1 88120		
28-11	8802-5000	Fuse assy	1			EA1 88300		
28-12	8861-5000	Fuse	2					
28-13	8650-5000	Stop switch comp	1			EA1 89100		
28-14	8661-5001	Stop switch spring	1			EA1 89121 -1		
28-14	8661-5000	stpo switch spring	1		Old type	EA1 89121		
28-15	8702-5000	Rectifier assy	1			EA1 89510		
28-16	8701-5011	Battery	1			EAE 87110		
28-17	8834-5000	Head lamp earth wire	1			EA1 81311		
28-18	0342-0510	Cross recd oval head screw	1			PRK 5×10	50	

MEMO

29) SERVICE TOOL · SPECIAL TOOL

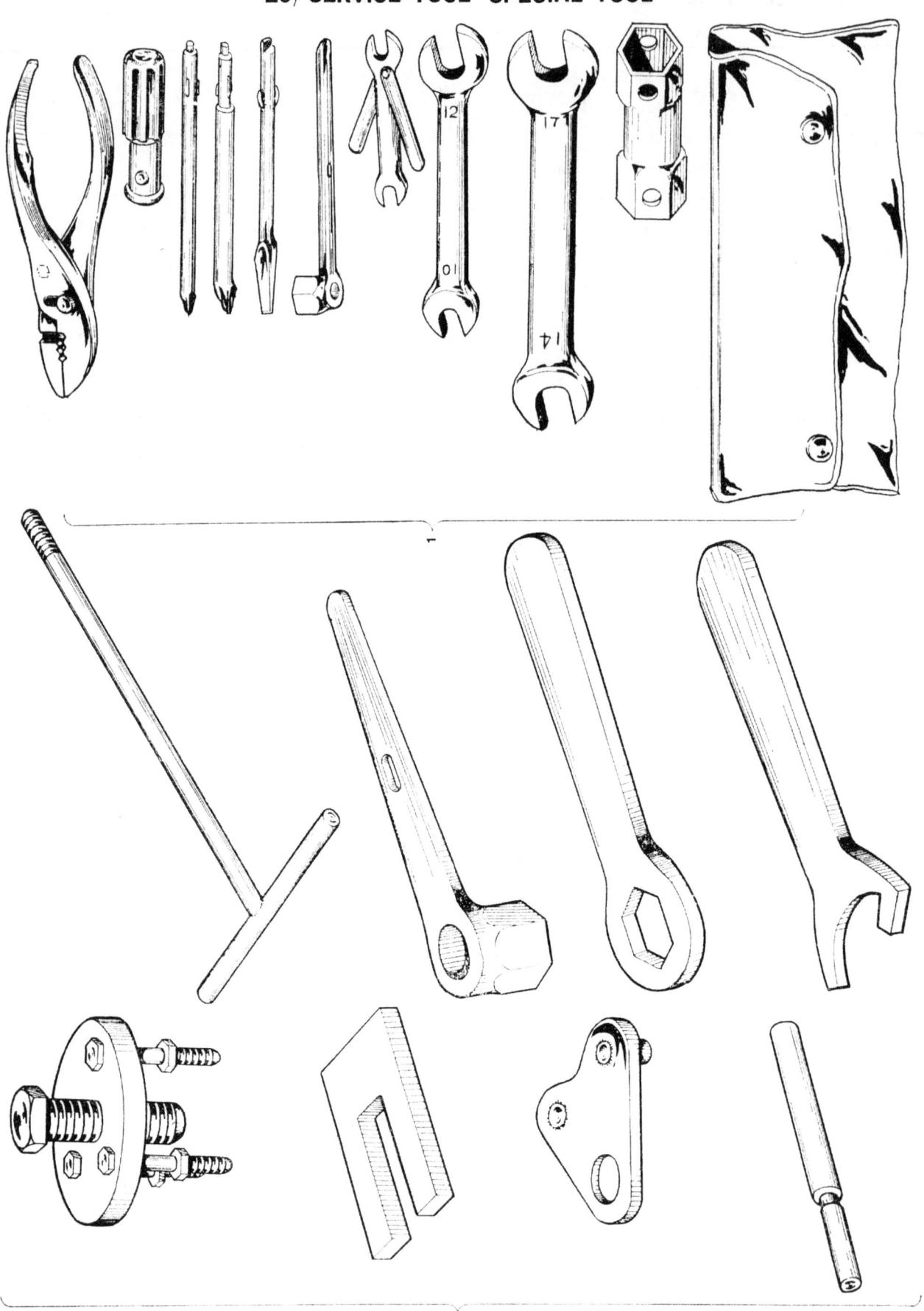

29) SERVICE TOOL · SPECIAL TOOL

Index No.	Part No.	Part Name	No. Req'd	Unit Price US $	Remarks			N. B.
					Serial No. From (MFG date)	Old Part No.	Min. Lot	
29-1	9201-5000	Tool kit	1			EA1 69100		
29-2	9300-5010	Special tool set	1			EA1 99100		

MEMO

30) EXCLUSIVE PARTS FOR U.S.A.

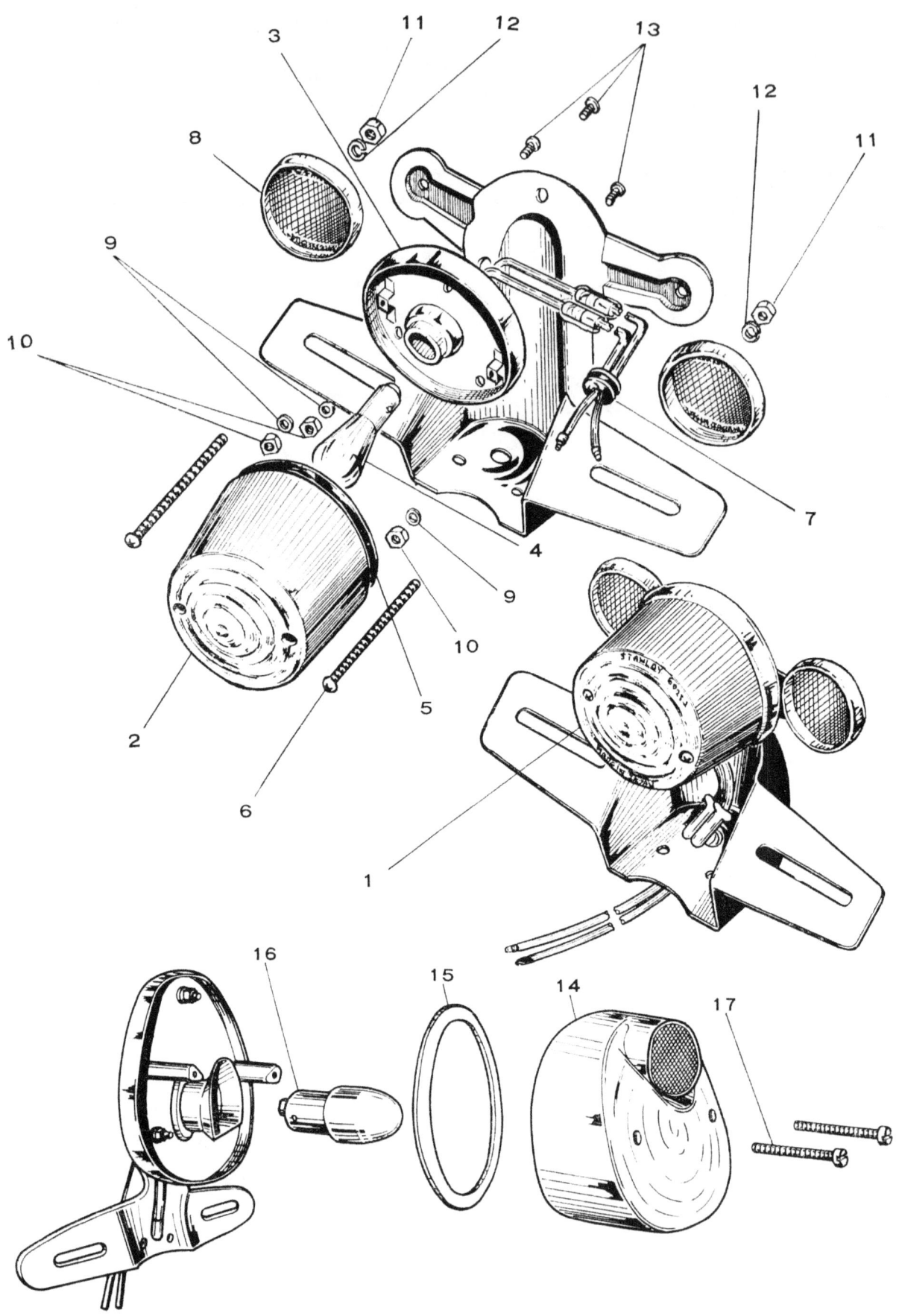

30) EXCLUSIVE PARTS FOR U.S.A.

Index No.	Part No.	Part Name	No. Req'd	Unit Price US $	Serial No. From (MFG date)	Old Part No.	Min. Lot	N. B.
30- 1	8202-5010	Tail lamp assy	1			EAE 83100		C. H. P old type abolished.
30- 2	8251-3020	Tail lamp lens	1			M 3513		
30- 3	8240-5010	Tail lamp base comp	1			EAE 83110		
30- 4	8252-3030	Tail lamp bulb	1			M 4515		
30- 5	8253-3020	Tail lamp gasket	1			M 4517		
30- 6	09534-102	3×55 Oval head screw	1			PRK 3×55	50	
30- 7	8256-3010	Tail lamp grommet	1			M 4518		
30- 8	8203-3010	Reflecter assy	2			M 4507		
30- 9	0411-0410	Plane washer A	2			HW 4	50	
30-10	0211-0400	Hexagon nut A	2			6N1 4	50	
30-11	0211-0500	Hexagon nut A	2			6N1 4	50	
30-12	0431-0513	Spring washer	2			SW 5	50	
30-13	0121-0410	Hexagon bolt B	3			6B 4×10	50	
		C. H. P New Type Tail lamp						
30-	8205-5011	Tail lamp assy	1					
30-14	8251-8000	Tail lamp lens	1					
30-15	8251-8000	Tail lamp Gasket	1					
30-16	8252-3030	Tail lamp bulb	1			M 4515		
30-17	0372-0330	Round head screw	2				50	
30-	6531-5021	Light luggage carrier	1					
		Other C. H. P Parts						
30-	3110-5011 CBK	Frame comp	1			EAE 31100 CBK		
30-	3110-5011 MB	Frame comp	1			EAE 31100 MB		
30-	6104-5020	Throttle grip assy	1			EAE 61200		
30-	6151-5020	Right switch case cover	1			EAE 61241		
30-	8810-5010	Wire harness comp	1			EAE 88110		
30-	8821-5000	Rear Wire harness	1			EAE 88120		
30-	8111-5020 CUR	Head lamp body	1			EAE 81110 CUR		
30-	8111-5020 MB	Head lamp body	1			EAE 81110 MB		
30-	8111-5020 CBK	Head lamp body	1			EAE 81110 CBK		
30-	8125-5020	Head lamp grommet	1			EAE 81112		
30-	8102-5020	Head lamp assy	1			EAE 81200		
30-	8140-5010 XC1	Head lamp rim comp	1			EAE 81210 -XC1		
30-	8150-5020	Head lamp lens comp	1			EAE 81220		
30-	8160-5020	Socket comp	1			EAE 81230		

31) EXCLUSIVE PARTS FOR TRAIL MODEL

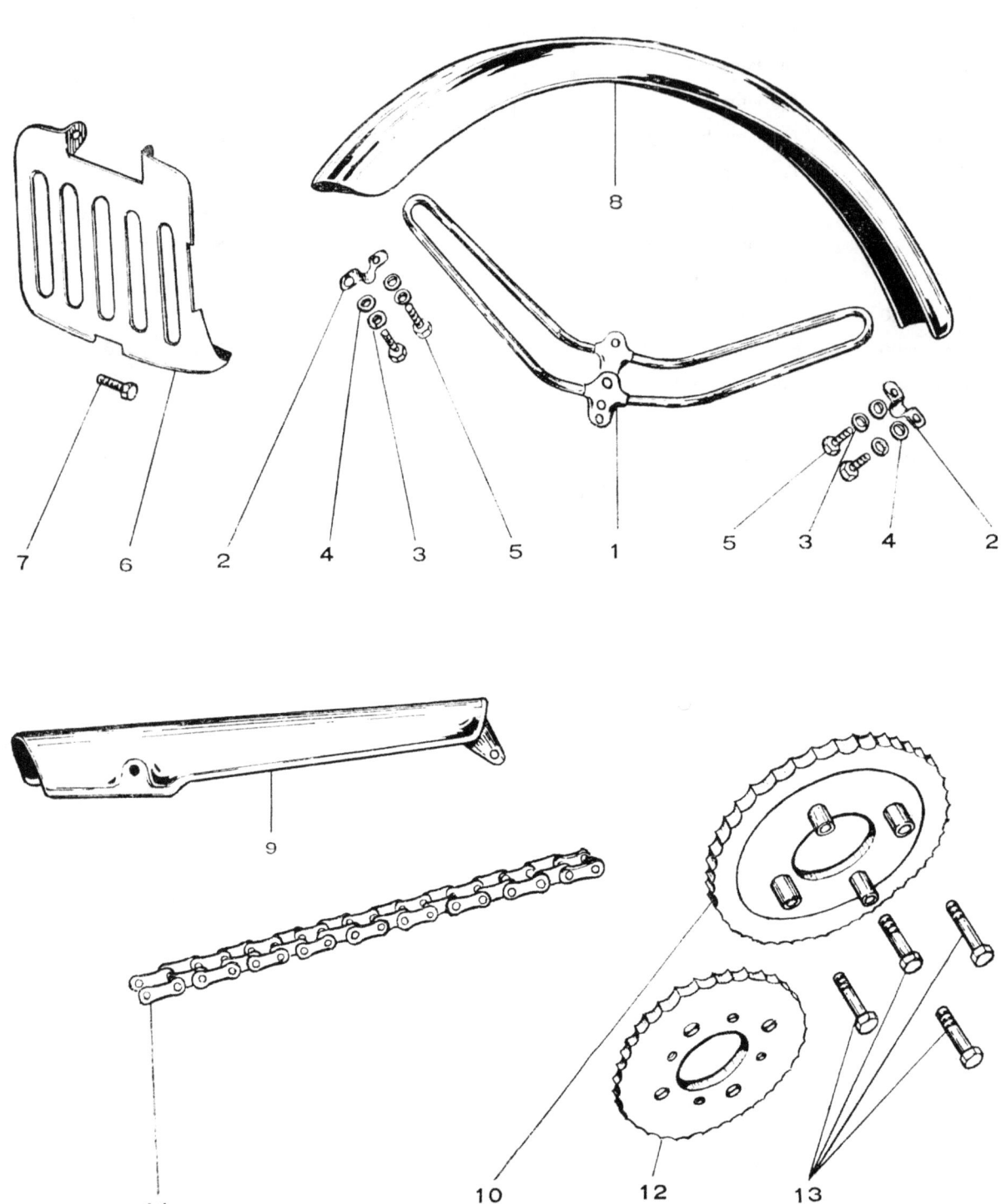

31) EXCLUSIVE PARTS FOR TRAIL MODEL

Index No.	Part No.	Part Name	No. Req'd	Unit Price US $	Serial No. From (MFG date)	Old Part No.	Min. Lot	N. B.
31- 1	4425-5011-XC1	Front fender stay	1			EAT1 42120 -1XC1		
31- 2	4428-5010	Front fender clamp	2			EAT1 42131		
31- 3	0431-0615	Spring washer	4			SW 6	50	
31- 4	0411-0613	Plane washer A	4			HW 6	50	
31- 5	0111-0614	Hexagon bolt A	4			6B 6×14	50	
31- 6	6761-5010	Engine protector	1			EAT1 39111		
31- 7	0121-0838	Hexagon bolt B	4			6B 8×38	10	
31- 8	4411-5501 XC1	Front fender	1			EAT1 42110 -1XC1		
31- 9	4751-5020	Half chain case	1			EAT1 45100		
31-10	7411-5010	Sub sprocket	1		47T	EAT1 72150 A		
31-11	7502-5010	Sub chain assy	1		For 47 T	EAT1 73000		
31-12	7416-5010	Main sprocket	1		34T	EAT1 72151 A		
31-13	0123-0816	Hexagon bolt B	4			EAT1 72159	50	
31-	6815-5040	Cover ornament	2					BS 90 T

MEMO

32) EXCLUSIVE PARTS FOR MODEL BS90M
(FRONT FENDER · CHAIN CASE · SPROCKETS)

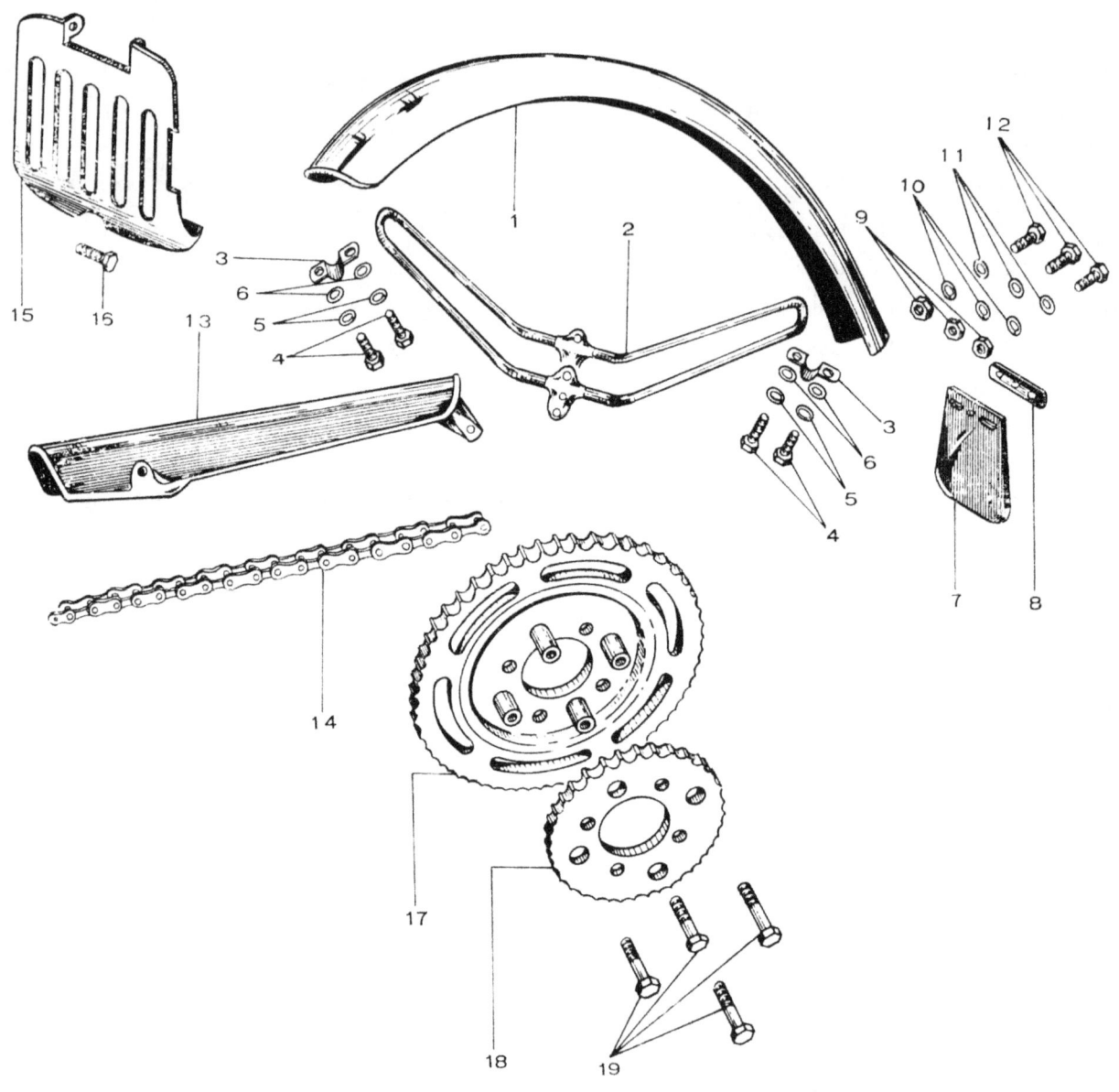

32) EXCLUSIVE PARTS FOR MODEL BS90M
(FRONT FENDER · CHAIN CASE · SPROCKETS)

Index No.	Part No.	Part Name	No. Req'd	Unit Price US $	Serial No. From (MFG date)	Old Part No.	Min. Lot	N. B.
32- 1	4411-5011 XC1	Front fender	1			EAT1 42110 -1XC1		
32- 2	4425-5011 XC1	Front fender stay	1			EAT1 42120 -1XC1		
32- 3	4428-5010	Front fender clamp	2			EAT1 42131		
32- 4	0111-0614	Hexagon bolt A	4			6B 6×14	50	
32- 5	0431-0615	Spring washer	4			SW 6	50	
32- 6	0411-0613	Plane washer A	4			HW 6	50	
32- 7	4451-5010	Front mud guard	1			EA1 91751		
32- 8	4452-5010	Mud guard band	1			EA1 91752		
32- 9	0211-0500	Hexagon nut A	3			6N1 5	50	
32-10	0431-0513	Spring washer	3			SW 5	50	
32-11	0411-0512	Plane washer A	3			HW 5	50	
32-12	0311-0510	Cross recd pan head screw	3			PNK 5×10	50	
32-13	4751-5303	Half chain case	1			EA13 45100		
32-14	7502-5020	Sub chain assy	1			EA13 73000		
32-15	6761-5010	Engine protector	1			EAT1 39111		
32-16	0121-0838	Hexagon bolt B	4			6B 8×38	50	
32-17	7411-5020	Sub sprocket	1		64 T	EA13 72150		
32-18	7416-5010	Main sprocket	1		34 T	EAT1 72151 A		
32-19	0123-0816	Hexagon bolt B	4			EAT1 72159	50	

MEMO

33) EXCLUSIVE PARTS FOR MODEL BS90M
(EXHAUST PIPE · MUFFLER · MUFFLER PROTECTOR)

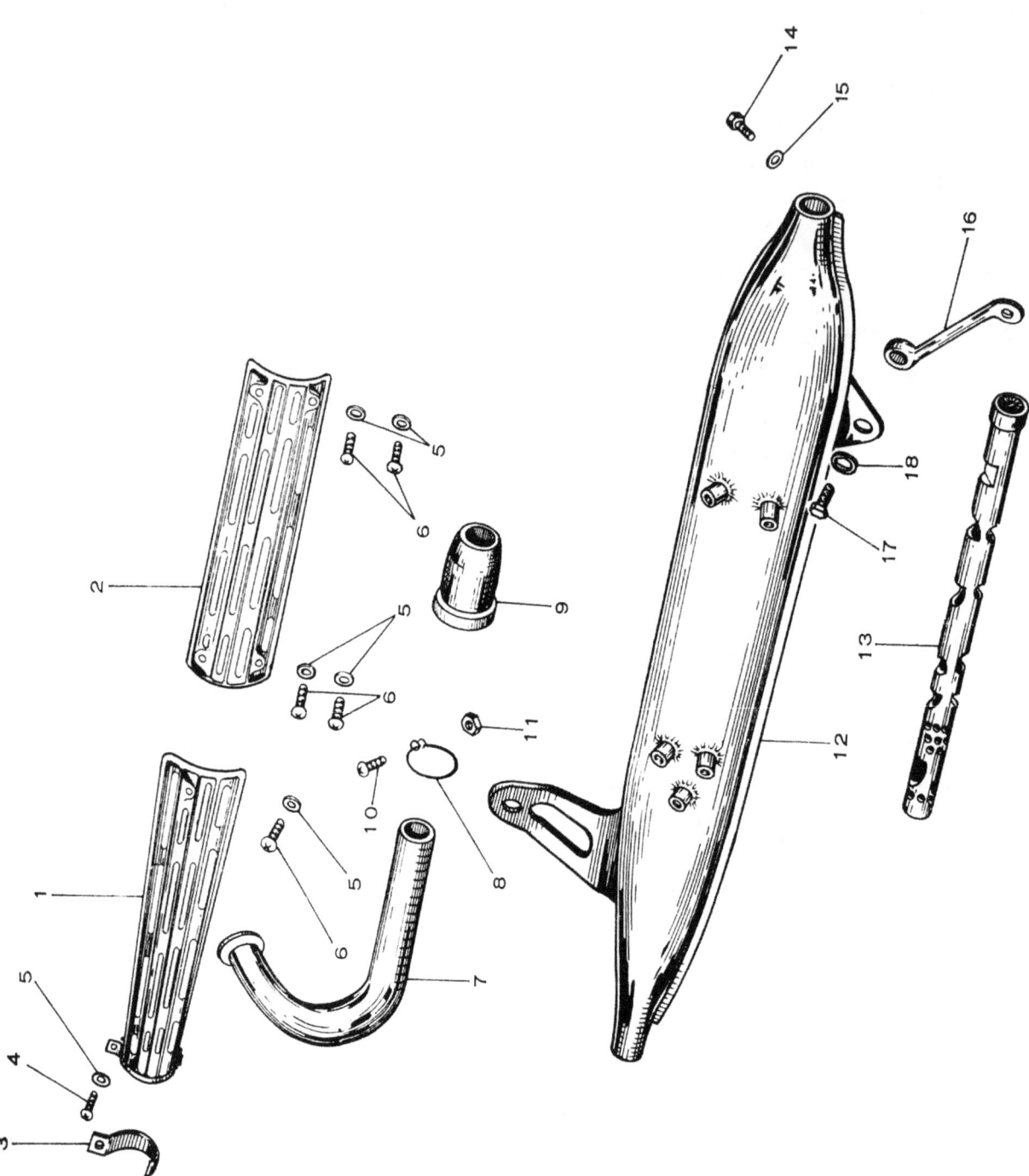

33) EXCLUSIVE PARTS FOR MODEL BS90M
(EXHAUST PIPE · MUFFLER · MUFFLER PROTECTOR)

Index No.	Part No.	Part Name	No. Peq'd	Unit Price US $	Serial No. From (MFG date)	Old Part No.	Min. Lot	N. B.
33- 1	6332-3210	Muffler protector	1		12B057127 (Feb. '66)			
33- 1	6332-5010	Front muffler protector	1		Old type	EA13 63327		
33- 2	6333-5010	Rear muffler protector	1			EA13 63328		
33- 3	6334-5010	Protector bracket	1		Spare part only	EA13 63329		
33- 4	0311-0610	Cross recd pan head screw	1			PNK 6×10	50	
33- 5	0411-0613	Plane washer A	6			HW 6	50	
33- 6	09531-102	6×6 cross recd pan head screw	5			PNK 6×6	50	
33- 7	6351-5050	Exhaust pipe	1		12B057127 (Feb. '66)			
33- 7	6351-5040	Exhaust pipe	1		Old type	EA13 63111		
33- 8	6364-5000	Muffler joint ring	1			EA1 63122		
33- 9	6362-5000	Muffler joint rubber	1			EA1 63121		
33-10	0311-0412	Cross recd pan head screw	1			PNK 4×12	50	
33-11	0211-0400	Hexagon nut A	1			6N1 4	50	
33-12	6301-5041	Muffler assy	1		12G011238 (July. '66)			
33-12	6301-5010	Muffler assy	1		Old type	EA13 63310		
33-13	6320-5020	Diffuser pipe	1		12B057127 (Feb. '66)			
33-13	6320-5000	Diffuser pipe	1		Old type	EA1 63313		
33-14	0121-0506	Hexagon bolt B	1			6B 5× 6	50	
33-15	0411-0512	Plane washer A	1			HW 5	50	
33-16	6335-5021	Muffler stay	1		12G011238 (July. '66)			
33-16	6335-5010	Muffler stay	1		Old type	EA13 63331		
33-17	0111-0612	Hexagon bolt B	1			6B 6×12	50	
33-18	0411-0613	Plane washer A	1			HW 6	50	
33-	3137-3210	Cover guide	1					
33-	6811-3211 CUR	Left cover	1					
33-	6811-3211 MB	Left cover	1					
33-	6811-3211 CBK	Left cover	1					
33-	6815-5050	Cover ornament	2					BS90M

MEMO

34) EXCLUSIVE PARTS FOR MODEL BS90M
(BRAKE PEDAL · FOOT REST)

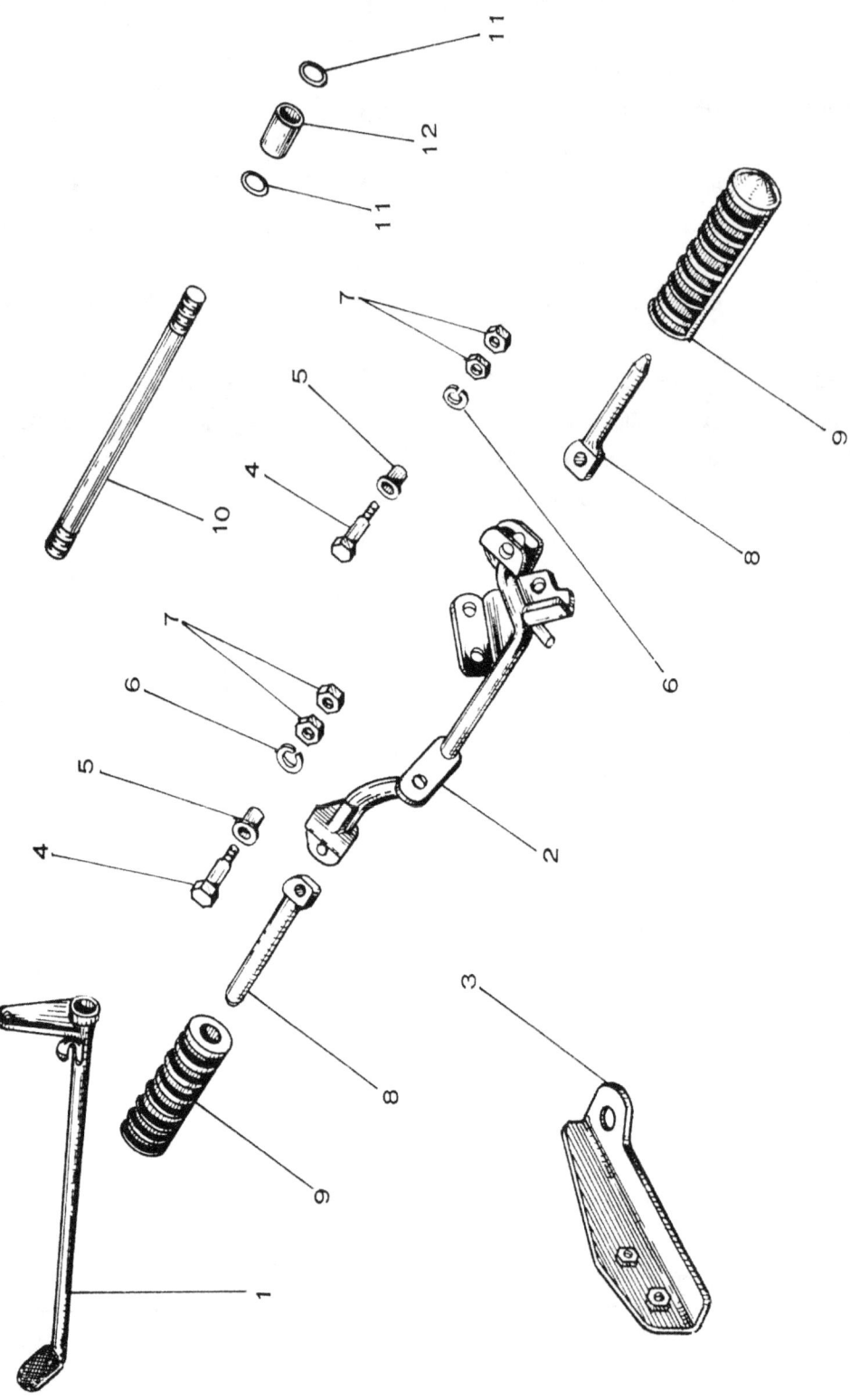

34) EXCLUSIVE PARTS FOR MODEL BS90M
(BRAKE PEDAL · FOOT REST)

Index No.	Part No.	Part Name	No. Req'd	Unit Price US $	Serial No. From (MFG date)	Old Part No.	Min. Lot	N. B.
34- 1	3810-5021	Brake pedal comp	1			EA13 61610		
34- 2	3710-5020 CBK	Foot rest bar comp	1			EA13 67110 -CBK		
34- 3	3336-5010	Stand stopper bracket	1			EA13 31417		
34- 4	3723-5010	Foot rest mounting bolt	2			EA13 67124		
34- 5	3722-5010	Foot rest mounting spacer	2			EA13 67122		
34- 6	0411-0818	Plane washer A	2			HW 8	50	
34- 7	0211-0800	Hexagon nut A	4			6N1 8	50	
34- 8	3711-5010	Foot rest bar	2			EA13 67121		
34- 9	3721-3002	Foot rest rubber	2			MO 8421 -2		
34-10	3415-5010	Rear cushion spacer	1			EA13 41422		
34-11	09541-107	10 plane washer	2			EA13 31432		
34-12	3389-5010	Rear cushion spacer	1			EA13 31433		
34-13	0211-1000	Hexagon nut A	1			6N1 10	50	
34-	09546-104	10 wave washer	1			EA13 67123	50	
34-	2581-5030	Gear change pedal	1					

MEMO

35) EXCLUSIVE PARTS FOR MODEL BS90M
HANDLE BAR · SEAT · CARRIER · REAR FRAME

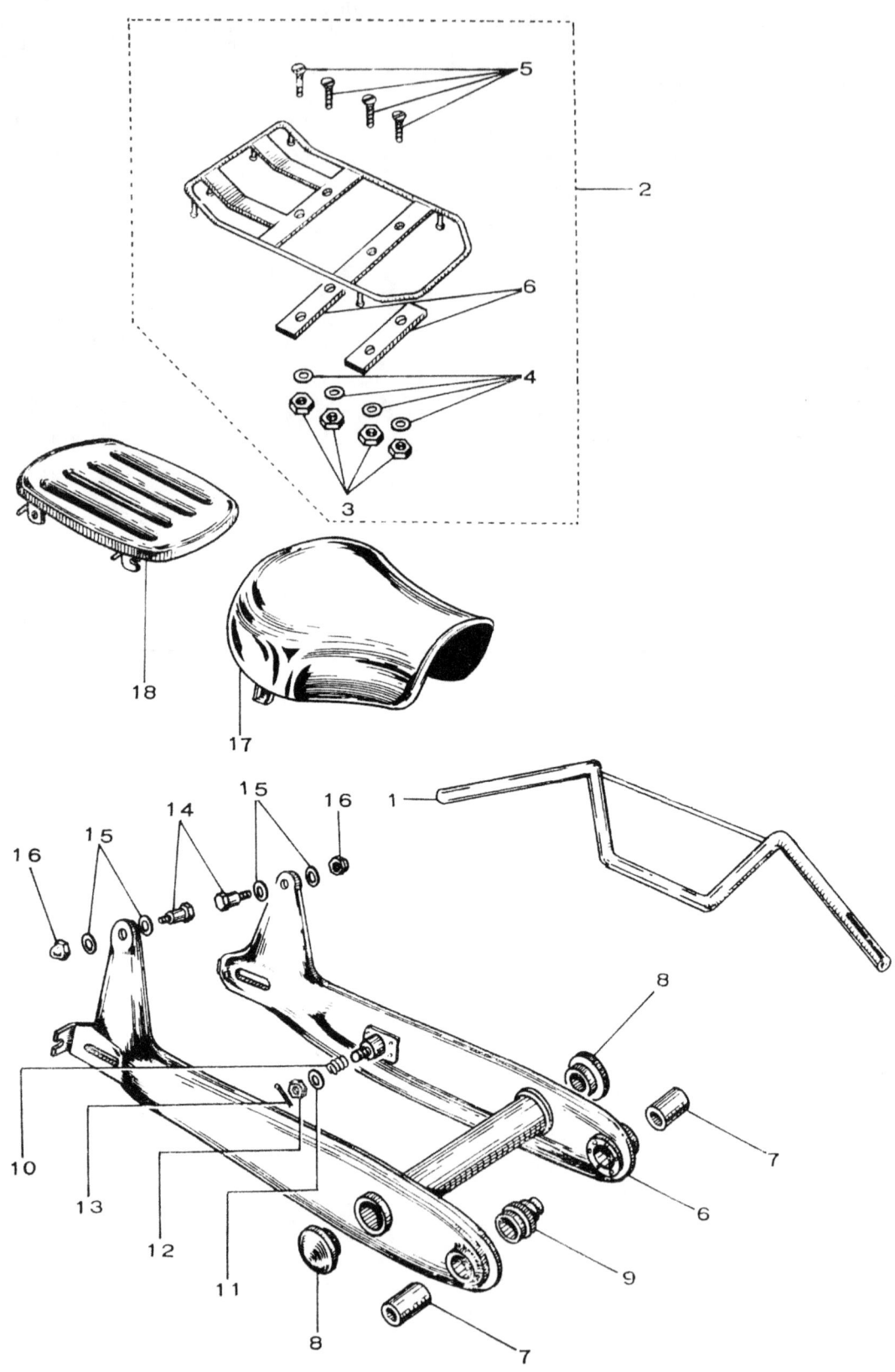

35) EXCLUSIVE PARTS FOR MODEL BS90M
(HANDLE BAR · SEAT · CARRIER · REAR FRAME)

Index No.	Part No.	Part Name	No. Req'd	Unit Price US $	Serial No. From (MFG date)	Old Part No.	Min. Lot	N. B.
35- 1	4511-5040	Mounting handle bar	1			EA13 43111		
35- 2	6541-5030	Heavy luggage carrier	1			EA13 91310		
35-	6548-5010	Setting carrier plate	2			EA11 91311		
35- 3	0211-0800	Hexagon nut A	4			6N1 8	50	
35- 4	0431-0820	Spring washer	4			SW 8	50	
35- 5	0381-0830	Flat head screw	4			SK 8×30	50	
35- 6	4810-3200 CUR	Rear fork comp	1			GB1 47110 -CUR		
35- 6	4810-3200 MB	Rear fork comp	1			GB1 47110 -MB		
35- 6	4810-3200 CBK	Rear fork comp	1			EA1 47110 -CBK		
35- 7	4851-5000	Rear fork bush	2			EA1 47211		
35- 8	4852-5000	Rear fork cap	2			EA1 47213		
35- 9	4853-3001	Chain protector	1			MO 3172 -1		
35-10	4854-5000	Torque rod spring	1			EA1 47212		
35-11	0411-0613	Plane washer A	1			HW 6	50	
35-12	0211-0800	Hexagon nut A	1			6N1 8	50	
35-13	0551-2020	Split pin	1			WP 20×20	50	
35-14	0123-1040	Hexagon nut B	2			6B 10×40	50	
35-15	09541-107	10 plane washer	4			EA1 31432	10	
35-16	09525-105	10 cap nnt	2			EA1 31428	10	
35-17	6410-5020	Seat comp	1					
35-18	6510-5000 CUR	Luggage carrier comp	1			EA1 65100 -UCR		
35-18	6510-5000 MB	Luggage carrier comp	1			EA1 65100 -MB		
35-18	6510-5000 CBK	Luggage carrier comp	1			EA1 65100 -CBK		

MEMO

36) EXCLUSIVE PARTS FOR MODEL BS90M
(CARBURETOR · FRONT FORK · REAR CUSION)

Index No.	Part No.	Part Name	No. Rdq'd	Unit Price US $	Serial No. From (MFG date)	Old Part No.	Min. Lot	N. B.
36- 1	1600-5030	Carburetor assy	1			EA13 16100		
36- 2	1635-5000 130	130 main jet	1			EA13 16141 130		
36- 3	1781-5030	Spark plug	1			EA13 17410		NGK. B-7HZ
36- 4	2151-5020	Left crank case cover	1		12H060263 (Aug. '66)	EA1 21431 -1		
36- 5	2153-5001	Dust cover A	1					
36- 6	4100-5020 CUR	Front fork assy	1			EA13 41000 -CUR		
36- 6	4100-5020 MB	Front fork assy	1			EA13 41000 -MB		
36- 6	4100-5020 CBK	Front fork assy	1			EA13 41000 -CBK		
36- 7	4121-5010	Main cushion spring	1			EA13 41171		
36- 8	4901-5010 CUR	Rear cushion assy	1			EA13 48100 -CUR		
36- 8	4901-5010 MB	Rear cushion assy	1			EA13 48100 -MB		
36- 8	4901-5010 CBK	Rear cushion assy	1			EA13 48100 -CBK		
36- 9	7251-5020	Front wheel tire	2		2.50-17	EA13 71410		

MEMO

37) EXCLUSIVE PARTS FOR MODEL BS90SP
(CYLINDER · PISTON)

Index No.	Part No.	Part Name	No. Req'd	Unit Price US $	Serial No. From (MFG date)	Old Part No.	Min. Lot	N. B.
37- 1	1121-5020	Cylinder	1			EA2 11211		
37- 2	1126-5010	Cylinder head stud	4			EA2 11212		
37- 3	1141-5010	Cylinder head gasket	1			EA2 11411		
37- 4	1341-5010	Piston	1			EA2 13310		
37- 5	1305-5010	Piston ring kit	1			EA2 13320		
37- 6	1431-5010	Potary valve cover	1			EA2 14131		
37- 7	2218-5010	Clutch spring	6			EA2 22118		
37- 8	2176-5010	Carburetor cover	1			EA2 21351		
37- 9	2177-5010	Carburetor cap	1			EA2 21353		
37-10	2178-5010	Carburetor cap ring	1			EA2 21355		
37-11	0313-0635	Cross recd pan head screw	3			PNK 6×35	50	

MEMO

38) EXCLUSIVE PARTS FOR MODEL BS90SP
(CARBURETOR)

Index No.	Part No.	Part Name	No. Req'd	Unit Price US $	Serial No. From (MFG date)	Old Part No.	Min. Lot	N. B.
38- 1	1600-5080	Carburetor assy	1					
38- 2	1611-5010	Mixing chamber body	1			EA2 16111		
38- 3	1614-5010	Throttle valve	1			EA2 16121		
38- 4	1615-5010	Jet needle	1			EA2 16122		
38- 5	1616-5010	Needle clip	1			EA2 16123		
38- 6	1617-5010	Spring seat	1			EA2 16124		
38- 7	1618-5010	Throttle valve spring	1			EA2 16125		
38- 8	1619-5010	Mixing chamber top	1			EA2 16126		
38- 9	1621-5010	Mixing chamber cap	1			EA2 16127		
38-10	1622-5000	Cable adjuster	1			EA1 16128		
38-11	1623-5000	Adjusting lock nut	2			EA1 16129		
38-12	1626-5010	Throttle stop rod	1			EA2 16131		
38-13	1627-5010	Throttle stop screw	1			EA2 16132		
38-14	1628-5010	Stop screw spring	1			EA2 16133		
38-15	0551-1010	Split pin	1			WP 1×10	50	
38-16	1631-5000	Pilot air screw	1			EA1 16135		
38-17	1632-3010	Air screw spring	1			E2 8135		
38-18	1635-5010 100	100 Main jet	1			EA2 16141 -100		
38-18	1635-5010 110	110 Main jet	1			EA2 16141 -110		
38-19	1633-5010	Needle jet	1			EA2 16142		
38-20	1634-5000	Pilot jet	1			EA1 16143		
38-21	1652-3100	Connecting union	1			GA1 16193		
38-22	1651-5000	Union bolt	1			EA1 16151		
38-23	1654-3100	Union gasket	1			GA1 16196		
38-24	1645-5000	Starter plunger	1			EA1 16161		
38-25	1646-5000	Plunger spring	1			EA1 16162		
38-26	1647-5010	Plunger cap	1			EA2 16163		
38-27	1622-5000	Cable adjuster	1			EA1 16128		
38-28	1660-3100	Float valve assy	1			GA1 16170		
38-29	1665-3100	Valve seat gasket	1			GA1 16173		
38-30	1666-5010	Float	1			EA2 16181		
38-31	1667-3100	Float pin	1			GA1 16182		
38-32	1656-5010	Float chamber body	1			EA2 16183		
38-33	1657-5010	Float chamber gasket	1			EA2 16184		
38-34	1613-5010	Clamp screw	1			EA2 16191		
38-35	0211-0600	Hexagon nut A	4			6N 6	50	
38-36	0311-0414	Cross recd pan head screw	4			PNK 4×14	50	
38-37	0431-0410	Spring washer	4			SW 4	50	

39) EXCLSIVE PARTS FOR MODEL BS90SP

Index No.	Part No.	Part Name	No. Req'd	Unit Price US $	Serial No. From (MFG date)	Old Part No.	Min. Lot	N. B.
39- 1	3110-5031 CUR	Frame comp	1					
39- 1	3110-5031 MB	Frame comp	1					
39- 1	3110-5031 CBK	Frame comp	1					
39- 2	6176-5040	Throttle wire	1			EA240 61520		
39- 3	6178-5030	Carburetor starter wire	1			EA240 61530		
39- 4	4810-5021 CUR	Rear fork comp	1			EA2 47100 -ICUR		
39- 4	4810-5021 MB	Rear fork comp	1			EA2 47100 -IMB		
39- 4	4810-5021 CBK	Rear fork comp	1			EA2 47100 -ICBK		
39- 5	4855-5010	Torque rod bolt	1			EA2 47214		
39- 6	5110-5011 CUR	Fuel tank comp	1					
39- 6	5110-5011 MB	Fuel tank comp	1					
39- 6	5110-5011 CBK	Fuel tank comp	1					
39- 7	5141-5010	Knee grip	1			EA2 51211		
39- 8	5142-5010	Knee grip	1			EA2 51212		
39- 9	8401-5030	Speedometer assy	1		Mile/H	EA21 61300		
39- 9	8401-5020	Speedometer assy	1		KM/H	EA2 61300		
39-10	6211-5010	Air cleaner element	1			EA2 62110		
39-11	6241-5010	Air pipe	1			EA2 62121		
39-12	6242-5010	Air pipe joint	1			EA2 62122		
39-13	6351-5010	Exhaust pipe	1			EA2 63111		
39-14	6430-5030	Sport seat comp	1			EA240 64100		
39-15	6821-5040 CUR	Right cover	1					
39-15	6821-5070 MB	Right cover	1					
39-15	6821-5040 CBK	Right cover	1					
39-16	7366-5010	Rear torque link	1			EA2 72191		
39-17	6301-5020	Muffler assy	1			EA2 63300		
39-18	6320-5010	Diffuser pipe	1			EA2 63313		
39-19	8205-5021	Tail lamp assy	1					
39-20	3428-5010	Frame handle	1					
39-22	6815-5010	Cover ornament	2					BS90SP

40) EXCLUSIVE PARTS FOR MODELS 90D/01, 90T/01 & 90M/01
OIL PUMP - CARBURETOR

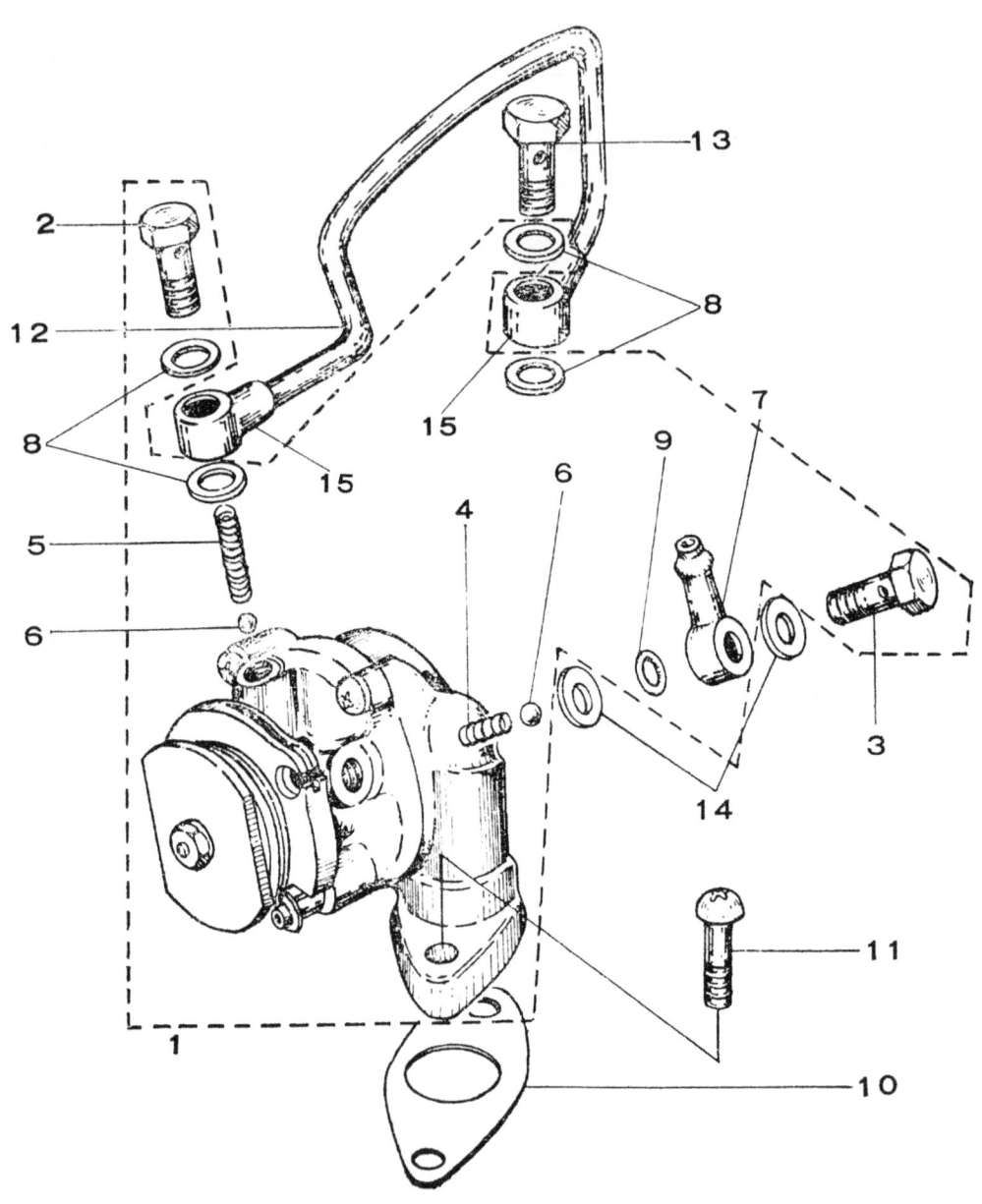

40) EXCLUSIVE PARTS FOR MODELS 90D/OI, 90T/OI & 90M/OI
(OIL PUMP · CARBURETOR)

Index No.	Part No.	Part Name	No. Req'd	Unit Price US $	Serial No. From (MFG date)	Old Part No.	Min. Lot	N. B.
40- 1	1501-5020	Oil pump assy	1					
40- 2	1564-5010	Union bolt	1					
40- 3	1572-5010	Union bolt	1					
40- 4	1568-5010	Check ball spring A	1					
40- 5	1569-5010	Check ball spring B	1					
40- 6	0611-0108	Ball	2			MO 5138	50	
40- 7	1571-5010	Union connector B	1					
40- 8	09065-103	6 aluminum gasket	4				50	
40- 9	09066-117	6 O ring	1				50	
40-10	1563-5010	Pump gasket	1					
40-11	0311-0516	Cross recd pan head screw	2			PNK 5×16	50	
40-12	1566-5011	Oil tube A	1					
40-13	1564-8000	Union bolt	1					
40-14	09065-103	6 aluminum gasket	2				50	
40-15	1565-8000	Union connecter	2					
40-	1412-5010	Rotary valve comp	1			EA2 14112		
40-	1430-5010	Valve cover comp	1					
40-	09066-111	10 O ring	1				50	
40-	1600-5070	Carburetor assy	1					
40-	1633-5030	Needle jet	1					
40-	1635-5000 130	130 Main jet	1			EA13 16141 -130		

MEMO

41) EXCLUSIVE PARTS FOR 90D/01, 90T/01 & 90M/01
(PUMP GEAR · KICK STARTER SHAFT · CRANK CASES)

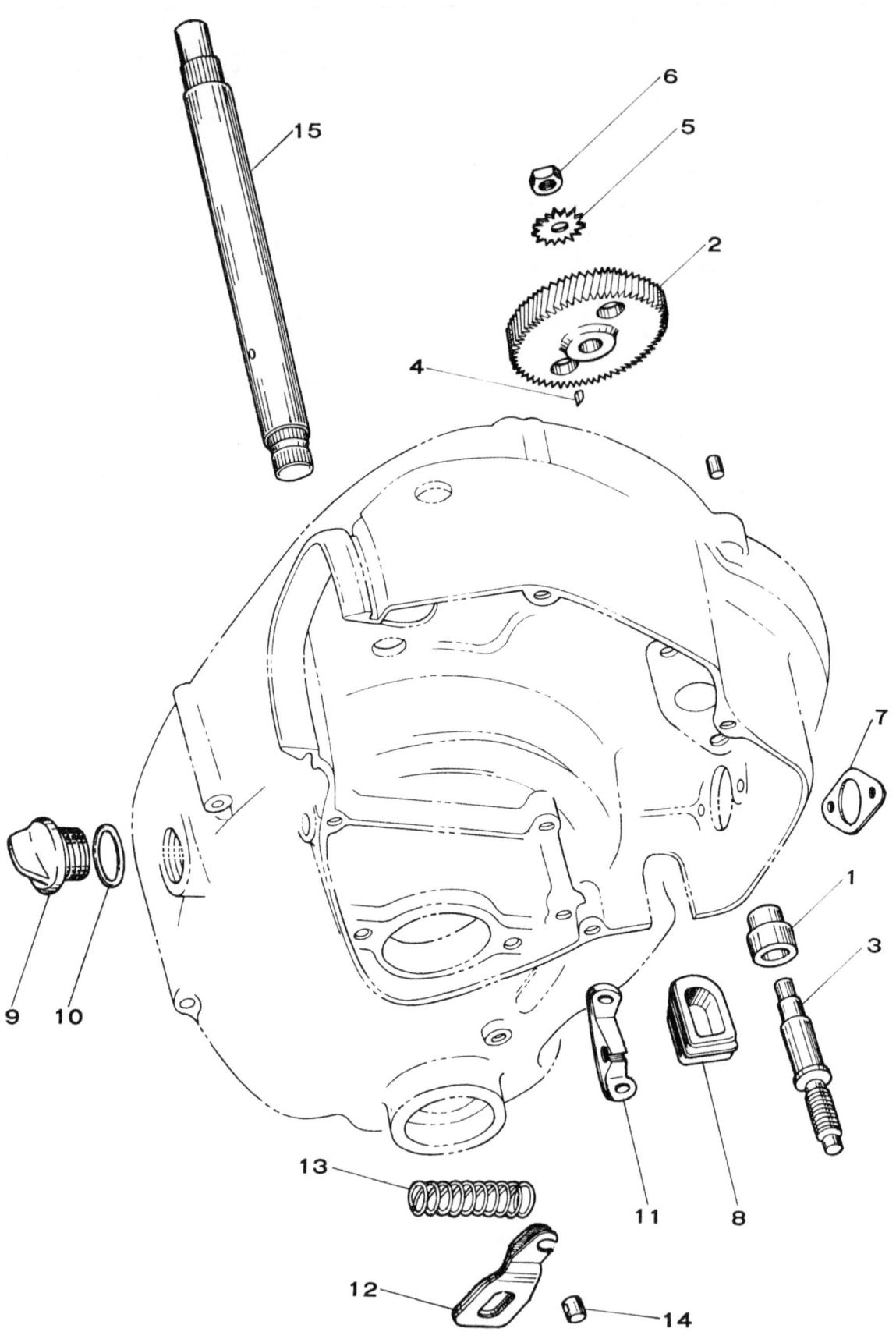

41) EXCLUSIVE PARTS FOR 90D/0I, 90T/0I & 90M/0I
(PUMP GEAR · KICK STARTER SHAFT · CRANK CASES)

Index No.	Part No.	Part Name	No. Rdq'd	Unit Price US $	Serial No. From (MFG date)	Old Part No.	Min. Lot	N. B.
41- 1	1513-5010	Worm shaft bush B	1					
41- 2	1552-5010	Pump gear B	1					
41- 3	1555-5010	Worm shaft	1					
41- 4	0671-2510	Woodruff key	1				50	
41- 5	0451-0815	External toothed washer	1				50	
41- 6	0231-0800	Hexagon nut C	1				50	
41- 7	2163-5010	Drain filter	1					
41- 8	1587-5010	Pump adjust screw cap	1					
41- 9	2165-8000	Oil filler plug	1					
41-10	09066-107	21 O ring	1				10	
41-11	1582-5012	Wire bracket	1					
41-12	2261-5010	Release arm	1					
41-13	2271-5010	Release arm return spring	1					
41-14	2275-5010	Release arm pin	1					
41-15	2621-3201	Kick starter shaft	1					
41-	2110-5010	Left crank case comp	1					
41-	2130-5010	Right crank case comp	1					
41-	2160-5010	Right crank case cover	1					
41-	2176-5020	Carburetor cover	1					
41-	2177-5020	Carburetor cap	1					
41-	2178-5010	Carburetor cap ring	1					
41-	2181-5010	Crank case gasket	1					
41-	2183-5010	Crank case cover gasket	1					
41-	2185-5010	Carburetor cover gasket	1					
41-	2264-8000	Release screw	1					

MEMO

42) EXCLUSIVE PARTS FOR MODELS BS90D/01, 90T/01 & 90M/01
FRAME · SEAT · COVERS

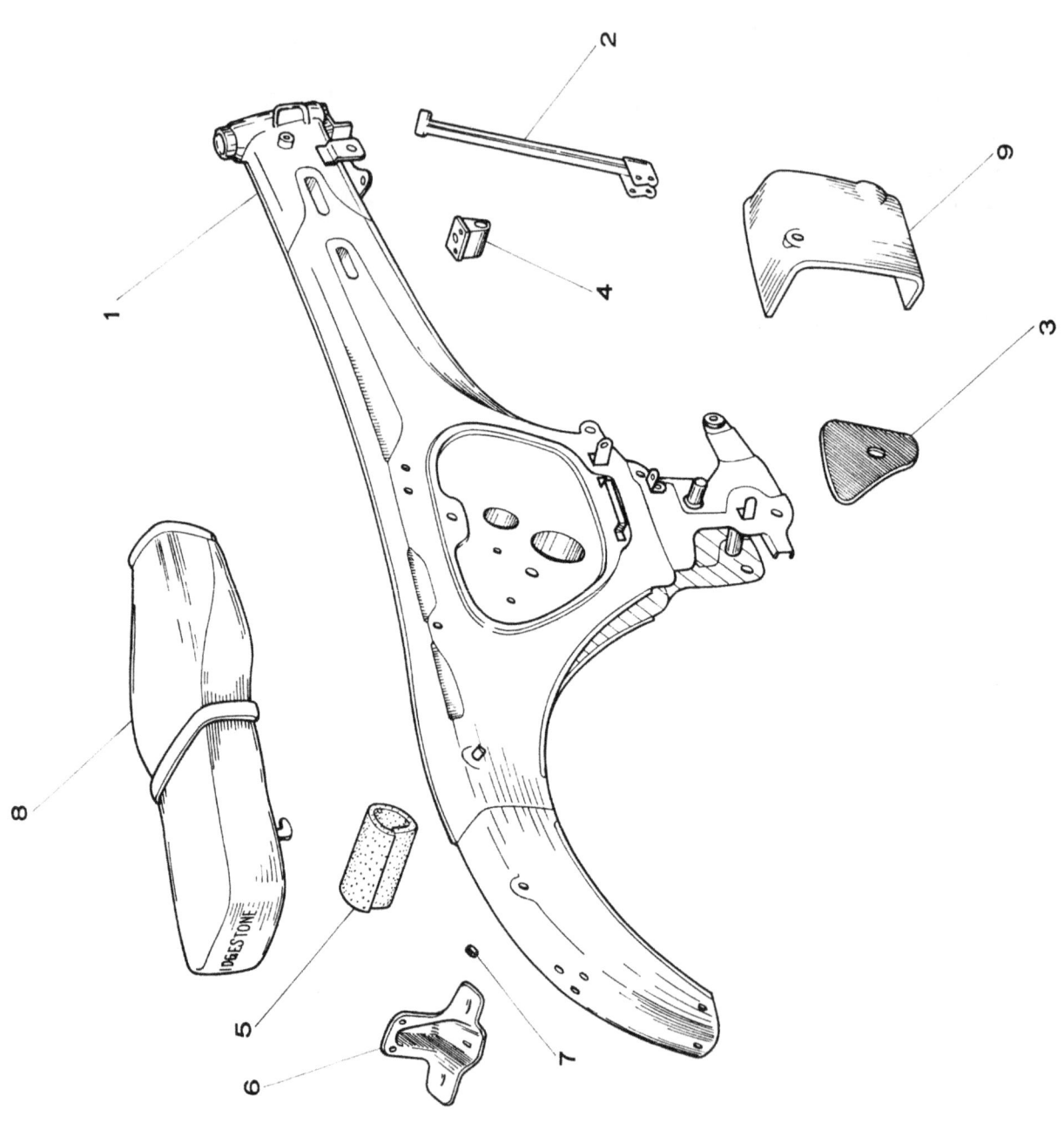

42) EXCLUSIVE PARTS FOR MODELS BS90D/OI, 90T/OI & 90M/OI
(FRAME · SEAT · COVERS)

Index No.	Part No.	Part Name	No. Req'd	Unit Price US $	Serial No. From (MFG date)	Old Part No.	Min. Lot	N. B.
42- 1	3110-5050 CUR	Frame comp	1					
42- 1	3110-5050 MB	Frame comp	1					
42- 1	3110-5050 CBK	Frame comp	1					
42- 2	3331-5010	Down tube	1					
42- 3	3451-5010	Oil tank cushion rubber	1					
42- 4	3433-5010	Handle lock	1					
42- 5	3427-5010	Tool set pad	1					
42- 6	3266-3200 CUR	License number plate bracket	1			GB1 31419 -CUR		
42- 6	3266-3200 MB	License number plate bracket	1			GB1 31419 -MB		
42- 6	3266-3200 CBK	License number plate bracket	1			GB1 31419 -CBK		
42- 7	3439-3200	Tail lamp wire grommet	1			GB1 31418		
42- 8	6460-5030	Dual seat comp	1					
42- 9	6821-5050 CUR	Right cover	1					
42- 9	6821-5050 MB	Right cover	1					
42- 9	6821-5050 CBK	Right cover	1					

MEMO

43) EXCLUSIVE PARTS FOR MODELS 90D/01, 90T/01 & 90M/01
(HEAD LAMP BODY · SPEEDOMETER · WINKER LIGHT)

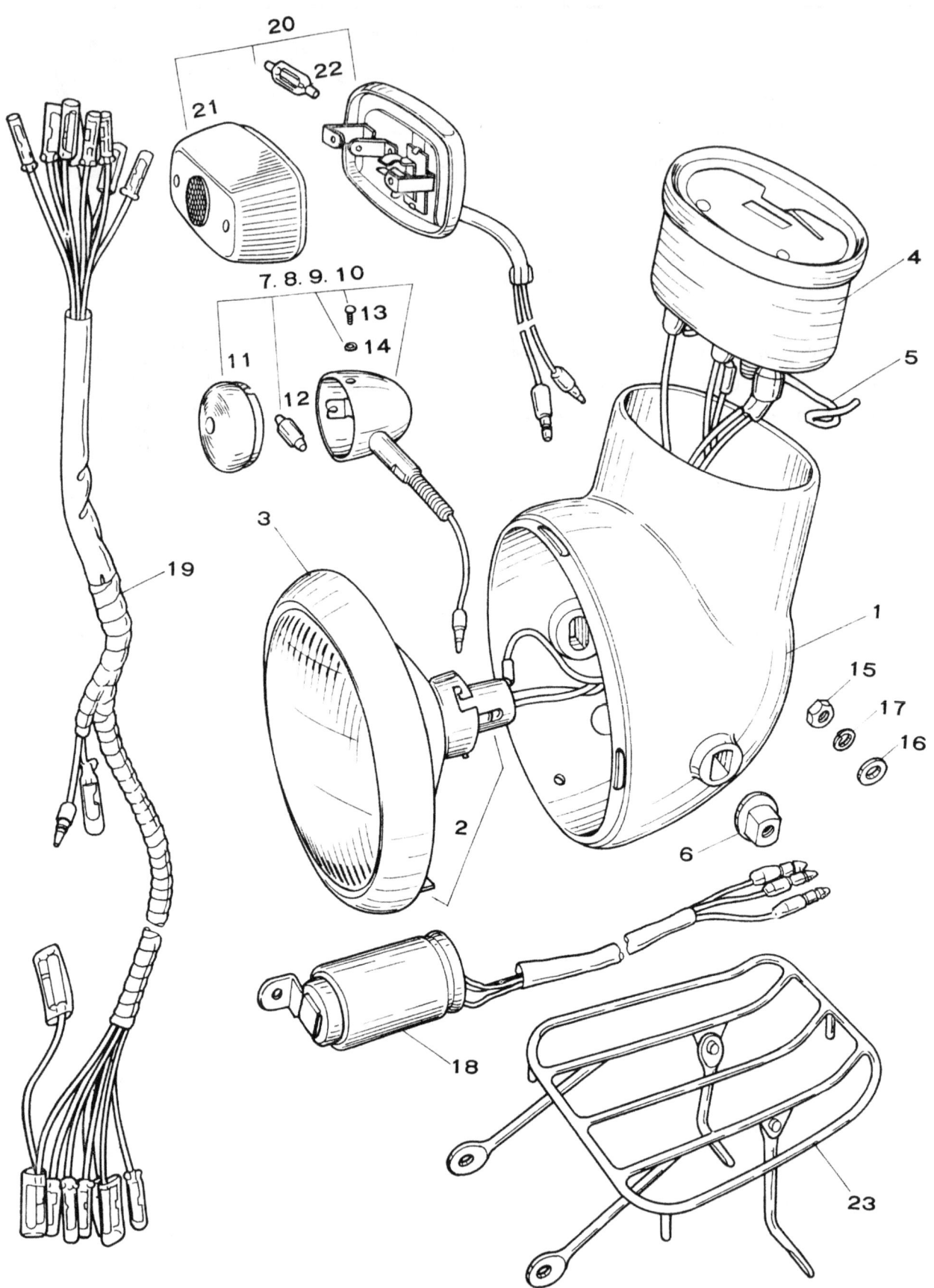

43) EXCLUSIVE PARTS FOR MODELS 90D/OI, 90T/OI & 90M/OI
(HEAD LAMP BODY · SPEEDOMETER · WINKER LIGHT)

Index No.	Part No.	Part Name	No. Req'd	Unit Price US $	Serial No. From (MFG date)	Old Part No.	Min. Lot	N. B.
43- 1	8111-5030 CUR	Head lamp body	1					
43- 1	8111-5030 MB	Head lamp body	1					
43- 1	8111-5030 CBK	Head lamp body	1					
43- 2	8102-5040	Head lamp assy	1					
43- 3	8140-5020	Head lamp rim comp	1					
43- 4	8401-5040	Speedometer assy	1		KM/H			
43- 4	8401-5050	Speedometer assy	1		Mile/H			
43- 5	8429-5020	Speedometer set spring	1					
43- 6	8126-3210	Lamp setting nut	2		17F009030 (June. '66) Abolished spare parts only			
43- 7	8301-5011	Left front winker assy	1					
43- 8	8302-5011	Right front winker assy	1					
43- 9	8303-5011	Left rear winker assy	1					
43-10	8304-5010	Right rear winker assy	1					
43-11	8331-3210	Front turn signal lens	4					
43-12	8332-3010	Winker bulb	4			M2 6233 -1		
43-13	0322-0308	Cross recd pan head screw	8				50	
43-14	0433-0307	Spring washer	8				50	
44-15	0231-0800	Hexagon nut C	2				50	
43-16	0411-0818	Plane washer A	2			HW 8	50	
43-17	0431-0820	Spring washer	2			SW 8	50	
43-18	8305-5011	Winker relay	1					
43-19	8810-5020	Wire harness comp	1					
43-20	8202-5030	Tail lamp assy	1					
43-21	8251-3200	Tail lamp lens	1			GB1 83121		
43-22	8252-5010	Tail lamp bulb	1					
43-23	6531-3220	Light luggage carrier	1			GB12 91200		

MEMO

44) EXCLUSIVE PARTS FOR MODELS BS90D/OI, 90T/OI & 90M/OI
OIL TANK · AIR CLEANER · CABLES

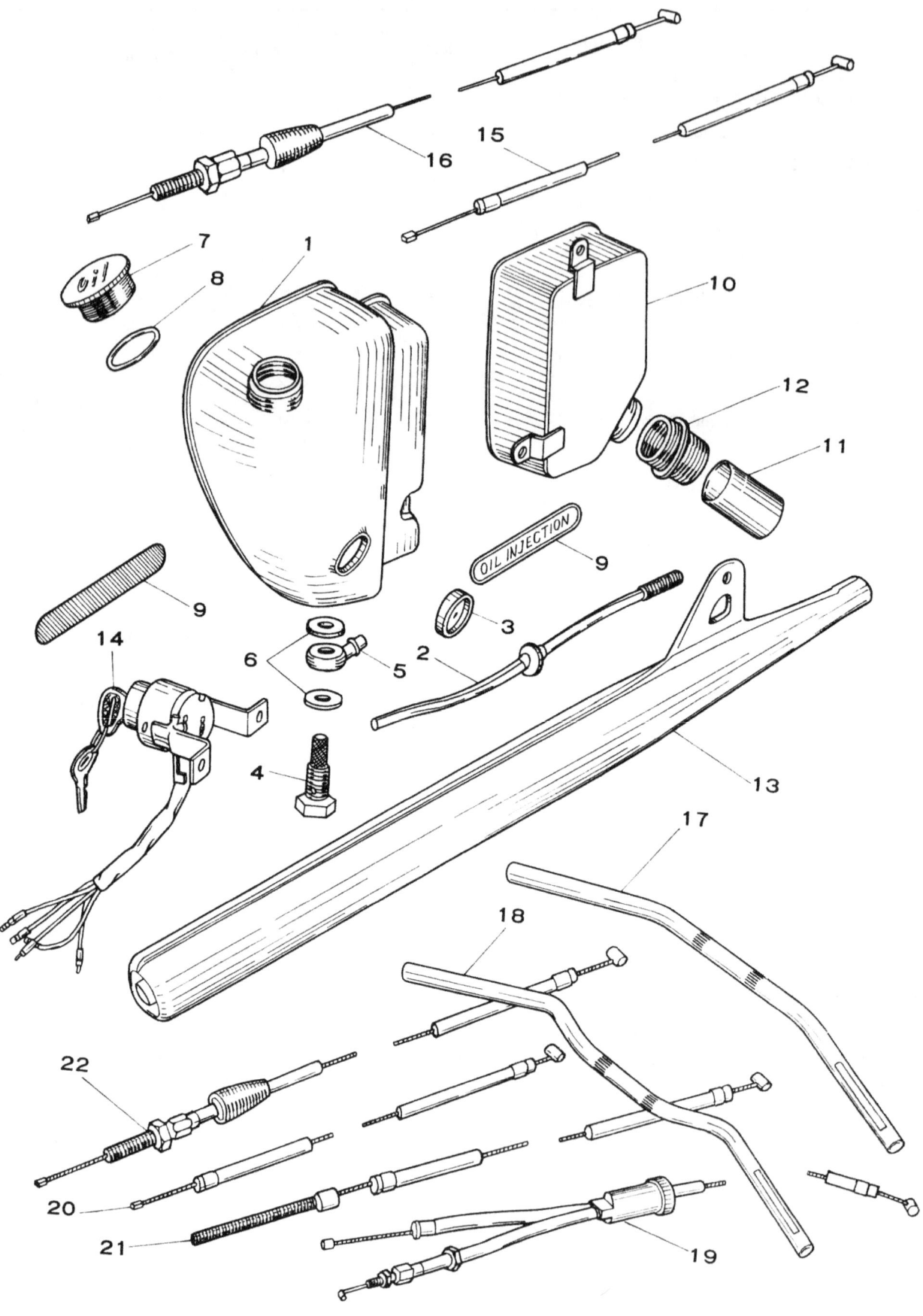

44) EXCLUSIVE PARTS FOR MODELS BS9OD/OI, 9OT/OI & 9OM/OI
(OIL TANK · AIR CLEANER · CABLES)

Index No.	Part No.	Part Name	No. Req'd	Unit Price US $	Serial No. From (MFG date)	Old Part No.	Min. Lot	N. B.
44- 1	5510-5010 CUR	Oil tank comp	1					
44- 1	5510-5010 MB	Oil tank comp	1					
44- 1	5510-5010 CBK	Oil tank comp	1					
44- 2	5533-5010	Oil tube C	1					
44- 3	5531-8000	Oil gauge	1					
44- 4	5532-5010	Oil tank filter	1					
44- 5	5534-5010	Union connector	1					
44- 6	09564-101	10 fiber gasket	2				50	
44- 7	5560-5010	Oil tank cap comp	1					
44- 8	09566-108	27 O ring	1				10	
44- 9	9116-5010	Oil injection label	2					
44-10	6211-5030	Air cleaner element	1					
44-11	6241-5020	Air pipe	1					
44-12	6242-5020	Air pipe joint	1					
44-13	6301-5030	Muffler assy	1					
44-14	8601-5020	Main switch assy	1					
44-15	6176-5071	Throttle wire	1					
44-16	6186-5040	Clutch wire	1					
		Exclusive parts for flat & down handle bar						
44-17	4511-3020	Down handle bar	1			M 1566		
44-18	4511-5010	Flat handle bar	1			EA1 91611		
44-19	6176-5120	Throttle wire	1					
44-20	6178-5010	Carburetor starter wire	1			EA1 91630		
44-21	6181-5010	Front brake wire	1			EA1 91640		
44-22	6186-5060	Clutch wire	1					

MEMO

45) EXCLUSIVE PARTS FOR BS90SP/01 (CARBURETOR · VALVE COVER · OIL PUMP)

Index No.	Part No.	Part Name	No. Rqd'd	Unit Price US $	Serial No. From (MFG date)	Old Part No.	Min. Lot	N. B.
45- 1	1600-5080	Carburetor assy	1					
45- 2	1430-5020	Valve cover comp	1					
45- 3	1501-5030	Oil pump assy	1					

Remarks: Other engine parts identical with those of BS90D/01 or BS90SP.

46) EXCLUSIVE PARTS FOR BS90SP/01 (FRAME · SEAT)

Index No.	Part No.	Part Name	No. Rqd'd	Unit Price US $	Serial No. From (MFG date)	Old Part No.	Min. Lot	N. B.
46- 1	3110-5080 CUR	Frame comp	1					
46- 1	3110-5080 MB	Frame comp	1					
46- 1	3110-5080 CBK	Frame comp	1					
46- 2	6460-5040	Dual seat comp	1					
46- 3	6176-5081	Throttle wire	1		For up-swept handle bar			
		Exclusive parts for Flat handle bar						
46-	6176-5130	Throttle wire	1					
46-	6178-5020	Carburetor starter wire	1			EA2 61530		

Remarks: Other parts are identical with those of BS90SP or BS90D/01

47) EXCLUSIVE PARTS FOR U.S.A (FOR BS90D/01, BS90T/01, BS90M/01 & BS90SP/01)

Index No.	Part No.	Part Name	No. Rqd'd	Unit Price US $	Serial No. From (MFG date)	Old Part No.	Min. Lot	N. B.
47- 1	3110-5060 MB	Frame comp	1		90T/01, 90M/01			
47- 2	3110-5060 CBK	Frame comp	1		90D/01			
47- 3	3110-5070 FAR	Frame comp	1		90SP/01			
47- 4	5110-5011 FAR	Fuel tank comp	1		90SP/01			
47- 5	4810-5021 FAR	Rear fork comp	1		90SP/01			
47- 6	5510-5010 FAR	Oil tank comp	1		90SP/01			
47- 7	8111-5020 FAR	Head lamp body	1		90SP/01			
47- 8	4100-5000 FAR	Front fork assy	1		90SP/01			
47- 9	4171-5000 FAR	Left fork cover	1		90SP/01			
47-10	4181-5000 FAR	Right fork cover	1		90SP/01			
47-11	4901-5030 FAR	Rear cushion assy	1		90SP/01			
47-12	6811-5030 FAR	Left cover	1		90SP/01			
47-13	6821-5050 FAR	Right cover	1		90SP/01			
47-14	8205-5011	Tail lamp assy	1		90D/01, 90SP/01			
47-15	8810-5010	Wire harness comp	1		90D/01, 90SP/01	EAE 88110		

VELOCEPRESS MANUALS - MOTORCYCLE

1930'S BRITISH MOTORCYCLE CARBS & ELEC COMPONENTS (BOOK OF)
1930'S BRITISH MOTORCYCLE ENGINES (OVERHAUL & MAINTENANCE)
1930'S BRITISH MOTORCYCLE GEARBOXES & CLUTCHES (BOOK OF)
AJS 1932-1948 SINGLES & TWINS 250cc THRU 1000cc (BOOK OF)
AJS 1945-1960 SINGLES 350cc & 500cc MODELS 16 & 18 (BOOK OF)
AJS 1955-1965 SINGLES 350cc & 500cc (BOOK OF)
ARIEL 1932-1939 PREWAR MODELS (BOOK OF)
ARIEL 1933-1951 (WORKSHOP MANUAL)
ARIEL 1939-1960 4 STROKE SINGLES (BOOK OF)
ARIEL 1958-1964 LEADER & ARROW (BOOK OF)
BMW R26 R27 (1956-1967) FACTORY WORKSHOP MANUAL
BMW R50 R50S R60 R69S (1955-1969) FACTORY WORKSHOP MANUAL
BRIDGESTONE 90 SERIES FACTORY WSM & PARTS CATALOGUE
BSA BANTAM ALL MODELS FROM 1948 ONWARDS (BOOK OF)
BSA SINGLES & V-TWINS UP TO 1927 (BOOK OF)
BSA SINGLES & V-TWINS UP TO 1935 (BOOK OF)
BSA SINGLES & V-TWINS 1936-1939 (BOOK OF)
BSA SINGLES & V-TWINS 1936-1952 (BOOK OF)
BSA OHV & SV SINGLES 250-600cc 1945-1954 (BOOK OF)
BSA OHV & SV SINGLES 250cc 1954-1970 (BOOK OF)
BSA OHV SINGLES 350 & 500cc 1955-1967 (BOOK OF)
BSA TWINS 1948-1962 (BOOK OF)
BSA TWINS 1962-1969 (SECOND BOOK OF)
DOUGLAS 1929-1939 PREWAR ALL MODELS (BOOK OF)
DOUGLAS 1948-1957 POSTWAR ALL MODELS FACTORY SHOP MANUAL
DUCATI 160cc, 250cc & 350cc OHC MODELS FACTORY SHOP MANUAL
HONDA 50 ALL MODELS UP TO 1970 INC MONKEY & TRAIL (BOOK OF)
HONDA 90 ALL MODELS UP TO 1966 (BOOK OF)
HONDA 125-150cc TWINS C/CS/CB/CA FACTORY WORKSHOP MANUAL
HONDA 250-305 TWINS C/CS/CB FACTORY WORKSHOP MANUAL
HONDA C100 SUPER CUB FACTORY WORKSHOP MANUAL
HONDA C110 SPORT CUB 1962-1969 FACTORY WORKSHOP MANUAL
HONDA TWINS & SINGLES 50cc THRU 305cc 1960-1966 (BOOK OF)
HONDA TWINS ALL MODELS 125cc THRU 450cc UP TO 1968 (BOOK OF)
J.A.P. ENGINES 1927-1952 & MOTORCYCLES 1934-1952 (BOOK OF)
LAMBRETTA 1947-1957 ALL 125 & 150cc MODELS (BOOK OF)
LAMBRETTA 1957-1970 LI & TV MODELS (SECOND BOOK OF)
MATCHLESS 1931-1939 ALL MODELS 250cc THRU 990cc (BOOK OF)
MATCHLESS 1945-1956 350 & 500cc SINGLES (BOOK OF)
MATCHLESS 1955-1966 350 & 500cc SINGLES (BOOK OF)
NEW IMPERIAL ALL SV & OHV FROM 1935 ONWARDS (BOOK OF)
NORTON 1932-1939 PREWAR MODELS (BOOK OF)
NORTON 1932-1947 (BOOK OF)
NORTON 1938-1956 (BOOK OF)
NORTON 1955-1963 MODELS 19, 50 & ES2 (BOOK OF)
NORTON 1955-1965 DOMINATOR TWINS (BOOK OF)
NORTON 1957-1970 TWINS FACTORY WORKSHOP MANUAL
NSU PRIMA 1956-1964 ALL MODELS (BOOK OF)
NSU QUICKLY 1953-1963 ALL MODELS (BOOK OF)
PANTHER 1932-1958 LIGHTWEIGHT MODELS 250 & 350cc (BOOK OF)
PANTHER 1938-1966 HEAVYWEIGHT MODELS 600 & 650cc (BOOK OF)
RALEIGH MOPEDS 1960-1969 (BOOK OF)
RALEIGH MOTORCYCLES 1919-1933 (BOOK OF)
ROYAL ENFIELD 1934-1946 SINGLES & V TWINS (BOOK OF)
ROYAL ENFIELD 1937-1953 SINGLES & V TWINS (BOOK OF)
ROYAL ENFIELD 1946-1962 SINGLES (BOOK OF)
ROYAL ENFIELD 1958-1966 250cc & 350cc SINGLES (SECOND BOOK OF)
ROYAL ENFIELD 736cc INTERCEPTOR FACTORY WORKSHOP MANUAL
RUDGE 1933-1939 (BOOK OF)
SUNBEAM 1928-1939 (BOOK OF)
SUNBEAM 1946-1957 S7 & S8 (BOOK OF)
SUZUKI 50cc & 80cc UP TO 1966 (BOOK OF)
SUZUKI T10 1963-1967 FACTORY WORKSHOP MANUAL
SUZUKI T20 & T200 1965-1969 FACTORY WORKSHOP MANUAL
TRIUMPH 1935-1939 PREWAR MODELS (BOOK OF)
TRIUMPH 1935-1949 (BOOK OF)
TRIUMPH 1937-1951 (WORKSHOP MANUAL)
TRIUMPH 1945-1955 FACTORY WORKSHOP MANUAL
TRIUMPH 1945-1958 TWINS (BOOK OF)
TRIUMPH 1956-1969 TWINS (BOOK OF)
VELOCETTE 1925-1970 ALL SINGLES & TWINS (BOOK OF)
VESPA 1951-1961 (BOOK OF)
VESPA 1955-1963 125 & 150cc & GS MODELS (SECOND BOOK OF)
VESPA 1955-1968 GS & SS (BOOK OF)
VESPA 1963-1972 90, 125 & 150cc (THIRD BOOK OF)
VILLIERS ENGINE UP TO 1959 INC. 3 WHEELERS (BOOK OF)
VILLIERS ENGINE UP TO 1969 (BOOK OF)
VINCENT 1935-1955 (WORKSHOP MANUAL)

VELOCEPRESS TECHNICAL BOOKS – MOTORCYCLE

CATALOG OF BRITISH MOTORCYCLES (1951 MODELS)
INDIAN PONYBIKE, BOY RACER & PAPOOSE ILL PARTS LIST & SALES LIT
MOTORCYCLE ENGINEERING (P.E. Irving)
SPEED AND HOW TO OBTAIN IT (Motor Cycle Magazine UK)
TUNING FOR SPEED (P.E. Irving)

VELOCEPRESS MANUALS - THREE WHEELER'S

BSA THREE WHEELER (BOOK OF)
VINTAGE MORGAN THREE WHEELER (BOOK OF)

VELOCEPRESS MANUALS - AUTOMOBILE

AUSTIN-HEALEY 6-CYLINDER WORKSHOP MANUAL
AUSTIN-HEALEY SPRITE & MG MIDGET WORKSHOP MANUAL 1958-1971
BMW 600 LIMOUSINE FACTORY WORKSHOP MANUAL
BMW 600 LIMOUSINE OWNERS HAND BOOK & SERVICE MANUAL
BMW 2000 & 2002 1966-1976 WORKSHOP MANUAL
BMW ISETTA FACTORY WORKSHOP MANUAL
CORVAIR 1960-1969 WORKSHOP MANUAL
CORVETTE V8 1955-1962 WORKSHOP MANUAL
FIAT 500 FACTORY WORKSHOP MANUAL 1957-1973
JAGUAR E-TYPE 3.8 & 4.2 SERIES 1 & 2 WORKSHOP MANUAL
JAGUAR MK 7, 8, 9 & XK120, 140, 150 WORKSHOP MANUAL 1948-1961
METROPOLITAN FACTORY WORKSHOP MANUAL
MGA & MGB OWNERS HANDBOOK & WORKSHOP MANUAL
MG MIDGET TC, TD, TF & TF1500 WORKSHOP MANUAL
PORSCHE 356 1948-1965 WORKSHOP MANUAL
PORSCHE 912 WORKSHOP MANUAL
TRIUMPH TR2, TR3, TR4 1953-1965 WORKSHOP MANUAL
VOLKSWAGEN TRANSPORTER, TRUCKS & WAGONS 1950-1979 WSM
VOLVO 1944-1968 ALL MODELS WORKSHOP MANUAL

VELOCEPRESS TECHNICAL BOOKS - AUTOMOBILE

FERRARI 250/GT SERVICE AND MAINTENANCE
FERRARI GUIDE TO PERFORMANCE
FERRARI OWNER'S HANDBOOK
FERRARI TUNING TIPS & MAINTENANCE TECHNIQUES
HOW TO BUILD A FIBERGLASS CAR
HOW TO BUILD A RACING CAR
HOW TO RESTORE THE MODEL 'A' FORD
MASERATI OWNER'S HANDBOOK
OBERT'S FIAT GUIDE
PERFORMANCE TUNING THE SUNBEAM TIGER
SOUPING THE VOLKSWAGEN
SOLEX CARBURETORS (EMPHASIS ON UK & EU AUTOMOBILES)
SU CARBURETORS (EMPHASIS ON UK AUTOMOBILES)
WEBER CARBURETORS (EMPHASIS ON ALFA & FIAT)

VELOCEPRESS BOOKS & GUIDES - AUTOMOBILE

ABARTH BUYERS GUIDE
COMPLETE CATALOG OF JAPANESE MOTOR VEHICLES
FERRARI 308 SERIES BUYER'S AND OWNER'S GUIDE
FERRARI BERLINETTA LUSSO
FERRARI BROCHURES AND SALES LITERATURE 1946-1967
FERRARI BROCHURES AND SALES LITERATURE 1968-1989
FERRARI OPP, MAINTENANCE & SERVICE H/BOOKS 1948-1963
FERRARI SERIAL NUMBERS PART I - ODD NUMBERS TO 21399
FERRARI SERIAL NUMBERS PART II - EVEN NUMBERS TO 1050
FERRARI SPYDER CALIFORNIA
HENRY'S FABULOUS MODEL "A" FORD
MASERATI BROCHURES AND SALES LITERATURE

VELOCEPRESS BOOKS – RACING

CARRERA PANAMERICANA - MEXICAN ROAD RACE (BOOK OF)
DIALED IN - THE JAN OPPERMAN STORY
IF HEMINGWAY HAD WRITTEN A RACING NOVEL
LE MANS 24 (THE BOOK THAT THE FILM WAS BASED ON)
VEDA ORR'S NEW REVISED HOT ROD PICTORIAL

AUTOBOOKS WORKSHOP MANUALS & BROOKLANDS ROAD TEST PORTFOLIOS

FOR A COMPLETE LISTING OF THE AUTOBOOKS & BROOKLANDS TITLES THAT WE CURRENTLY HAVE AVAILABLE, PLEASE VISIT OUR WEBSITE.

Please visit our website

www.VelocePress.com

for a complete up-to-date list of titles, descriptions, and secure online ordering using PayPal.

www.ingramcontent.com/pod-product-compliance
Lightning Source LLC
Chambersburg PA
CBHW080434230426
43662CB00015B/2275